Watersheds 4

Ten Cases in Environmental Ethics

Fourth Edition

LISA H. NEWTON
Fairfield University

CATHERINE K. DILLINGHAM
Fairfield University

JOANNE CHOLY
Fairfield University

THOMSON ™

WADSWORTH

Australia • Canada • Mexico • Singapore • Spain
United Kingdom • United States

THOMSON
WADSWORTH

Publisher: *Holly J. Allen*
Philosophy Editor: *Steve Wainwright*
Assistant Editors: *Lee McCracken, Barbara Hillaker*
Editorial Assistant: *John Gahbauer*
Technology Project Manager: *Julie Aguilar*
Marketing Manager: *Worth Hawes*
Marketing Assistant: *Andrew Keay*
Advertising Project Manager: *Laurel Anderson*
Executive Art Director: *Maria Epes*

Print/Media Buyer: *Lisa Claudeanos*
Permissions Editor: *Kiely Sisk*
Production Service: *Matrix Productions*
Copy Editor: *Lauren Root*
Cover Designer: *Yvo Riezebos*
Cover Image: "View from Old Ragg, Shenandoah," *Mark Oatney/Getty Images*
Compositor: *Cadmus*
Printer: *Webcom*

For more information about our products, contact us at:
Thomson Learning Academic Resource Center
1-800-423-0563

For permission to use material from this text or product, submit a request online at
http://www.thomsonrights.com.
Any additional questions about permissions can be submitted by email to
thomsonrights@thomson.com.

Library of Congress Control Number:
2004113469

ISBN 0-534-52126-6

Thomson Higher Education
10 Davis Drive
Belmont, CA 94002-3098
USA

Asia (including India)
Thomson Learning
5 Shenton Way
#01-01 UIC Building
Singapore 068808

Australia/New Zealand
Thomson Learning Australia
102 Dodds Street
Southbank, Victoria 3006
Australia

Canada
Thomson Nelson
1120 Birchmount Road
Toronto, Ontario M1K 5G4
Canada

UK/Europe/Middle East/Africa
Thomson Learning
High Holborn House
50/51 Bedford Row
London WC1R 4LR
United Kingdom

Latin America
Thomson Learning
Seneca, 53
Colonia Polanco
11560 Mexico
D.F. Mexico

Spain (includes Portugal)
Thomson Paraninfo
Calle Magallanes, 25
28015 Madrid, Spain

To the land,
and to our grandchildren's future

Contents

Preface

We would much rather read books than write them. The only reason to write a book is that you need something to teach with and there's nothing there, or it's there in such scattered and inconvenient form that you can't use it for a large class. Such is the case with the classic cases of environmental ethics—the "defining moments" when human technology trips over itself and sprawls into an ungainly heap of poisoned soil, polluted water, and human injury and death, with no one to explain it or pay for it. In such moments we can focus the student's wandering attention on the real problems of environmental complexity, the biological, economic, and legal issues underscored by the damage irrevocably done to real people and the land they depend upon. For our own purposes alone, then, we had to assemble the snippets of newsprint that hold the information for these cases; it was a short step to put the cases together in a book for our colleagues.

This edition reflects a new urgency about current events. The first edition focused in particular on the classic stories—Love Canal, the tropical rainforest, the Exxon Valdez—that had brought environmental consciousness to the fore in the 1970s. The second and third editions kept many of those cases, adding others—genetically modified organisms, antibiotic resistance—as they became central to environmental disputes. This edition also retains the cases that have shown themselves to be more than ordinarily useful, while adding others—the controversy over chlorine chemistry, biodiversity and the practices that sustain it, alternatives to fossil-fuel-based energy—that are now emerging and will be central to the environmental dialogue in the years approaching. The most recent political developments throw into strong light the need for all students, all citizens, to understand these issues and understand them well. In a context of clear danger to the land that sustains us, it is impossible to overestimate their importance. We have found the use of cases an enormous help in the classroom. A case is a story. We deal with theories in our classrooms, but we anchor our theories in stories, for if a theory cannot find illustration in the things that actually happen to us, the theory is bound for the dustheap. Stories are easy to remember, fun to talk about, and the foundation of insight. In the case of these classic stories, known to all, that insight is generalizable and valuable for the foreseeable future. Assembling them for practical use each semester has made our work considerably easier for us. We trust it will do the same for you.

We would like to thank our editors for their patience and helpful suggestions in the course of the preparation of this manuscript. We are also grateful to the reviewers for their constructive comments: Joseph L. Chartkoff, Professor of Anthropology, Michigan State University; Ari Santas, Philosophy, Valdosta State University; Gene S. Helfman, Institute of Ecology, University of Georgia; Craig T. Jordan, University of Texas at San Antonio. Above all we gratefully acknowledge the help and support of God and our families, without whose forbearance and support the completion of this project would not have been possible.

Lisa H. Newton, Joanne Choly, and Catherine K. Dillingham

Armistice Day: November 11, 2004

Introduction

THE NATURE OF THE PROBLEM

The natural world seems to be deteriorating around us, and it seems to be our fault. We are uncertain about the extent of the deterioration, the means that would reverse it, and the prospects for human life in the future if those means are undertaken. We are not sure that we have the political will to pay for what those means would cost, and we have more than a suspicion that the costs may be unthinkably high.

These have been bad times for environmental consciousness and conscience. When the first edition of *Watersheds* came out in 1992, we had just elected a vice-president for the United States who had written a book, an excellent one, on the relation between civilization and the natural environment, strongly urging protection of our remaining natural resources and wiser policies on energy use and consumption.[1] When the third edition hit the shelves, we had apparently elected (depending on your meaning of "elected") a president whose first environmental act was to urge the opening of the Arctic National Wildlife Refuge for oil exploration. His next was to renege on his promise to reduce carbon dioxide emissions. This action ignited a firestorm, but its energy may have been only in the newsprint; attacks on the Clean Water Act followed, along with the rescinding of all of his predecessor's protections of the forests.[2] At the writing of this edition, that administration has just been returned to power in the nation's capital, and the depression in the environmental community is palpable.

The environmental movement itself has been fragmented by self-indulgent "anarchist" actions staged by less responsible partisans, campaigns of dubious validity and scientific worth on the part of its most dedicated leadership, and frankly deceptive campaigns (with names like "Wildlife Studies Association" and "GreenWorld") funded by mining and utility companies. What seemed to be a determined and intelligent national movement from the first Earth Day to the 1990s now seems lost. The very passion that newly converted environmentalists—or just alarmed citizens—bring to the discussion of environmental policy can work against effective action, by antagonizing the quieter sorts of citizen and by encouraging cynicism if the worst predictions do not immediately come true. Attempts to produce good scientific proofs on the state of the environment, for the sake of the public, run into the perpetual dilemma of popular science: when the projections are accurate and responsible, they tend to be misunderstood and distorted by press and politics; when they are simplified for popular consumption, they tend not to be strictly true and often cause alarm. That alarm itself is new: it is a type of formless apprehension that may define the century to come. We are frightened, and we do not know how frightened we should be; this is not the best condition in which to formulate policy.

So the first assignment for any work on the environment is to clarify questions, sort out fact from judgment and opinion, analyze terrors into workable tasks, and focus emotion through the lens of logic into practical policy. That happens to be, since Socrates, the traditional assignment of the discipline of Philosophy. The question that lies before the people of the world, especially of the more developed parts, concerns the search for moral imperatives: What is to be done? What are our duties in this new and confusing age—to ourselves, our children, other nations, to all living things, to the planet? What policies should we adopt to promote the greatest happiness of the greatest number of human beings in the long run? Must that happiness be balanced against the welfare of the biosphere? May we put the happiness of our own fellow citizens in some privileged place in the calculation? What type of human being will we have to be to carry these new imperatives into practice? While we work to change the relationship between our very recently evolved civilization and a natural world that has been evolving over eons of time, how will we have to change our accounts of human virtue, aspiration, and self-realization?

These are the classic questions of ethics. The crises of the environment, the headline catastrophes, have posed new ethical questions, and those questions have spawned a new literature, indeed a whole new academic discipline. For while the first effect of environmental catastrophe, accomplished or impending, is to throw all policy and prudence into question, the second is to throw all philosophy into question. Let us take those questions one at a time.

First, disaster demands reevaluation of all policies effective at the time. Decisions that seemed prudent and cost effective at the time they were made—decisions to build a school over an old dump (as happened at Love Canal), to prune excess manpower from a little-used oil-spill response team (that Alyeska was supposed to maintain to clean up oil spills in Prince William Sound), to defer maintenance on some backup safety systems at the chemical factory (as happened in Bhopal)—suddenly seem terribly unwise, indeed criminally negligent. Our response is, appropriately, to develop more stringent and far-reaching policies, to introduce new probability calculations into business prudence, and, in effect, to transfer some of the costs of cleaning up a disaster to the safety preparations before it happens, hoping to avoid the balance of the costs entirely. The debate (if so polite a word is appropriate to describe the aftermath of an environmental catastrophe) is centrally ethical: it is a debate on the appropriate balance between individual rights and the common good, between short-term and long-term benefit, and among the interests of all parties to the activity. We have a field, Applied Ethics, that encompasses all such ethical inquiries as they relate to practical issues; a new field, Environmental Ethics, includes these inquiries as relate to the interests of the biosphere itself.

Second, that ethical approach raises conceptual problems that go beyond policy and prudence. The next effect of environmental catastrophe is philosophical inquiry—especially when the event is generalized to the ongoing catastrophe of the last days of the twentieth century: an end to all frontiers, the threat to the last wilderness, the incredible rate of consumption of nonrenewable resources, the depletion of the ozone layer, and the extinction of species. Although we always knew that we would make mistakes, and that accidents would happen, and that humans through carelessness or venality might cause isolated disasters, only recently has it occurred to us that our entire approach to the natural world could be a disaster in itself and a crime—not just imprudent but conceptually and morally wrong, like slavery. Maybe humans should not be treating Nature as a mere thing, to be exploited without limit. Maybe Nature is part of our community, like us, requiring respect and nurture rather than mindless "use." It is beginning to dawn on us that resources are not unlimited; it is possible that they are not even "resources," in the sense of material available for use, for "taking." Maybe we will have to learn to live as a part of all life, subordinate to the natural workings of the natural world that sustains us, if we are to continue to live at all.

This philosophical doubt on the environmental front has occasioned some genuinely original inquiry. One of the most interesting moves in philosophy since the dawn of this newer, more acute, environmental consciousness, has been "ecofeminism," a fusion of environmentalism with feminism, which distinguishes approaches based on *life taking* (the exploitation of "resources") from those based on *life giving* (partnering with Nature) and argues for the superiority of the latter. Another interesting move identifies all living matter as part of the biosphere (occasionally personalized as "Gaia"), a nurturant, life-giving superorganism, in which we live and of which we form an integral part, and which is our only means to flourish as fully realized persons. Whatever destroys this organism, destroys humanity; as long as we continue to imagine Nature as "things" to be commandeered to our purposes and conceive of living organisms other than ourselves as "objects," the destruction will continue; the human imperative for survival therefore demands a total revision not only of our uses of nature but of our imaging and conceptualizing of the natural world. This organic approach is one of several that presently form the "deep ecology" movement.

The field of philosophy has expanded, very recently, to include careful treatments of the new philosophical approaches to the natural environment. These developments in philosophy, fascinating as they are, will receive very little attention in this book. Beyond the superfluity of one more theoretical analysis, it turns out to matter very little when the cod disappear from Georges Banks and the cloud of poison rolls over Bhopal, whether we approach the problems from the perspective of ecofeminism or deep ecology, or, for that matter, from Kantian or Utilitarian perspectives. Sound policy—policy that brings the costs of predictable malfunctions forward, into the setting up of the economic arrangements in the first place—is what is needed, and rigorous enforcement of that policy. It should be noted, that in the course of developing that policy, we will have to go deeper than the immediate surface "causes" of the incident that has focused our attention, to examine the political and economic practices that made it inevitable. These inquiries can be penetrating, even radical: for example, to develop a policy that will be effective in preventing the depletion of fisheries, we will have to reexamine our entire pattern of assault on natural resources and the underlying attitude of disrespect that eventuates in the terrible waste of life in the natural world. Similarly, to develop a policy that will prevent the destruction of the ancient groves in the Pacific Northwest, we may have to bring into question the whole institution of private property in land.

Nothing should prevent the student, or instructor, from going beyond the concerns of public ethics raised by these cases to fundamental considerations of the moral and metaphysical status of Nature and its relation to the humans that, temporarily, inhabit it. While attempts to deal directly with the distortions of our national and international life caused by short-sighted energy policies will not be helped by bouncing the problem back to the conceptual level—indeed, they may be significantly hindered by such redirection—ultimately, we will have to engage in just such reconceptualization. As then Senator (later vice-president, now Professor) Al Gore put it in *Earth in the Balance*,

> The strategic nature of the threat now posed *by* human civilization to the global environment and the strategic nature of the threat *to* human civilization now posed by changes in the global environment present us with . . . challenges and false hopes. Some argue that a new ultimate technology, whether nuclear power or genetic engineering, will solve the problem. Others hold that only a drastic reduction of our reliance on technology can improve the conditions of life—a simplistic notion at best. But the real solution will be found in reinventing and finally healing the relationship between civilization and the earth.

THE REASON AND PLAN FOR THIS BOOK

Al Gore's formulation raises the most serious aspect of the environmental crisis. We may be very good at developing new technologies, or at least new wrinkles in existing technologies, but there lies the problem: we have never thought of the earth as anything but the raw materials for our technologies, and we are total flops at reinventing and healing relationships, whether in our families, our communities, our nation, or the peoples of the world. Adding the planet Earth to our list of failed relationships only takes us further out of our depth. The question is not, yet, how to "solve" the problem of the environment, but how to get a handle on it, how to think about it, how to begin to comprehend its complexity.

That's where this book comes in. Faced with global dilemmas of indescribable complexity, demanding not new gadgets to solve immediate problems but new ways of relationship to the globe itself, we look for microcosms in which the dilemmas may be faithfully reproduced, but limited as to time and place and so easier to grasp. Each one of these cases is a "defining moment," in Al Gore's formulation, that "focuses media coverage and political attention, not only on the environment itself, but also on the larger problems for which it is a metaphor. . . . " When we debate environmental problems on the global level, we find we cannot agree on anything—not on the facts, nor the prospects for the future, nor on the ethical and political principles that should govern any solution. But on concrete cases, like the radioactive tanks at Hanford, the death of the fisheries, or the gas explosion at Bhopal, we can reach certain very basic agreements—at least, that whatever happened is bad and should not happen again in the future—and we can use such agreement as the foundation for further explorations of the issues. If nothing else, a knowledge of the headline cases—the lunch-table conversation cases, the cases that are broadly known—can supply common coinage for an ongoing discussion.

The book aims to be useful to a variety of purposes, academic and otherwise. It is primarily designed as a supplement to all college and graduate level courses in Environmental Ethics, Business Ethics, Ecology, Environmental Law, Social and Legal Environment of Business, Energy and the Environment, or Environmental Economics. Five or six academic departments are represented right there; perhaps the cases will prove sufficiently interesting to extend that range. These stories are not, after all, the private property of any academic elite or theoretical approach. They are, for better or worse, the property of all of us, as unwitting and unwilling indirect agents of their occurrence, and as heirs, with our children, of their consequences. We had best get to know them well.

NOTES ON THE TEXT

We have tried to keep all chapters to a length convenient for reading and discussing in the course of a single class assignment, concluding with some questions for reflection to encourage synthesis of the material and general insights on ethics and the environment and, if appropriate, a short list of books and articles for further reading. A more complete bibliography will be found after the Epilogue.

NOTES

1. Al Gore, *Earth in the Balance: Ecology and the Human Spirit* (Boston: Houghton Mifflin, 1992).

2. "Bush, in Reversal, Won't Seek Cut in Emissions of Carbon Dioxide," *New York Times,* 14 March 2001, p. A1. See also Douglas Jehl, "Bush Defends Emissions Stance: Ties His About-Face on Carbon Dioxide to an 'Energy Crisis' ", *New York Times,* 15 March 2001, p. A23; Letters column, *New York Times,* 16 March 2001; Andrew Revkin, "Bush's Shift Could Doom Air Pact, Some Say," *New York Times,* 17 March 2001, p. A7; Editorial, "Environmental Rollbacks," *New York Times,* 8 April 2001.

1

Of Greenhouses
and Freezers

The Perils of Global
Climate Change

INTRODUCTION: HOLLYWOOD AT ITS BEST

A helicopter freezes and falls from the sky; the pilot tries to get out and freezes solid, starting with his chin, as we watch. Northern Europe, Canada, and Siberia disappear. A chain of tornadoes devastates Los Angeles while a tidal wave engulfs New York City to the height of about 40 feet and then freezes under the endless snowfall. Timber wolves, escaped from the zoo, pursue three plucky teenagers around the wreckage of a frozen freighter while their companions wait anxiously in the New York Public Library, burning books. The president of the United States takes a long last look around the Oval Office and heads for Mexico, where his government huddles in exile, only to die in the storm. *Now* will you take global warming seriously?

The Day After Tomorrow, one of 2004's summer blockbusters, takes global warming and turns it into disaster-flick entertainment, coming in, on its opening weekend, only slightly behind *Shrek 2,* which was about an endearing green monster who lives in fairyland. Fairyland has always been far preferable to our own world, now and in the past, but the world that *The Day* pictures for our immediate future is horrible beyond measure. A new ice age begins, not with slowly dropping temperatures, but as a result of the disruption of the ocean currents caused by the growing percentage of greenhouse gases in the atmosphere. We had always expected that global "warming" would be just that—the slow upward creep of the average temperature of the latitudes of the earth until the temperate zones became tropical and the tundra turned balmy.

Not so: all we really know about the forces that can change our climate is that they will disrupt the patterns now in place, frustrate our expectations, and give us weather that we cannot predict from all our experience of human history (roughly the last 40,000 years, especially the last 10,000, since the beginning of agriculture). What do we humans tend to do when confronted with radical unpredictability? Nothing; we can't handle it. We retreat to absolute denial that it is happening (the Bush Administration's politically preferred response, in general[1]), or better yet, to fairyland, in the theater next door.

Is the science of *The Day After Tomorrow* valid? Not really. Radical changes in climate have been shown (from the ice cores drawn from Greenland and Antarctica, foregrounded at the beginning of the film) to occur in decades, or in less than a century. That's very fast. But ice ages do not come upon us overnight (or pursue young heroes down the halls of the library, giving hilariously changed meaning to the notion of "glacial" speed). How important is the warming trend, the steady move toward climate change? *National Geographic,* not given to science fiction and horror stories, devoted their September 2004 issue to global warming, at the political risk, acknowledged by the editor, of the canceled subscriptions of those in favor of the Bush Administration's response (or the retreat to fairyland).[2] What do we really know? Let us begin at the beginning.

THE CURRENT CONCERN
OVER GLOBAL WARMING

The "greenhouse effect" is the (imperfect) analogy used to explain the atmospheric phenomena that keep our planet warm enough to sustain life. Our atmosphere allows about half the incoming solar radiation to reach the earth's surface. The balance is either directly reflected back into space or absorbed and held (for a while). The energy that does get through is either bounced back as heat or is used to do work (e.g., photosynthesis and evaporation fuel our climate), degraded to heat energy, and then returned to the atmosphere. Here is where the greenhouse effect kicks in: some gases in the atmosphere, notably water vapor and carbon dioxide, have the capacity to hold onto that heat for a while, just as the glass panes in a greenhouse do. Without this heat-holding action the earth's surface would cool to about $-18°$ C ($-4°$ F) instead of maintaining an average temperature of $14°$ C ($57°$ F), and there would be no life as we know it. The current concern is not that the greenhouse effect exists—we wouldn't be here if it didn't—but that it is possibly being exacerbated by anthropogenic (man-made) increases in the effective gases, threatening a disruption to the equilibrium between incoming and outgoing energy and to average global warming. Carbon dioxide is the gas most at fault in the climate changes. Carbon is abundant in the biosphere and is the central element of all living things. Usually the carbon in the air, primarily in the form of carbon dioxide, is in balance with the stored carbon in the earth, especially in the woody stems of plants. Through photosynthesis, green plants from bacteria to California redwoods take carbon dioxide from the air, combine it with water, convert the mixture into various forms of carbohydrates consumed by the plant or stored in its stems and leaves, and release the extra oxygen into the air. Animals, including us, evolved well after this process was established. We live on the oxygen and consume the plants. As long as we just eat the fruits and leaves of the plants, as we did back when we were foragers, we will release no more carbon into the atmosphere than is taken up. Balance is achieved.

At various points during the evolution of plants, and of some of the early animals, whole bogs would sink, with all animals in them, down below the folds of the earth, and in the pressure of that earth, they would lose all but their carbon, or carbon attached to hydrogen only. These reservoirs of organic material, purified by pressure, became the concentrated fuels we know as coal, oil, and their accompaniment, natural gas (methane). All this remained locked in the earth, with no way of returning to the atmosphere.

But since the dawn of agriculture, humans have been adding carbon, hence carbon dioxide, to the atmosphere through deforestation (releasing the stored carbon in the trees) and the burning of wood and charcoal. (To be sure, forest fires have been around since there were forests, but they tend to flash through major groves, consuming understory brush and leaving most of the carbon locked in the standing trunks of living or dead trees—and they were nowhere as persistent as humans.) Just from that, the balance was upset, but the wood and charcoal burning by less than a million humans worldwide was unlikely to cause any major climate damage. The Industrial Revolution changed all that.

Since the beginning of the factories, when the world had just acquired its billionth human being, humankind has been adding tremendously to the natural amounts of carbon dioxide entering the atmosphere, primarily through the burning of those fossil fuels, locked in the earth and inaccessible until a little over a century ago. In 1988, atmospheric scientist James Hansen surprised the world, including the scientific world, by concluding that "this evidence is pretty strong that the greenhouse effect is here"; since then, more evidence has been pouring in that the planet is warming, and warming very quickly.[3] For instance, in early 2002, a chunk of the Antarctic ice shelf the size of Rhode Island broke off and drifted into the ocean; Dr. Theodore A. Scambos, a glaciologist at the National Snow and Ice Data Center, told the *New York Times* that it was probably the effect of global warming.[4] The ice shelf, Larsen B, 1,200 square miles, had disintegrated and collapsed in only 35 days, a rate of decay not seen in 12,000 years. Careful studies of the ranges of birds and animals show that they are already responding to global warming by shifting toward the poles—at a rate of about 4 miles per decade. Spring events—nesting, mating, and migrating—are happening 2 days earlier per decade.[5]

By the end of 2003, the American Geophysical Union had issued a position statement that concluded, "Scientific evidence strongly indicates that natural influences cannot explain the rapid increase in global near-surface temperatures observed during the second half of the twentieth century."[6] In the same month, two prominent U.S. government scientists, Dr. Thomas Karl of the National Atmospheric and Oceanic Administration (NOAA) and Dr. Kevin Trenberth of the National Center for Atmospheric Research, concluded not only that human causes accounted for the rise in global temperature but also that "in the absence of climate mitigation policies...the likely result is more frequent heat waves, droughts, extreme precipitation events and related impacts... wildfires, heat stress, vegetation changes and sea-level rise."[7] The next month, a 19-member research team prepared a report for *Nature* on the danger of mass extinctions, concluding that more than a million species could be extinct or nearly so by the middle of the twenty-first century unless rapid countermeasures were taken.[8] The American West could dry out completely, as the snowpack decreases and the spring runoff begins earlier.[9]

The NOAA 2003 climate report confirmed that 2003 equaled 2002 as the second hottest year on record, trailing 1998. The five hottest years on record are all since 1997, and the ten hottest are all since 1990. The stakes are getting higher: extreme heat events killed 20,000 in Europe and 1,500 people in India during 2003.[10]

Can anything be done about it? James Hansen, Director of the NASA Goddard Institute for Space Studies, he who startled the scientific world with his global-warming claims in 1988, remains optimistic. The human race can stop the warming, but we have to act now. We must improve our energy efficiency and increase our use of renewable energy sources, and we must not delay—even a one-degree Celsius increase could trigger the beginning of the end of the Greenland ice sheet, releasing enormous amounts of fresh water into the North Atlantic.[11] And that, as we recall, was the beginning of the end of the Northern Hemisphere in *The Day After Tomorrow.*

So the data are there—the greenhouse is closing in on us. No miraculous reversal has come to our aid. The next questions are, what would be the consequences of uncontrolled global warming (in addition to the Ice Age chasing us down the halls of the New York Public Library...) and how can we get a grip on the causes of global warming in the United States? We will examine these issues and conclude with a consideration of the problems and promises of the Kyoto Protocol.

THE LITANY OF DISASTER

The predicted consequences of global warming are, by now, known well: From the warming alone, we can expect flooded coastal areas due to melting glaciers and an increase in ocean volume not only from the addition of fresh water from the melting ice caps but also because, like many other substances, water expands as it gets warmer. The level of the sea will rise. Not surprisingly, the world's island nations (the Seychelles, for instance) are the most vociferous advocates of reducing greenhouse gases. We should recall that 25 percent of the world's population lives less than 1.1 meters above sea level. (In our own country, the city of New Orleans has similar concerns.)

Beyond the simple warming and melting, we can expect some of the unpredictability suggested in *The Day,* and we may look for increased frequency and severity of storms, droughts, heat waves, as well as changes in precipitation that cause floods. This flooding effect may already have begun; it is difficult to track because deforestation, which also causes global warming, is the most immediate cause of floods. When the trees that anchor the soil are gone, the rest of the organic matter goes too; the next heavy rain simply courses down the slopes where they once stood with nothing to absorb or stop it. That causes the floods.

The dwellers in the affected zones will also change. We may look for an increase in tropical diseases in temperate zones due to migration of insect vectors. We expect changes in ecosystems and therefore, as noted earlier, species extinctions due to changes to habitat. We expect "bleaching" of the coral reefs—the strange loss of color, due to loss of symbiotic algae, of reefs around the world. Indeed this prediction is already a reality: the reefs are bleaching worldwide. One of the healthiest reefs off the Dutch Island, Bonaire near Venezuela, is now bleached; and the International Society for Reef Studies has found the "most geographically widespread bleaching ever recorded." Coral reef bleaching has been observed "all over the Caribbean." It is strongly suspected to extend to the oceanic reefs.[12]

But predictions and forecasts about climate are difficult, some say impossible, because of its complexity and natural variability. For example, the data for the late 1990s are certainly complicated by the El Niño and La Niña effects on temperature. Also, consider the consequences of positive feedbacks, such as warmer temperature = more evaporation = more water vapor (potent greenhouse influence) = more warming. D. Rind, in the journal *Science* comments, "Climate, like weather, will likely always be complex: determinism in the midst of chaos, unpredictability in the midst of understanding."[13]

Meanwhile, although we have no way of knowing the cause, frog populations are declining in Costa Rica, 59 bird species in southern Britain have changed their range, 34 butterfly species in Europe have changed their range, the Mexican Jay in Arizona has an earlier breeding season, and the Michigan wolf and moose populations are in decline. For that matter, reindeer, moose, deer and caribou populations are declining in Canada, Norway, the United Kingdom, the United States, and Greenland.

Diseases are also spreading, in patterns that would be predicted with a warming climate. Marine sickness in the oceans is increasing, "from sardines to seals," and human tropical diseases are moving both north and south.[14] The models that predicted the spread of malaria are being verified. Since 1990, outbreaks "have occurred during hot spells in Texas, Florida, Georgia, Michigan, New Jersey, and New York."[15] Dengue fever, another tropical disease that affects 50–100 million people, has now been identified in Buenos Aires and northern Australia. Factors other than global warming can change the range of the disease vectors, changes in mosquito control policies, for example, but, "The case for a climatic contribution becomes stronger however, when other projected consequences of global warming appear in concert with disease outbreaks."[16]

Of course, the trick is to prove that these events *are* caused by an increase in greenhouse gases and resultant warming rather than by naturally occurring events. One lab experiment does support the connection between coral bleaching and carbon dioxide buildup, showing that increased concentration of the gas inhibited a reef's growth, thereby making it more vulnerable to other threats.[17]

One of the most influential studies about the consequences of global warming to the United States was released in June 2000. The study, commissioned by Congress, was conducted by scientists from government agencies, universities, private organizations, and industry; and had 300 independent reviewers. Predictions include Atlanta summers in New York City and Houston summers in Atlanta, increased crops in some farmlands, decreased in others, decreased salmon migration, less snow in California, increased storms and coastal erosion, and a longer shipping period in Alaska as lanes stay open.[18] But the uncertainties remain, says Thomas Karl, co-chair of the committee of experts: "We don't say we *know* there's going to be catastrophic drought in Kansas. . . . What we do say is 'Here's the range of our uncertainties.' "[19] Indeed one climate model used in the study predicted drier soil in the Midwest over the next century, another predicted wetter soil.[20] Bob Herbert, in an op-ed in the *New York Times,* commenting on that study, suggested that some "benefits" could accrue to the United States because of global warming (maybe I could grow oranges in my back yard, say).[21] But Michael Oppenheimer, a senior scientist at Environmental Defense, warns that regardless of some temporary benefits, the climate will continue to warm, so that "today's winners are likely to be tomorrow's losers. . . ." and that "Global Warming is a problem that cannot be looked at from the point of view of a few individuals in a few isolated places. . . . If the climate in general is hurting large swatches of humanity. . . there is no way any particular group. . . can escape from what is happening in the world as a whole. We are too interconnected for that."[22]

Climatologists have long predicted that global warming would be most evident at the poles; the data have supported that prediction. Antarctica has gotten the most attention over the years, presumably because it was already in the public eye because of the yearly appearance of the "ozone hole" (a gap in the stratospheric ozone layer appearing each spring over Antarctica, apparently caused by chlorofluorocarbons from our refrigerators and air conditioners). And sure enough, while the global average temperature has increased by more than 1° F since the Industrial Revolution, the average temperature in Antarctica has risen 5° F in the last 50 years.[23] Large chunks of ice have been breaking off glacial shelves over the last decade. Such events do not affect sea-level rise, because these ice masses are already in the water, *but* the West Antarctic ice sheet is considered unstable; the possibility of its breaking off into the ocean causes grave concern about sea-level rise and coastal flooding.[24]

Changes in the Antarctic scene are not limited to ice cover, however. In the last 25 years the Adelies penguins have declined from 15,200 breeding pairs to 9,200. Their prey, as well as the prey of whales and seals is krill, the larvae of which live at the bottom of the ice. The loss of krill due to diminishing ice could wreak havoc in the food chain that leads from algae to krill to penguins to seals to the mighty whales.[25]

Meanwhile, in the Arctic, the ice has been getting thinner and the water warmer, as noted earlier. An old hand at Arctic research is reported to have exclaimed, "Oh my God, where did all the ice go?" when his research vessel arrived at the expected latitude. It should have been at 71°–72° N, and they didn't see it until they reached 75° N. NASA Goddard Space Flight Center reports that the Arctic sea ice declined by more than 5 percent between 1978 and 1998. That won't raise the sea level, of course, since the Arctic ice is already floating in the ocean. (When the ice melts in your drink, it doesn't overflow.) But one concern, as an example of positive feedbacks, is the albedo effect, the reflection of sunlight by the ice. With melting ice and more exposed ocean, the oceans absorb more of the light and warms accordingly, affecting currents and weather and increasing the melting.[26] Another concern is "Arctic oscillation": pressure changes over the North Pole that result in increased winds that tend to break up more ice. John Wallace, a meteorologist at the University of Washington predicts that if the trend continues "we may be on the verge of an ice free Arctic Ocean in the summer."[27] A number of observers doubt that the Arctic changes can be due to natural causes. One has found that the probability of the ice decrease being caused by natural variability is less than 2 percent for the last 20 years, another that the chance of ice loss since 1993 being of natural origin is 0.1 percent.[28]

Besides the poles, attention is also being paid to Greenland, the ice sheet of which contains a large part of the planet's fresh water. Since the Greenland ice sheet is entirely on land, any melting will indeed cause the sea level to rise; in fact, "if the whole ice sheet were to melt, sea level would rise by 7 m."[29] Recent NASA studies show that whereas the central high-altitude regions remain fairly constant, the low-altitude edges of the sheet (the margins) have been thinning "by almost 300mm annually, primarily due to increased melting . . . changes that are contributing to rising sea levels.[30]

Yes, but why isn't the whole situation worse than it is? Underscoring the unpredictability of the changes in the global climate is the mysterious mismatch between the amount of carbon produced and the amount we can find. We can measure (within a fair guesstimate) how much carbon dioxide we throw into the atmosphere each year; we know, sort of, how much "greenhousing" that amount should do; and we can measure the temperature. From the beginning of global-warming awareness, there have been major discrepancies between the amount of carbon dioxide we produce through burning fossil fuels, the amount of carbon dioxide in the atmosphere, and the amount of warming that should have been produced because of the accumulating greenhouse gases.

Given the amount of carbon dioxide and other greenhouse gases that we pump into the atmosphere, very little atmospheric warming has been observed, only a little more than 1° F. Climate modelers have hypothesized that much of the warming has been trapped in the oceans, but that's hard to prove. Now a definitive study of millions of ocean measurements taken over many years has demonstrated that the world's ocean basins have warmed an average of 0.06° C between 1955 and 1995, close to the increase that had been predicted. These findings imply that the heat stored in the oceans will eventually reach the atmosphere, perhaps resulting in an increase of the upper level of predictions to 4.5° C by the year 2100.[31]

And where has all the carbon dioxide gone? One estimate is that less than half the carbon dioxide emitted by human activity remains in the atmosphere, the rest is stored either in the land or the water. But this buffering effect has its limits:

> Oceans and forests are absorbing, at least for now, roughly half of the eight billion tons of carbon that humanity is pouring into the atmosphere each year. Even photosynthesizing bacteria living in a New Zealand thermal pool do their part absorbing CO_2.... The continued ability of sinks to absorb carbon may vanish if global warming persists. Higher water temperatures would reduce the ability of oceans to dissolve CO_2, limiting the carbon available to phytoplankton, the aquatic plants that begin the food chain for creatures ranging from whales to sea urchins.... Increased odds of drought and fire threaten the health of terrestrial sinks like a cedar forest.... With rising temperatures, decomposition would quicken, releasing carbon faster from [decaying animal and vegetable matter].[32]

NATIONAL POLICY OPTIONS

What can, or should, the United States attempt to do, on a policy level, about global climate change? There seem to be four answers available in national conversations, which can be summed up as (a) in effect, nothing; (b) not much; (c) lots; and (d) don't try to solve anything on the national level—re-engage with the Kyoto Protocol and the Kyoto process to define concerted global action.

Let's take a look at these options. In the discussion that follows, options (a), (b), and (d), derive in large part from (and echo the tone of) a 2004 Council on Foreign Relations Policy Initiative, *Climate Change: Debating America's Policy Options,* by David Victor.[33]

Making a Market for Climate Protection

We are a nation that believes, strongly, in the free-market system and the liberty of individuals and corporations to choose those courses of action that will maximize their economic welfare on the market. (We believe that if everyone makes such choices, and competition is allowed to flourish, everyone will become wealthier, or at least as wealthy as he or she can get in a free society.) The Kyoto framework is unrealistic at least in part because it seeks to impose a governmental authoritative top-down structure on the workings of the free market, an effort doomed to failure. The best way to build a regulatory system is bottom-up, essentially by educating the rest of the world to adopt a new form of "currency"—the emissions quotas that can be transferred at will across borders, permitting economies that are growing more slowly to raise capital by selling quotas to economies in sturdy growth. Most important, we must establish this regime in the United States first, so that we may experiment with the provisions and market mechanisms and find the ones that work. Given the incentives to reduce pollution contained in such a system, whatever problems there may be with greenhouse gases (this model does not dwell on the science or consequences of the warming process) will be well on their way to solution as the rest of the world joins us. At no point will any player in the solution be asked to sacrifice vital interests or in fact to do anything except maximize return on investment. This course has the advantage of preserving the free market, preserving freedom of action for the United States, and cementing alliances with economic forces throughout the world. It is highly innovative and presents the appearance of decisive action. It has the disadvantage of causing annoyance to those who believe in authoritative solutions, and it is sufficiently complex as to present the risk of politically embarrassing failure.

Adaptation and Innovation

The following suggestion modifies the previous one's reliance on free-market innovations. After all, the federal government is not entirely helpless or lacking in influence amid the operations of the free market. Possibilities for stimulating innovation and adaptation exist within the free-enterprise system. Mechanisms embedded in systems of taxation and subsidy can provide incentives for change in the direction of cleaner technologies. The science of climate change is not sufficiently certain to justify large investments in emissions control or indeed any remedial devices, but there is no harm in encouraging voluntary programs to reduce emissions and providing some financial incentives to develop innovative technologies. Innovative approaches may be tried that will allow an industry to continue emissions at its present rate if it will (for instance) pay Bolivia to preserve a portion of its rainforest to balance the carbon in the atmosphere. The statement of this position adds the assumption, that if climate change does take place, it will be no more drastic than other variations in the weather that we have absorbed over the generations; no serious concern or redirection is warranted. This course has the advantages of minimal disruption of economic activity, and it focuses on U.S. interests only; "it does not attempt to appeal to wooly notions of international justice by speculating about the dangers of climate change in developing countries"[34] Its major disadvantage is that, in effect, it doesn't do anything. Unfriendly commentators might describe its burden as "let them eat pollution."[35] Allies, working on controls of their own, might be annoyed to find that the largest supplier of emissions has no intention of adding its efforts. Worse yet, if climate change does have demonstrably untoward results, an administration that has dismissed the dangers as negligible will have lost the credibility necessary to impose the controls that will turn polluting industries around in midstride and start toward a solution to the problem.

The Manhattan Project Approach

On this approach, the problem of climate change must be reconceived, taken from the lap of the gods and seen as a problem created by human conduct—amounting to a vast unconsented experiment with human and environmental health, which is best reversed immediately. To that end, an appropriately radical initiative, along the lines of the Manhattan Project that produced the atomic bomb in the 1930s and early 1940s, must be undertaken, enlisting all of the American people in the effort. Taxes on carbon should be levied immediately, to the point where it becomes economically advantageous for people to purchase smaller homes, to secure better insulation for their drafty houses, and to abandon their SUVs once and for all in favor of smaller cars, preferably hybrids. Conservation and recycling measures should become part of the daily round of American life, encouraged by subsidies for the use of recycled materials and taxes on the use of virgin materials. Conservation of paper, and encouragement of the use of post-consumer-waste recycled paper, should spare the remaining forests in the Western Hemisphere for their historic function of sequestering carbon dioxide. Subsidies should bolster our infant solar electricity and wind power industries. A goal should be set, of replacing one half of our use of fossil fuels with alternative energy sources by 2020, and of replacing all fossil fuel use by 2050. Meeting that goal will require a substantial engineering of the family car and the factory, but in hydrogen cell technology, assuming that the hydrogen is obtained by electrolysis of water and not from natural gas, that engineering can be accomplished—indeed, already has been. Right now hydrogen cell technology is not economical for general use, but appropriate incentives will make it so. By 2075, disregarding a few backyard barbecues on Saturday night, we may be close to an emissions-free society. That will not solve every problem in the world—other nations may still be contributing to the greenhouse gases—but at least the United States will not be contributing to the problem. There should be no reason why we cannot at that point sell the technology we have developed to other nations that need it, creating an enormous number of jobs in the new energy economy, and end with a society that is as prosperous as it is healthy. The advantage to this course is that it gets the job done, by the time-tested method of enlisting the collective energies of an informed and inspired public. This is the sort of thing that Americans are best at. The disadvantage is that there will be political storms to rival those of *The Day After Tomorrow* in the process of getting the measures in place. The process of change will, admittedly, call forth a level of political leadership that has not been seen for a while, but the result will be worth the attempt.

CAN INTERNATIONAL AGREEMENTS
COOL OFF THE GREENHOUSE?

The fourth alternative moves the nation back to the global community to address the problem. At one level, after all, there is little point to relying on state or federal law to solve a global problem. To be sure, the slowing of U.S. emissions, especially from our vast herd of SUVs and our huge midwestern power plants, will have to be part of any solution. But the first step should be to get a global handle on the problem, a global strategy that every nation in the world can implement, a concerted effort in which we Americans may join.

There are several advantages to concerted action. First, a commitment to act in concert permits the recruitment of the best scientists and engineers in the world to establish the scientific dimensions of the problem and design approaches that will actually solve it. Second, however long and arduous the process of solution may be, the knowledge that other nations are participating in the effort—at the least, not sabotaging it by increasing their own emissions to match any U.S. decreases—will make it politically easier for the citizens of all nations to accept whatever sacrifices are necessary. Third, in the end, there will be no significant lowering of emissions unless all nations participate; even now, rapid industrial development in China, for instance, threatens to dwarf any U.S. and European efforts to get emissions under control.

Yes, but in this fractious world, can global agreements ever work? Sometimes they can.

Typical of international agreements that might be developed to address the problems of global warming is the Montreal Protocol, designed to halt the destruction of the ozone layer. The Kyoto Protocol, adopted many years after Montreal, was designed on the same model to control greenhouse gases. The problems are very similar, on the surface at least—both have to do with climatic and atmospheric changes that are truly global in nature—the documents apparently addressed them sensibly, but one seems to be working and one does not. It is too simple to blame the Bush administration for refusing to cooperate with Kyoto. Let's take a look at both global initiatives and see what may have determined the difference.[36]

The Montreal Protocol on Substances that Deplete the Ozone Layer took effect on January 1, 1989, after some years of negotiations. It has been amended at least five times since then, to permit inclusion of special circumstances. Essentially, the signatories agreed to limit and then end the manufacture and sale of the chlorofluorocarbons (CFCs) that had been found to cause the deterioration of the ozone layer (with all manner of qualifications to permit small producers to continue manufacture as necessary for development). In general, it worked, although given the uncertainties of data on the ozone layer we will have to wait for a few more years for the victory party. The protocol had certain things going for it: the CFCs had a few sources, easily identifiable, and their manufacturers were actively seeking (and finding) products that could be substituted for the CFCs. As a result, the Montreal Protocol had little political opposition. The governments were moderately interested in implementing the agreements, and the citizens had no reason or means to oppose. The practice of manufacturing and selling CFCs was modified in the boardroom; the customers had no choice but to accept the substitute.

Greenhouse gases are not like this. The technology of change for greenhouse gases is far more difficult and diffuse and will be harder to develop. The Kyoto Protocol, developed in early December 1997 pursuant to the Framework Convention on Climate Change constructed in Rio de Janeiro in 1992, attempted to secure agreements to bring the emissions of greenhouse gases back to 1990 levels in the developed nations. Less developed nations were held to a different standard, to allow them to develop their industrial capacity. To cut emissions in this country, we would have to force all our overage coal-burning plants to install new technology or emission control devices; we would have to cut emissions from our automobiles by 20 percent; we would have to cut back on the use of inefficient diesel engines, which comprise the bulk of our construction equipment. The economic impact would be real, and felt by everyone. Especially sensitive areas, like the make, weight, and use of the family automobile, would be especially heavily affected. Citizens would be directly in the line of its fire. The Kyoto Protocol was a political bombshell the moment it hit the table, and an oil-friendly administration's decision to pretend that it isn't there is entirely understandable.

An agreement to decrease the noise, size, and operation of automobiles is unacceptable in the developed world, or at least, citizen acquiescence is going to be problematic. In the developing world, governments profiting hugely from environmentally destructive operations may be disinclined to enforce regimes they see as imposed upon them. Recall that states have power over their citizens only to the extent that they can deliver the goods. Control of distribution of natural resources is part of that power. Agreeing to conserve the resources *or* allowing foreigners to dictate the nature and pace of their distribution, by themselves, will significantly cut that power. Not even the developed nations can institute new systems of property rights, not without a fight. And there are indicators that Kyoto, especially, may be on the wrong side of every political agenda imaginable. China, for one, has pledged to its prospering citizens, long restricted to bicycles, that they will be an automobile nation soon. That means paving over cropland, which until now has absorbed carbon dioxide (while feeding its citizens), with the miles of roads and parking lots that will be required, manufacturing most of the automobiles in factories that historically have not been environmentally friendly, and then turning thousands, no, millions of cars loose on the new roads to foul the air. Persuading Americans of the value of small green cars and low-emissions manufacturing may be a piece of cake compared to persuading the Chinese.

How, generally, are international agreements supposed to be enforced? There simply are no international law enforcement mechanisms that can be imposed as a matter of right on unwilling people. One enforcement mechanism is trade sanctions, which could in theory be spelled out in the original agreement. If all-purpose sanctions can be used against "rogue" states to limit their nuclear capability, surely they can be used to enforce environmental agreements. It should be noted that trade sanctions are not very effective. In fifty years of trying, the U.S. has not been able to bring down the communist government of Cuba by the most severe embargoes. Indeed, it has been argued, that trade sanctions only made that government stronger and more popular with its people. The World Trade Organization has shown itself to be effective to some extent in enforcing the reduction of subsidies and of import quotas and tariffs as barriers to trade, but only among nations that have a strong interest in the furthering of that trade.

The rest of the enforcement would probably be carried out by CSOs (civil society organizations), also called NGOs (nongovernmental organizations), through publicity, demonstration, boycott, sit-in, and whatever other means might occur. In the absence of world government, we will have government by Greenpeace. The result could be messy.

It may be too soon to write off Kyoto, even as Europe falls behind in meeting its commitments and the United States withdraws from the process altogether. In a plenary address to the American Association for the Advancement of Science at their annual meeting in Seattle, Washington, on February 13, 2004, Sir David King, the chief scientific adviser to the British government, emphasized that the international community has to work together to reduce carbon emissions and, as quickly as possible, develop alternative energy sources to the burning of fossil fuels. He pointed out that lowering emissions is not necessarily bad for the economy: "Between 1990 and 2000, Great Britain's economy grew by 30 percent, employment increased by 4.8 percent, and our greenhouse gas emissions intensity fell by 30 percent."[37] John Browne, Lord Browne of Madingley, Group Chief Executive of the British Petroleum Company PLC, argues similarly that although climate change is a frightening possibility, it is entirely possible to reduce emissions without losing economic strength. Kyoto, therefore, could be viewed as a process, not a product, a general and future-oriented move toward greater efficiency, greater cooperation, and greater wisdom in forecasting effects—a move that can survive a few fits and starts.

CONCLUSION

In many ways, the problem of global warming (or, if one prefers, the problem of unpredictable ice-age acceleration) is a classic environmental problem, on the model of the Reserve Mining case of the 1970s, in which vast amounts of sand and gravel were dumped into Lake Superior, tailings from a beneficiation enterprise to extract usable iron from low-grade ore. The tailings, which may have contained asbestos, left a plume of matter in the lake, which serves as water supply for many cities. The situation was undesirable, but was it dangerous? The case was in and out of court for years, eventuating in a decision that the company could no longer dump its tailings in the lake.[38] But all the issues were there. The company was carrying on business in standard ways, obeying all laws, not doing anything accepted as harmful to public health or safety. The organizations that monitor the lake complained that all sorts of invisible damage were being done to the ecosystem. There was no lawful way to resolve the matter, so it stayed in the courts for years. What finally resolved it was a judge-made change in the burden of proof. Until that point in the legal proceedings, the assumption had been that the company had a perfect right to dump its tailings in the lake unless it could be shown that it was doing damage. Afterward the assumption was that a lake has a right not to be dumped into unless the company can show that its operations are safe, for the public health, for the trout fry, for the future of the entire Great Lakes. In a sense, this case ushered the Precautionary Principle, made famous in the Rio Declaration, into American law.

What would that principle do to the greenhouse gas problem? It would require that all greenhouse gas–emitting operations be closed down immediately and not permitted to start up again until they could prove that no substance for which they could be held responsible would damage public health or the environment, now or in the future. It would be a long time before that could be proved. Until that time, we are left with our own very imperfect political process to discern the problems, articulate them, and engage the national dialogue in their solution.

QUESTIONS FOR REFLECTION

1. How should we balance the need for economic progress, or at least stability, and the large but uncertain threats of climate change?

2. Why is the effect of global warming on the poles so worrisome?

3. Suppose it could be shown that global warming would hurt no human being but that half the other mammalian species in the world, unable to adapt to changed conditions, would slowly die out and become extinct. Would that be enough reason to take drastic action to slow global warming?

4. What can we, as human beings living in the the world, do to make international agreements more effective?

NOTES

1. However, attitudinal change has been observed. See Andrew C. Revkin, "U.S. Report, in Shift, Turns Focus to Greenhouse Gases," *New York Times,* 26 August 2004, p. A18. Stay tuned.

2. See From the Editor.

3. Richard A. Kerr, "Hansen vs. the World on the Greenhouse Threat," *Science* (June 1989): 1041.

4. *New York Times,* 20 March 2002, p. A1. More information can be found at the NSIDC website.

5. Terry L. Root, "Fingerprints of Global Warming on Wild Animals and Plants," *Nature* 42 (January 2003): 7–42.

6. American Geophysical Union, "Human Impacts on Climate," 16 December 2003.

7. Thomas Karl and Kevin Trenberth, "Modern Global Climate Change," *Science* 302 (December 2003): 1719–23.

8. "Extinction Risk from Climate Change," *Nature* 427 (January 2004):145–48.

9. "As the West Goes Dry," *Science* 303 (February 2004): 1124–127.

10. NOAA annual climate report for 2003; NOAA, January 2004.

11. James Hansen, "Defusing the Global Warming Time Bomb," *Scientific American* (March 2004).

12. Janet Raloff, "Sea Sickness," *Science News* 155 (January 1999): 72, and "White-out," *Scientific American* (April 1999): 30.

13. Daniel Rind, "Complexity and Climate," *Science* 284 (April 1999): 105. See also, Richard Monastersky, "Fickle Climate Thwarts Future Forecasts," *Science News* 155 (February 1999): 133, and Richard A. Kerr, "Big El Niños Ride the Back of Slower Climate Change," *Science* 283 (February 1999): 1108.

14. Jason Dick, "Global Warming," *Amicus Journal* (Winter 2000): 13.

15. Loc. cit.

16. Paul R. Epstein, "Is Global Warming Harmful to Health?" *Scientific American* (August 2000): 50.

17. Richard Monastersky, "Carbon Dioxide Buildup Harms Coral Reef," *Science News* 155 (April 1999): 214.

18. Andrew C. Revkin, "Warming's Effects to Permeate U.S.," *New York Times,* 12 June 2000, p. A1.

19. Loc. cit.

20. Richard A. Kerr, "Dueling Models: Future U.S. Climate Uncertain," *Science* 288 (June 2000): 2113.

21. Bob Herbert, "Cold Facts of Global Warming," *New York Times,* 10 July 2000, p. A19.

22. Oppenheimer, quoted in ibid.

23. David Helvarg, "On Thin Ice," *Sierra,* November–December, 1999, p. 38.

24. Richard Monastersky, "Disappearing Ice Down South, *Science News* 155 (April 1999): 271, and "Plumbing Antarctica for Climate Clues," *Science News* 156 (November 1999). For a detailed discussion of the West Antarctic Ice Sheet, see Michael Oppenheimer, "Global Warming and the Stability of the West Antarctic Ice Sheet," *Nature* 393 (April 1998): 325.

25. Henry Fountain, "Two Gigantic Icebergs Break Free from the Antarctic Ice Cap," *New York Times,* 11 April 2000.

26. Richard Monastersky, "Sea Change in the Arctic," *Science News* 55 (February 1999): 104.

27. Quoted in Richard A. Kerr, "A New Force in High-Latitude Climate," *Science* 284 (April 1999): 241.

28. "Skating on Thinning Ice," *Science* 286 (December 1999): 1813, and Richard A. Kerr, "Will the Arctic Ocean Lose All Its Ice?" *Science* 286 (December 1999): 1817. (For more information on the topic, see "Understanding Earth's Dynamic," *Science* 288 (June 2000): 1983–2007.

29. Dorthe Dahl-Jensen, "The Greenland Ice Sheet Reacts," *Science* 289 (July 2000): 404.

30. Stephen Perkins, "Greenland's Ice Is Thinner at the Margins," *Science News* 158 (July 2000): 54.

31. Richard A. Kerr, "Globe's 'Missing Warming' Found in the Ocean," *Science* 287 (March 2000): 2126.

32. Tim Appenzeller, "The Case of the Missing Carbon," *National Geographic* (February 2004): 92–117.

33. New York: Council on Foreign Relations, 2004. The Council on Foreign Relations actually presents only options (a), (b), and (d), considering option (c) to be unrealistic or politically undesirable. Possibly mindful of the Bush Administration's difficulties in crafting sentences in English, the volume helpfully provides the president with a memorandum outlining the choices, and three speeches, one for each favored alternative, just waiting to be blown up on a teleprompter. Our discussion of (c) is drawn from many sources, some of them contributory to Chapter 9 in this text, on alternative energy.

34. Ibid., p. 68.

35. Ibid., p. 69.

36. The sources for this discussion are United Nations documents, primarily from the United Nations Environment Programme.

37. David King, "Global Warming: The Imperatives for Action from the Science of Climate Change," *Science* (January 2004).

38. You can read all about the case in the first edition of *Watersheds,* published in 1990.

2

Genetically Modified Organisms

The Complex Difficulties of Frankenfood

INTRODUCTION: A HUNGRY WORLD

Shelley Hurt, in the Spring–Summer 2004 issue of the *Miller Center Report,* presents the central paradox of the conflict over the introduction of genetically modified organisms (GMOs) into the food supply, referred to generally as the GMO wars: Plantings of genetically modified crops have increased from 4.2 million acres in 6 countries in 1996 to 109.2 million acres in 13 countries in 2000, a 26-fold increase in 5 years; in the United States, plantings have increased from 3.7 million acres in 1996 to 74.9 million acres in 2000, a 20-fold increase.[1] In 2003, 140 million acres of genetically modified crops were planted in the United States alone. These are the crops that are supposed to feed the world. Yet during that same period, according to a November 2003 United Nations Food and Agriculture Organization (FAO) report, chronic hunger increased significantly, to afflict more than 842 million persons worldwide.[2] The problem is not rapidly expanding population. The population of the world has grown, but a report from the Institute for Food and Development Policy attests that "during the past 35 years, 'per capita food production has outstripped population growth by 15 percent,' and the UN's FAO states that the world has produced enough food to feed the growing world population since 1974."[3] So why are people still hungry? The problem is serious—as President Jimmy Carter pointed out, "There can be no peace until people have enough to eat"[4]—and it is tragically ironic, as the United States tries diets and surgery and magic to lose weight in a nation increasingly obese.

There is clearly a failure, a major life and death failure, in distribution of food worldwide; the painful suggestion is that GMOs are contributing to this failure rather than working toward its remedy.

The story that follows finds itself on the strange interface between the American business system, the world's production of food, and the age-old hubris that insists that Nature can be conquered, packaged, and bought and sold for the purposes of the human conquerors. There are times when the conquest has worked, more times that it has not, and the GMO controversy may turn out to be the cautionary tale for our time.

LAW AND ORDER:
THE PROSECUTOR'S TALE

Nowhere is American business less attractive than when it goes on the offensive against an individual farmer. There is no logical reason why that should be so; the farmer is a businessman like any other, one who just happens to make his profits off the sale of the produce of his land. Every American business has the right to carry on its affairs and seek its profits, within legal limits. So what is morally objectionable about a bank, with a loan in default, seizing the collateral for that loan, even if that collateral is a farmer's land? It's just that every time the bank forecloses on the poor farmer's home, as portrayed so poignantly in, for instance, *Grapes of Wrath,* we want, all of us, to tear the banker into very small shreds. It must be something about the way the scene is played out in those movies. Or maybe it's something about the human relationship to the land, the rooted relationship that has evolved for more than 10,000 years, which at some deep level does not recognize the power of a piece of paper from an alien commercial system. The GMO story of recent years starts with prosecutions that throw into question the profound relationship of the farmer to his land and to his crops and that place American business in a very strange position. Most important, they call into question the customary operations of the natural world, and place the integrity of all ecosystems in jeopardy. If the preservation of the work of natural systems is part of our concern, we will have to pay attention to the curious saga of agricultural DNA and its legal owners. Let us begin with the tale of Percy Schmeiser.

Percy Schmeiser has been a farmer for more than 50 years in Bruno, Saskatchewan, Canada, raising rapeseed, or canola, from which derives a very useful vegetable oil. In October 2002 he and his wife Louise celebrated their fiftieth wedding anniversary; that's about how long they had been operating that farm. He is well known in his community, and well liked, serving as mayor of the town of Bruno from 1966 to 1983 and later as a member of the legislative assembly for his district. He was a conventional, scientific farmer, using chemicals as they seemed to be useful and studying his crop of canola each year to identify the best plants from which the next year's seed would be saved, as farmers have done for millennia. He never bought Monsanto, Inc. canola seed, which had been genetically modified to withstand spraying with Roundup Ready, a popular herbicide; he had no need or desire for it.[5]

In 1998 Monsanto suspected that Schmeiser might have planted its Roundup Ready canola, because a farmer in his general area had reported that after Schmeiser had sprayed with Roundup (prior to planting that year's crop), canola plants remained standing in or near his fields. (Unattractive footnote: Monsanto rewarded farmers who "snitched" on their neighbors who had "stolen" Monsanto seed.) Promptly, Monsanto employees entered Schmeiser's property and without permission took samples of suspicious plants. Sure enough, some of them turned out to carry the patented DNA that Monsanto owned. So Monsanto sued Percy Schmeiser for infringement of patent. It alleged that Schmeiser had illegally purchased Roundup Ready seed from local farmers in 1997 (instead of purchasing directly from Monsanto, as its contracts required) and then saved some of that seed for the 1998 crop. It didn't want much from the aging farmer: just $205,000 in legal fees, $105,000 in profits that Schmeiser must have made on the crop, $13,500 ($15 an acre) for technology fees, and $25,000 in punitive damages—about $400,000 in all.

What had happened? Well, seeds blow around. Given the geography and weather of Saskatchewan, Percy Schmeiser had no difficulty figuring out what must have happened. The wind blows all the time up there, especially in the winter. The ground freezes over, becomes a sheet of ice, and anything that's loose on the ground—like seed spilled from a truck, or from the neighbor's harvester—blows until it hits an obstacle, and that might be 100 miles. In Schmeiser's case, 100 miles was not necessary: his neighbor (probably the person that turned him in) had bought seed from Monsanto in 1997 and grown canola in fields bordering Schmeiser's, with not so much as a fence separating them.[6]

All the GMO canola found on Schmeiser's property was growing in ditches along the sides of fields (natural resting places for windblown seed) and in the field immediately bordering those ditches. It wasn't rocket science to figure out how it got there, and if this had been a standard case in torts, alleging intentional wrongdoing, Schmeiser would probably have prevailed. But patent law is unique. It was specifically created in the nineteenth century for cases in which many inventors were working on the same problem. The first person who solved the problem would run to the patent office with a diagram of the solution and would be awarded the sole right to make a profit on the device (or method, or whatever) for the next 7 years. His competitors, not knowing of his success, might very well stumble on the same solution but would find, to their chagrin, that they could make no profit from it. The point of the law was that the first inventor owned it, and no matter how much richer and more powerful his competitors were, they could not simply appropriate it and claim it as their own (defending themselves, in some later court, with the claim that they "did not know" it had been discovered before). The downside to awarding a patent—disabling later inventors—was offset by a strong benefit: anyone in the same line of work could use the patented design, which was now publicly known, by simply paying royalties to the patent holder, and could use the design to leapfrog the technology to the next level. Essentially, the patent freed the time of all the other inventors to make advances that would benefit the public, while rewarding the first. It's a good system. (Note: The patent is the opposite of the "trade secret." A patent is deliberately made public to aid in the advancement of technology; a trade secret is deliberately kept private to protect it from competitors. If you figure out a trade secret—legally, that is, by simple ingenuity or reverse engineering—you can use it all you want without paying royalties. But a patent is public, and no matter how innocently you acquire it, it's not yours to use without paying the inventor: even if you found it first, he patented it first.)

All this works well for gizmos, but what about plants—self-replicating, randomly distributed by the wind, uncontained since plants began? Monsanto claimed that every study they had done showed that canola seed *never* blew across property boundaries, but how many of those studies had been done in Saskatchewan? Meanwhile, what is Schmeiser owed for the destruction of a seedline that he had been cultivating for 50 years? There are other laws that apply to this situation, after all. If I raise purebred cocker spaniels, and I am so pleased with one of my sires that I patent his DNA and charge enormous stud fees to the owner of any bitch impregnated by him, what are my rights when he gets over the fence one night and impregnates one of your best purebred Welsh corgis? Might *you* not have a suit against *me?* But patent law, as it is written and interpreted, might very well come down on my side.

Incidentally, law aside, Schmeiser seems to have been right about the tendency of genetically modified seed to migrate. In February 2004, the the Union of Concerned Scientists (UCS) released a study entitled *Gone to Seed,* documenting contamination of the seeds of traditional crops with DNA from GMOs; their laboratory tests of random samples of common seeds showed the presence of patented DNA. On the whole, the record of containment of bioengineered organisms is not good. As early as 2000, GM Starlink corn, approved for animal feed but not for human, was found in Mexican food, and mixed seed from Canada was mistakenly distributed in Europe. In 2001, illegal GM corn was found in Mexico, where laws forbid its introduction in order to protect the wild landraces. No one knows how it got there. By 2002 organic farmers in Saskatchewan were suing Monsanto because of the modified canola that had got Percy Shmeiser in so much trouble; it was in their fields too, and they knew very well they had not bought it. In the same year, GM corn was found amid the soybeans in Nebraska. In the newest case, GM pollen has been contaminating the organic papaya plantations in Hawaii, and GM bentgrass (used on golf courses) was found dispersed 13 miles from a test field. There are rumblings about prohibiting or carefully limiting the use of GM crops because of the danger of spread, but

> The biotechnology industry and some scientists and lawyers say that the flow of genes from modified crops to other plants, while inevitable, will not be a . . . problem. For one thing, they say, genes have flowed naturally from crop to crop and from crop to weed for eons. "Since pollen flow has happened all along, you have to look and see if it's caused problems in the past, . . . The answer is no."[7]

The New York Times was upset by this conclusion, editorializing that if there are any problems at all with safety, this failure of containment is genuinely alarming.[8]

In the end, on May 21, 2004, the law vindicated Monsanto: Monsanto had a patent, the patented device (or in this case, substance) had been found in Schmeiser's field, and Monsanto's patent was valid. But, there would be no damages; Percy Schmeiser did not owe any of those appalling sums of money. Who won? Both claimed victory, and as far as the law was concerned, both parties deserved to: Monsanto for protecting its patent, Schmeiser for not being bankrupted four times over by the damage payments. (He still has his own legal fees to pay.)[9]

Percy Schmeiser was not the only victim of Monsanto's prosecutions. As Schmeiser's case was wandering through the Canadian courts, a 61-year-old Mississippi farmer, Homan McFarling, was waging his own battle in the United States. McFarling had indeed willingly bought seeds from Monsanto and had signed the contracts that came with them, requiring that he keep his fields open for inspection, that he retain no seed for later planting, that he ensure that none of his seeds cross boundaries into neighbor's fields, that he buy new seed from Monsanto in the future, and that he report any neighbors who might be seen using Monsanto's crops without permission. He saved some of his seed anyway, contrary to the contract, was sued, and was required to pay Monsanto $780,000 in damages for the profits he had cost them. Apparently he had no idea what the fine print in the contract said. His net worth approximates $75,000, after a lifetime of very hard work, and a sensible court declared the judgment "unenforceable." That does not get McFarling off the hook, however. He will not have to pay $780,000, but it's up to a Missouri court to determine what he will pay.[10]

Where did this controversy come from? What are "GMOs," and what are the implications of having them patented and on the market? The business world is most interested in the opportunities and challenges presented by the patenting of GMO technology, permitting Monsanto to assert and defend "ownership" rights in any crops that may descend from plants modified by that technology. The ecological world is most interested in the existence of GMOs themselves and their evident unchecked spread throughout the natural environment. What effects may they have, and what precautions are appropriate to mitigate the dangers they may pose? In the sections following, we will track the origins of GMOs, the political explosion that attended their introduction into the market, and the possible future of a technology that poses risks that are simply not foreseeable.

THE ORIGINS OF GENETIC MODIFICATION
OF PLANTS

It all began quietly. That crops could be engineered to resist weed killers—saving farmers, in the case of genetically engineered tomatoes, potentially $30 per acre each season by reducing the need for hand or mechanical tilling—was announced in March 1986, in a two-page article in *Science*, authored by

Marjorie Sun. The Department of Agriculture was expected to announce very soon its approval of the first outdoor tests of the engineered plants. The article discussed the potential of such a development, especially the business opportunities that awaited the chemical companies who engineered seeds resistant to their own herbicides. There was some discussion of the risk of vertical monopolies as chemical companies acquired seed companies to create the fit they were looking for; there was some talk of the possible environmental problems if farmers became less careful with herbicides; there was a concern over regulation by the EPA (Environmental Protection Agency). None of the concerns seemed to be serious.[11] As for the possibility that people might not want to eat foods known to be genetically modified, that issue was never raised. No one suspected this might be the case at the time.

The need for improvement in the world's agriculture was a well-recognized cause of concern. Up to 40 percent of the world's crops are destroyed as they grow or before they leave the field. Right now it takes one hectare, 2.5 acres, to feed four people, according to Maria Zimmerman, who is in charge of agricultural research for the sustainable development department of the United Nations Food and Agricultural Organization. According to a projected increase in demand, stemming from a higher population living at a higher standard of living, in about 20 years that hectare will have to support six people. Working harder will not get the job done; technology has to help. We have the technology. "Scientists can now tell with precision which of 50,000 genes in a plant governs a particular trait. If it is beneficial, they can take that gene out of one species—something that wards off a common insect, for instance—copy it and stick it into another organism, to protect it. That organism, and its offspring, will then have a genetic structure that lets them resist such pests."[12]

By the end of that year, MIT's prestigious *Technology Review* had reported the development of new (at the time) and safer herbicides, especially Monsanto's glyphosate, with other contributions from DuPont and Cyanamid. But these are broad-spectrum herbicides, lethal to all plants, which had spurred research to engineer crop plants that will not suffer from the herbicide. The article notes a huge potential payoff should such plants be developed.[13] A year and a half later, Jane Brody reported new developments in hormone production: designer livestock, created by altering hormones produced by genetic engineering, can create cows with more beef and less fat.[14] The most impressive advance to date was announced a year after that—plants that contained their own insecticide. Understandable enthusiasm greeted the plants with *Bacillus thuringiensis* (Bt), a natural insect-killer, engineered into them. There were muted worries there might be health and safety problems, both for humans and the environment, if more exotic forms of molecule were to be used and got loose; the danger that bugs might get immune to Bt surfaced even then.[15] Environmentalists fought the use of bioengineered Bt, partly on the conservative principle that we should not change nature, but partly on behalf of the organic farmers, who would use nothing else and were worried about acquired resistance. When it came to cotton, however, they had to concede that biotech is better than the alternative. *Forbes*, a business booster, treated the cotton issue as a success story. In a 1990 article (entitled, of course, "The Lesser of Two Weevils"), *Forbes* reported that cotton farmers in the United States had put 100 million pounds of agricultural chemicals on their crop each year for the last several years, most of it insecticide. Monsanto's cotton, with Bt engineered into it, resists bugs without all the spraying, saving the environment. The article noted signs that cotton pests were beginning to show resistance to the sprayed stuff, which fate may well await Bt.[16] But for the time being, agribusiness in the form of Monsanto, the cotton farmers, and the environment, all profited from the new developments.

THE UNEXPECTED POLITICAL BACKLASH

Tomatoes may have led the way to the present impasse. In 1993, John Seabrook, writing in the *New Yorker*, introduced the Flavr Savr, a tomato developed by Calgene. Almost everyone was enthusiastic about the long-lived tomato, especially Wall Street. But the beginnings of organized opposition signaled less enthusiasm from other communities. Jeremy Rifkin, president of the Foundation on Economic Trends and an anti-technology activist of long standing, well known in technological circles for unflagging opposition to biological research and change, was already organizing a boycott against it. Seabrook went on to mention that the Mycogen Corporation was even then developing a corn with Bt in it that would be helpful in cutting the use of pesticides (which amounted to 25 million pounds of chemicals per year on corn alone in the United States). Jeremy Rifkin opposed this development as well, as did Environmental Defense (formerly, the Environmental Defense Fund, the first strictly environmental organization to enter the fray), both citing the possibility of cultivating insect resistance to Bt. The Rhone-Poulenc firm, meanwhile, wanted to make money selling its bromoxynil herbicide, so it was helping Calgene develop a bromoxynil-resistant cotton plant. That meant, in the activists' understanding, more herbicide use. (The growers disagreed, pointing out that if they didn't have to worry about the crop dying from the herbicide, they could use it once, thoroughly, and have done with it. The activists, most notably Rebecca Goldburg of Environmental Defense, pointed out that when the local weeds acquired the herbicide resistance, you'd have to use all kinds of *other* herbicides to get rid of them.)[17] Meanwhile, in the Flavr Savr, there is an antibiotic to cut down on bacterial attack. Just as regular exposure to an insecticide will lead to insecticide-resistant insects, so regular exposure to an antibiotic will lead to antibiotic resistance among the microbes, and that development can be very costly in terms of human health. Clearly there were threats, or possible threats, to human and environmental welfare in the development of these new organisms. As has happened most frequently in the last quarter century, calls for further testing, and opposition to the use of GMOs until the testing was completed, came not from governments but from nongovernmental organizations (NGOs; also called Civil Society Organizations, or CSOs).

Jeremy Rifkin saw the whole development as a move to help the drug and chemical manufacturers cash in on the food business. "What we're seeing here is the conversion of DNA into a commodity, and it is in some ways the ideal corporate commodity—it's small, it's ownable, it's easily transportable, and it lasts forever. . . . Genetic engineering is the final enclosure movement. It is the culmination of the enclosure of the village commons that began five hundred years ago. As we Americans have developed as a society and we have moved from an agricultural to a pyrochemical to a biotechnical culture, we have seen that whoever controls the land or the fossil fuels or, now, the DNA, controls society."[18]

By the middle of 1998, the battle was joined. Michael Specter wrote an extensive and thoughtful article on the European rejection of GMOs in the summer of that year. Beginning with a quote from a traditional farmer in Germany, denouncing the U.S. attempts to "change the basic rules of life" by genetic engineering, he drew out the opposition's credo: "Here we are going to live like God intended." Why is Europe so conservative about its food, he wondered, and he came up with three logically independent answers.

- First, because Europe has many small farmers, who are threatened by the new agribusiness crops; these farmers are too small to buy into the revolution and will be driven out of business if it is successful.

- Second, Europe has a strong environmental movement, the "Green Party" of most European nations, especially Germany. This movement is committed to the preservation of the natural species and therefore to opposition to the introduction of new ones, especially species that, spreading through the wild, might threaten natural species. Because the movement had its birth opposing chemical pollution, it is reflexively antibusiness.

- The third and most telling reason is "recent history": "The shadow of the Holocaust is dense and incredibly powerful still," said Arthur Caplan, the American ethicist now at the University of Pennsylvania. "It leaves Europe terrified about the abuse of genetics. To them the potential to abuse genetics is no theory. It is a historical fact."[19]

How did the Holocaust get into the soybeans? Are GMOs really that great a change from traditional crops? Joseph Zak, under contract to the American Soybean Association to calm Europeans, minimized the impact of the change, putting it in the line of all advances in agriculture, including, for instance, "when we moved to breeding to make a better product." Another observer came closer to the source of the fear, pointing out that Europeans see genetic modification as "tampering with their food" and that the perception of manipulation "drives people crazy."[20]

In the fall of 1998, *The Ecologist* devoted an entire issue to the controversy. Entitled *The Monsanto Files: Can We Survive Genetic Engineering?* and featuring on its cover the skeleton of a horse half buried in the endless sand of a lifeless desert, it waged a scathing attack on Monsanto specifically. "This is the company that brought us Agent Orange, PCBs and Bovine Growth Hormone; the same company that produces Roundup, the world's biggest selling herbicide, and the highly questionable 'Terminator Technology.' ... Can we allow corporations like Monsanto to gamble with the very future of life on Earth?" The issue continues with allegations of threats to health from every GMO on the market— hormone-produced milk, the herbicide Roundup, and all the dioxins and PCBs that Monsanto has sown into the environment from its varied operations.[21]

Most interesting in the criticism of GMO technology and products are the parallels drawn between the threats to health posed by GMOs and those posed in the United Kingdom by episodes of "mad cow disease," or bovine spongiform encephalopathy (BSE), which is a prion disease, not a product of genetic engineering (nor is it genetic). What does BSE have to do with the GMO controversy? The parallels are there.

- First, profit-oriented innovations led farmers in Britain to include the offal of slaughtered animals in feed for their herds of beef cattle, and that is how (in all likelihood) the cows became infected in the first place;

- Second, even when infected cattle staggered and fell before the television cameras of three continents, scientists plausibly argued that such disease could not possibly affect humans, so British beef was quite safe; accordingly, its distribution was not regulated very strictly;

- Third, after scientists and government regulators had promised it wouldn't happen, some people who ate that beef became very sick and some died.

All this proves what? That fooling around with nature in order to make more money is a very bad idea (feeding herbivores offal essentially moves them up on the food chain, and there was no reason to think that their systems could handle that move); that science is not always right; and that government regulation often dances to the tune of the commercial interests that support the election campaigns. Essentially, the BSE issue served to undermine the authority of regulatory mandates and scientific pronouncements, and that undermining turned out to be very important in the outcome of the GMO debate.[22] We'll see those cows again.

Of course the objections were answered. No less a personage than former-president Jimmy Carter argued the safety and acceptability of GMOs, "everything from seeds to livestock." Protesting the regulations proposed for adoption by signatories to the Biodiversity Treaty forged at the 1992 Earth Summit at Rio de Janeiro, Carter argued that the requirement that recipient nations approve, item by item, the importation of any GMOs, would leave food and vaccines rotting on docks all over the world. A farmer himself, Carter points out that "for hundreds of years virtually all food has been improved genetically by plant breeders," by the simple techniques of selective breeding. There is no evidence of any harm from genetically engineered products; some evidence of much benefit does exist; and if the technology is halted at this point, the real losers will be the developing nations and the poor of the world.[23] But just as science and regulators had failed to be totally effective, Jimmy Carter's influence made little difference. The controversy continued. In October 1998,

Michael Pollan wrote an extensive account of a potato (New Leaf Superior), from development of the new vegetable to planting it in his own garden; the controversy that enveloped it, including a gripping account of his own uneasiness with this unregulated, unexplained organism, foreshadows all later problems with this technology.[24]

In the middle of 1999, the volume of the war increased noticeably. Popular literature was beginning to notice the GMO controversy, and the consumer movement sided with the environmental activists.[25] Meanwhile a new controversy erupted. Monsanto had engineered a new kind of gene, instantly dubbed the "terminator gene," one that would make sure that its bioengineered plants had no progeny. Why do this? An unsigned editorial in *The Economist* explained:

> Terminator is a set of genes that act as a series of molecular switches. These switches are set off by a chemical signal sprayed on genetically tinkered seed. Although the plant springing forth from that seed is healthy and can go about its business of producing grain, say, quite normally, the grain that it produced will not grow if planted, because the activated terminator gene has killed off the seed's reproductive bits. This means that farmers who want to grow a plant with the same genetically engineered traits next season have to go back to the company for more seeds.[26]

That was the point, of course: "terminator" technology would make it physically impossible for Homan Sparling to grow patented crops from saved seed, and Monsanto would not have to waste time in prosecutions. Predictably, a new uproar greeted the news. First, how mean of Monsanto to deprive poor farmers of the developing world the possibility of saving their seeds! More ominously, would these genes spread, by pollen, to the fields of neighboring farms? If they did, would they inject themselves into the seeds of traditional crops, making it impossible for farmers planting them to save their traditional seeds from year to year? How would these farmers know that their seeds were contaminated until a new crop planted simply failed to germinate, and their family starved? What new death spores was science (for profit) loosing on the world?[27]

The publicity was immense. Still in development, and long in advance of being used anywhere, terminator genes were already being blamed for crop failures all over the world. The Rockefeller Foundation, which sponsors agricultural projects across the world, strongly objected to their use. Monsanto formally promised not to commercialize the genetic engineering of seed sterility. "Given its parlous public image, Monsanto must be hoping that its move will buy it a little goodwill. The terminator technology has raised such interest in the industry, and caused such an outcry in society, because it is a neat and potentially powerful way for biotechnology firms such as Monsanto to protect the intellectual property locked in genetically modified seeds."[28] As Laura Tangley pointed out,

> More than 1.4 billion people, most of them in poor, developing countries, rely on farm-saved seed as their primary seed source and are unable to afford repeated annual expenditures for new seeds. Terminator seeds, if they ever worked, could be a real threat to world food security. Monsanto,

Tangley points out, is not the only company working on them. "The battle highlights the difficulty of protecting intellectual property when the products are sophisticated genetic technologies. Monsanto and other firms have said the terminator is a legitimate way to recoup the billions of dollars they have poured into developing bioengineered crops with traits such as insect resistance.[29]

That's a good point. The controversy underscores the difference between developed-world and undeveloped-world patterns of agriculture. Yearly buying of new seeds is the way farmers do business in the United States now. The hybrid seeds that farmers use to produce the wonder crops to which we modern folks have become accustomed do not breed true—do not produce the uniform crop we expect—so they have to buy new seeds each year. But in poorer countries, farmers often recycle whatever seeds they have, hybrid or not. They have no choice. But patents do not expire at the border, and patents are the law. How *do* we protect intellectual property in such a complex area? Or is that the wrong question? Maybe the question is, should DNA be intellectual property at all? After all, Monsanto is responsible for very little of the DNA of wheat, corn, tomatoes, or soybeans. Most of it came with the earth, the created and evolved natural wealth of edible plants that make it possible for humans to live on this earth. We did not "invent" that wealth, anymore than we created the rainfall and sunlight the crops need to thrive. Maybe we simply have no right to go "patenting" and creating "property rights" in the stuff of life itself.

In May of 1999 new fears were raised, as engineered corn was alleged to be dangerous to Monarch butterflies.[30] Suddenly, wrote John Carey, covering science from Washington for *Business Week*,

> foes of bioengineering in the food supply have their own potent symbol: the beloved monarch butterfly. In mid-May, Cornell University researchers reported that pollen from corn altered to slay corn-borer pests can land on neighboring milkweed plants, where it can kill monarch butterfly caterpillars. The finding has biotech foes exulting. "The monarch butterfly experiment is the smoking gun that will be the beginning of the unraveling of the industry," says Jeremy Rifkin . . . The findings cast genetically altered food plants in a new light. They may benefit farmers and consumers, but now opponents have evidence that there could be worrisome ecological effects on other species.

It was a silly controversy from the beginning. The study was artificially set up, the caterpillars were fed carefully isolated Bt pollen in the lab, and the findings are impossible to verify. Most monarch butterfly larvae die anyway from one cause or another, and you'll never get a statistically significant finding that more are dying from nibbling on altered pollen; most of their milkweed doesn't grow anywhere near cornfields to begin with; and the monarch is not at all endangered in its northern range. But both Greenpeace and the Union of Concerned Scientists are now asking the EPA to pull the seeds off the market.[31]

"If the current British furore over genetically modified foods were a crop not a crisis," chortled *The Economist* in June 1999,

> you can bet Monsanto or its competitors would have patented it. It has many of the traits that genetic engineers prize: it is incredibly fertile, thrives in inhospitable conditions, has tremendous consumer appeal and is easy to cross with other interests to create a hardy new hybrid. Moreover, it seems to resist anything that might kill it, from scientific evidence to official reassurance. Now it seems to be spreading to other parts of Europe, Australia and even America. There, regulators will face the same questions that confront the British government: how should the public be reassured, and how can the benefits of GM foods be reaped without harm, either to human beings or to the environment?

At least, the U.K.-based Economist consoled us, the United States doesn't have to deal with the Prince of Wales, who had taken a very public position against GMOs. The editorial went on to point out that this unforeseen consumer backlash "threatens to undermine both this new technology and the credibility of the agencies that regulate it." That, it recalled, was the major effect of the fallout from Mad Cow disease (those cows again).[32] By repeated infections of scandal and general suspicion (fanned by NGOs) that government is in league with the biotech industry, food fears seem to have developed a resistance to official reassurance, much as insect species develop resistance to pesticides.

Through the summer and fall of 1999, the media continued its barrage, tracking the continuing battles in Europe,[33] tracking the damage to U.S. farmers from the boycott,[34] studying the potential for GMOs to spread to the wild,[35] questioning the ability of bioengineered crops to feed the world as claimed,[36] chronicling the new kinds of crops being brought on to the genetically modified line (including leaner pigs, extra-meaty hogs, and "Enviropigs," porkers with replicated mouse genes that produce manure with less phosphorus),[37] and most ominously, tracking the growing trend in the United States to demand proof that genetically modified food is really safe.[38] By October, Monsanto found itself answering claims that its central weed killer, Roundup (glyphosate), caused cancer. Apparently a "confidential" report by the European Commission (EC) had concluded that it had "harmful effects" on mites and arthropods that consume harmful insects. Humans exposed to glyphosate, according to the Channel 4 news that broadcast the report, are three times as likely to get non-Hodgkin's lymphoma. The report was a low blow to Monsanto: general acceptance of Roundup Ready is essential if Roundup crops are to be marketed. Monsanto spokespeople dismissed the scientific basis of the studies, pointing out that they were conducted in 1995, were badly designed then, and had never been taken seriously.[39]

But the resistance to GMOs is not that easy to dismiss: "Increasingly, genetically 'improved' crops are trading at deep discounts, while European processors have been willing to pay premiums of as much as $1.50 a bushel for non–genetically modified crops. In September, the huge U.S. grain-processing corporation, Archer Daniel Midland (ADM), advised American grain farmers to begin segregating genetically modified and non–genetically modified crops. At the same time, the two main U.S. baby food manufacturers, Gerber Products and H. J. Heinz, declared they would no longer use genetically modified corn or soybeans in any of their products." More problems were foreseen for canola farmers, who do not segregate their crops.[40]

"The problem is as much about public perceptions as it is about science," comments Barry Came, echoing a theme that underlies the entire conflict.

> In Europe, the anti–GM battle has been waged against the backdrop of a series of European food scares that began with BSE, or "mad cow" disease, in Britain [here those cows are again], and has escalated with scandals over carcinogenic dioxins in Belgian poultry and dairy products and the use in France and elsewhere of sewage slurry in animal feeds. The aggressive stance of U.S.-based agribusiness giants has not helped. The U.S. government, responding to pressure from the powerful agribusiness lobby in Washington, has taken the Europeans to court at the World Trade Organization, winning successive decisions against Europe's restrictions on Caribbean bananas and growth hormone additives in beef. The Americans have threatened similar challenges to European resistance to the free import of genetically engineered grains. . . . The combined effect has been to shatter Europeans' confidence in what they are eating and drinking as well as fostering deep resentment about the unrestrained power of U.S. multinational corporations. "There has been an unprecedented, permanent and irreversible shift in the political landscape," Greenpeace's Lord Melchett told Shapiro last week. "People are increasingly aware and mistrustful of the combination of big science and big business."[41]

To avoid the EC boycott, ADM has demanded that all its suppliers segregate genetically modified grain from "natural" grain. Consider the dilemma of farmer Dave Boettger: he has 280 acres, half in genetically modified crops. ADM will pay eight cents a bushel more for the natural product. But if testing reveals even a tiny amount of altered genes in the higher-priced shipment, he has to pay ADM to dump the whole load. Pollen blows over all his fields; he can make no guarantees that none of the genetically modified pollen blew into a natural field. Now, how does he sell his crop?[42]

In the middle of the debate on genetically modified foods generally, consideration should be given to two instructive cases concerning milk, whose production has been enhanced by hormones, and salmon that has been genetically engineered to grow more quickly. The issues are identical, involving the same doubts, reassurances, and ultimate activist boycotts. The cases are instructive because each pertains to an area of agriculture where abundance, even surplus, gives the human race an unaccustomed luxury of picking and choosing.

Again, the business press reported it: an unsigned item in the *Economist* in July 1999 described a meeting of the Codex Alimentarius Commission, a joint body of the Food and Agriculture Organization (FAO) and the World Health Organization (WHO). "At issue is a genetically engineered version of bovine growth hormone called rbGH, known in Europe as rbST. According to its manufacturer, Monsanto, approximately 30% of American dairy cattle are injected with rbGH at some stage in their lives, raising their milk yields by roughly 10%. Although both America's Food and Drug Administration (FDA) and Codex's scientific advisory committee on food additives (JECFA) consider it safe, many national governments and consumer groups beg to differ."[43] The same pattern—of reassurance by all appropriate scientific bodies, and of rejection of that reassurance by activist groups that no one could have anticipated—shows up here, with the same result. There has been a moratorium on hormone-enhanced milk products in Europe since 1990. Canada joined in this one, in January 1999. What's wrong with the hormone? Veterinaries cite side effects for the cows—lameness, fertility problems. And there is a 25 percent greater chance of developing mastitis. The mastitis worries public-health experts, not because it causes pain to the cow but because it is treated with antibiotics, which get into the milk and therefore into us, "leading to worries about allergic reactions and antibiotic resistance."[44] Then the consumer groups took up the question. The September 1999 issue of *Consumer Reports* pointed out that not just corn and potatoes are genetically engineered. Milk "may come from cows injected with Monsanto's recombinant bovine growth hormone, Posilac, to boost milk production. Monsanto says that roughly 30 percent of the nation's cows are in herds that get this hormone, produced by genetically engineered bacteria. And 60 percent of all hard-cheese products today are made with Chymogen, a biotech version of an enzyme from calves' stomachs that helps separate curds from whey."[45]

This time the United Nations was not on Monsanto's side. In August of 1999 the United Nations Food Safety Agency endorsed the European Union's (EU) moratorium on Monsanto's genetically engineered bovine somatotropin (BST). The FDA had ruled in 1993 that BST is safe; at present it is used in 30 percent of U.S. dairy cattle. However, Europe and Canada disagree.[46] Prominent in this issue is the offhand remark in the *Economist,* that there was plenty of milk to go around (for those who could afford to buy it). On the one hand, what benefit then flows to the public and the consumer if cows' bodies are flogged to produce yet greater quantities of surplus milk? On the other hand, is this whole food fight a product of generous times in the developed world, where no real need for more food is felt and we can afford to be fastidious?

In the summer of 1998 Dr. Rebecca Goldburg of Environmental Defense raised the issue of "transgenic" fish. AquaBounty Farms, of Waltham, Massachusetts, was preparing to commercialize a kind of Atlantic salmon with an engineered growth hormone. Genetic engineering seemed a logical next step in the phenomenal growth of aquaculture; as the demand for fish worldwide increases and the wild fisheries deteriorate under the pressure of overfishing, we will have to depend on the fish farms to get the fish to the table. AquaBounty "claims that its transgenic Atlantic salmon can grow as much as 400 to 600 percent faster than the nontransgenic ones."[47] That's the good news. The bad news, Goldburg insists, comes when the transgenic fish escape from the rearing facilities and join the native fish. What could go wrong? Her list is interesting: ". . . fish containing a new growth hormone gene might displace wild fish if they outcompete the natives for food or spawning sites, since the transgenic fish would be larger and grow faster than wild fish at a given age. Genes for freezing tolerance might expand the geographic range of engineered fish, allowing them to compete with new, more northerly (or southerly) species and potentially reducing populations of these fish."[48]

Why is this bad news? Our transgenic fish turn out to be bigger, stronger, and better in the evolutionary competition, so they displace some of the weaklings. Why is this wrong? It is wrong not on any anthropocentric ethic (centered on human rights and interests), but as a violation of the integrity of the ecosystem—its ability to persist in its natural way, undisturbed by the introduction of alien organisms. The introduction of transgenic organisms into the mix is like introducing kudzu or zebra mussels—an exotic species likely to destroy the ecosystem by displacement of its natural residents, who have lived in symbiotic harmony for eons. That is why it is wrong.

At least in this piece, Goldburg does not take on the other scenarios that are entirely possible with the untested transgenic species. Others do: If wild females preferred genetically engineered males, (as Goldburg argues, since they seem to prefer larger mates) and if young engineereds are ultimately unable to survive in the wild, escape could wipe out the entire wild species.[49] It is also entirely possible that there is a virus out there to which the wild species are immune by now but to which the transgenics will be susceptible—again, if they mate with the wild females, wiping out the species. In any case, it is not expected that salmon will be the last fish to be commercialized in transgenic form, nor that the trip of the transgenics from the breeding pen to the table will be free of controversy.[50]

THE FUTURE OF GMOs

Were GMOs ever a good idea to begin with? There seems to be more here than meets the eye. Europeans are not normally less rational than Americans; there is no a priori reason why Europeans should be terrified of food that we have been eating for years without apparent harm. Three factors in the profoundly hostile European reaction are worth mentioning, because they lead to global considerations that will have to be addressed before we go much further.

First, it is possible that Europeans have a preference for what is known as the "precautionary principle": the conservative principle according to which no new thing is to be accepted until it has been proved beyond a reasonable doubt to be safe and better than what is currently available. Americans, on the other hand, more trusting of novelty, may be inclined to go with a risk-benefit calculation, placing the new idea on a par with the old and comparing them for safety and advantage. So Americans may shrug off an unknown innovation while Europeans greet it with skepticism.

Second, even if Europe had in this case decided to go with a risk-benefit calculation, weighing whatever risks there might be with the benefits of genetically altered food, no one ever suggested to them that there were any consumer benefits. Monsanto did not think any risks were associated with the foods. But were there any benefits? All the benefits mentioned were for the growers, who could cut dramatically their costs for chemicals and labor and so make a bigger profit. Presumably some of the profit would be passed on to consumer, but the corn that benefited went mostly to hog and cattle feed (to other producers, not to consumers), and the rape plants were all ground up for canola oil, which went into processed food not to be sold on the shelves. At no point did the consumer get in on the cost savings, and no one ever suggested that these genetically modified foods were healthier, safer, or better tasting.[51]

Third, there is the question of the small farmer. Europe has many small farmers, and they make up a powerful political force. Genetically modified crops, with the high expense for seed and the economies to be realized in savings on large-scale tillage, are not for the small farmer, whose profit is in niche markets. Genetically modified crops, like all large-scale agribusiness, do best in depopulated areas like the Great Plains in the United States, where small towns turn to ghost towns as the Atlantic and Pacific coasts gain population. In the United States, the small farmer is not a political force; the "farm vote" is cast by the enormous automated farms that have inherited the heartland (not to mention the legislators whose campaigns were financed by ADM and Cargill). Is this move to agribusiness, away from the small farmer, a good idea?

The plight of the small farmer is of global significance. The question has force in the United States, where the "family farm," has at least sentimental value; carries political weight in Europe; but is of terrible moment in the developing world. In India, the Philippines, and other nations of Africa, Asia, and South America, the search for "market access" has given priority to huge plantings of single crops for export only. Ironically, the large farms, owned by multinational corporations, often share the region with the farmers they displaced, now without enough food to feed their children.[52] Ultimately, the issue of whether it is better for the environment, for the consumer, and for the farm family, to carry on agriculture through small local farms providing local markets with a variety of crops, or through huge monocultures supplying global markets through worldwide transportation networks, is larger than we can consider here. But it's worth thinking about.[53]

What future is in store for genetically modified food? As we (the authors) write, both sides of the dispute are in motion. A cover story in *Time* on the new "golden rice," genetically modified to contain beta-carotene (vitamin A) proclaims, "This rice could save a million kids a year," and proceeds to present a convincing argument for the assertion, based on the extent and consequences of malnutrition in the developing nations. The article rehearses the by now familiar arguments against uncritical acceptance of genetic modifications, and does a nice job of capturing the European suspicions of multinational companies bearing gifts of new products. But its focus on Ingo Potrykus, professor of plant science at the Swiss Federal Institute of Technology, who worked for years to develop the rice, puts a human face on the development of transgenic organisms for the first time. Potrykus really does want to save the world, or at least to feed a significant portion of its children with a more nutritious diet. Before the world writes off GMOs as an idea whose time will not come, someone, Potrykus argues, has to explain why it is not necessary to save those children from blindness and depressed immune systems.[54] On the other hand, Michael Pollan, botanist extraordinary and author of several excellent pieces on GMOs, nature and agriculture,[55] is not alone in pointing out that the rice growers of the developing nations would have all the nutrition they needed if they simply left the brown hulls on the rice (the nutritious "brown rice" available in the supermarket), instead of polishing it to get the culturally favored white rice. Their nutrition could be enhanced immediately if they would just plant vegetables on the margins around the rice fields; if we Americans really want to help them, maybe we could give them the seed for the vegetables. (As Bill McKibben points out, the farmers prefer eating rice with vegetables, which they grew before the new agricultural plans forced them into monoculture of rice.)[56] Even if they will not eat brown rice or grow vegetables, there are already very inexpensive vitamin supplements on the market, and a tenth of the annual publicity budget for "golden rice" could easily bring every child in the developing world to nutritional adequacy. Golden rice seems to have been developed more for public relations reasons than nutritional ones; it may be, Pollan suggests, "the world's first purely rhetorical technology."[57]

All things considered, the GMOs may not be worth the hassle. If they could feed a hungry world, obviously they (or their patent holders) would have a moral claim on us. (Such is the claim, for instance, for the next generation's "self-cloning" corn, currently under development in Mexico.[58]) But there is no evidence that they can; as a matter of fact, they seem to make the problem of hunger worse. For they need large tracts of land for a large yield, which alone would justify the investment in expensive seed. In the developed world, such investment may well make sense, since the high-priced crops are going to feed higher-priced livestock or food-processing industries. Neither of those have anything to do with hunger (90 percent of the nutritional value of the grain is lost if it is fed to livestock; similar fractions are lost when it is processed into oil for luxury foods, themselves unnecessary and unavailable to the poor). But in the less developed world, there are no vast tracts of land available for these crops. The only way to get the land is to displace the subsistence farmers that lived there. Those farmers may be hired by the new agribusiness establishments to work in the fields from which their families have been evicted (for very low wages), but they will not be able to buy the crops they are cultivating, which are primarily for export, and they will not be able to continue farming on whatever marginal lands are left over. The ironic result of agricultural progress is hunger in the developing world, while Americans become fat and food is discarded in truckloads from the supermarket. If we want to help developing nations, we might want to smooth the way to the market for their traditional crops, so that their work would raise their income as well as give them enough food to eat.

The integrity of the natural environment is also threatened by the GMOs. There is real worry about the spread of the genetically modified creatures into the wild. Among the plants, as the UCS study showed, there is no way to prevent traditionally wind-pollinated crops from spreading their seed across the farmlands neighboring those in which they are planted. In the wrong places, this cross-pollination could threaten the continuity of the landraces of grain— maize and wheat especially—to which we turn when new diseases threaten our crops. There is no way to keep modified salmon caged indefinitely without some escapes, and escapes could threaten the wild species, as valuable in their way as the landraces of corn and wheat that we count on.

Possibly the worst result of the GMO plantings anywhere is the destruction, by the introduction of large-scale agriculture, of the wildlife corridors and mini-habitats along the borders of the fields of the small farms. The economics of GMOs do not permit the nonintensive agricultural methods that are available with the native species, where habitats can be left untouched and fields can lie fallow to regenerate themselves. What the agribusinesses forget is that the earth, like any organism, needs time to rest and restore its original balance of nourishment for plants, be they cultivated or wild. The best course for the future of the earth lies in a restoration of the balance that agribusiness is destroying, and it is not clear that the agenda of restoration is compatible with the widespread use of genetically modified crops.

QUESTIONS FOR REFLECTION

1. Proponents of genetically modified foods often claim that GMOs are the only way to feed a hungry world. Can you see how that might be true? Give arguments. Can you see why it might be false?

2. How would we ever determine if GMOs are "safe" for human consumption? Can you design research that would show that they definitely are (or are not) safe?

3. What are the implications of this "food fight" for the way agriculture is carried out in the world? What desirable effects follow from the use of GMOs? What undesirable consequences for the society seem to follow?

4. We live by folk tales and myths as much as by facts. Write a science fiction story (short) about GMOs that get out of hand. Is it difficult to do?

5. Is there such a thing as a "violation of nature," apart from any harm to human beings? Do GMOs violate nature? Why or why not?

NOTES

1. Pew Initiative on Food and Biotechnology, "Genetically Modified Crops in the United States," *Factsheet* (August 2003), cited in Shelley L. Hurt, " 'Seed Wars': The Promises and Pitfalls of Agricultural Biotechnology for a Hungry

World," *Miller Center Report* 20, no. 1 (Spring-Summer 2004): 31.

2. Hurt, " 'Seed Wars,' " p. 29.

3. Ellen Hickey and Anuradha Mittal, eds., *Voices from the South*

(May 2003), cited in Hurt, " 'Seed Wars,' " p. 29.

4. President Jimmy Carter, "First Step toward Peace is Eradicating Hunger," *International Herald Tribune* (17 June 1999), cited in Hurt, "'Seed Wars,' " p. 34.

5. For the basic outlines of this story, see the interview with Percy Schmeiser, "Percy Schmeiser: The Man That Took On Monsanto," *The Ecologist* 34(4): S30–S34.

6. Most of this information was from Percy Schmeiser's website, http://www.percyschmeiser.com.

7. Andrew Pollack, "Can Biotech Crops Be Good Neighbors," *New York Times,* 26 September 2004, Week in Review section, p. 12.

8. Editorial, "The Travels of a Bioengineered Gene," *New York Times,* 30 September 2004.

9. Simon, Bernard, "Monsanto Wins Patent Case on Plant Genes," *New York Times,* Saturday, 22 May 2004, pp. C1, C4.

10. The story is told on http://www .mindfully.org/GE/GE4/Monsanto-vs-Homan-McFarling5dec02.html, cited in Hurt, " 'Seed Wars,' " p. 32.

11. Marjorie Sun, "Engineering Crops to Resist Weed Killers," *Science* 231 (March 1986): 1360–1361.

12. Michael Specter, "Europe, Bucking Trend in U.S., Blocks Genetically Altered Food," *New York Times,* 20 July 1998, pp. A1, A8.

13. Charles M. Benbrook and Phyllis B. Moses, "Engineering Crops to Resist Herbicides," *Technology Review* (November–December 1986): 55ff.

14. Jane E. Brody, "Quest for Lean Meat Prompts New Approach," *New York Times,* 12 April 1988, pp. C1, C4.

15. Amal Kumar Naj, "Can Biotechnology Control Farm Pests? Specialty Plants May Cut Need For Chemicals," *Wall Street Journal,* 11 May 1989, p. B1.

16. Gary Slutsker, "The Lesser of Two Weevils," *Forbes* (15 October 1990): 202–203.

17. Rebecca Goldburg, "Biotechnology's Bitter Harvest: Herbicide–Tolerant Crops and the Threat to Sustainable Agriculture," Biotechnology Working Group of the Environmental Defense Fund, 1990, available online at various websites.

18. John Seabrook, "Tremors in the Hothouse: The Battle Lines are Being Drawn for the Soul of the American Consumer as Agribusiness Launches the First Genetically Altered Supermarket Tomato," *New Yorker,* Brave New World department, 19 July 1993, pp. 32–41 (quote at 38–39).

19. Michael Specter, "Europe, Bucking Trend in U.S., Blocks Genetically Altered Food," *New York Times,* International section, 20 July 1998, pp. A1, A8.

20. Cited in ibid., p. A8.

21. *"Rethinking Basic Assumptions,"* The *Ecologist* 28(5): entire September–October 1998 issue.

22. The Mad Cows have given birth to a floating panic about such mysterious brain disease. Consider: the U.S. government plans to destroy nearly 400 sheep because there is a chance that they <u>may</u> have been exposed to Belgian sheep that <u>may</u> be infected with some variant of BSE (as opposed to scrapie, a disease of the same family which often shows up in sheep and is not transmissible to humans). Carey Goldberg, "U.S. Planning to Destroy Sheep at Risk of an Infection," *New York Times,* 18 July 2000, p. A12. If that's not enough, consider "mad squirrel disease," the flap over which is chronicled by Burkhard Bilger in "Letter from Kentucky: Squirrel and Man," *New Yorker,* 17 July 2000, pp. 59–67.

23. Jimmy Carter, "Who's Afraid of Genetic Engineering?" Op-Ed, *New York Times,* 26 August 1998.

24. Michael Pollan, "Playing God in the Garden," *New York Times Magazine,* 25 October, 1998, p. 46ff.

25. Ralph Nader wrote the Foreword to *Genetically Engineered Foods: Changing the Nature of Nature: What You Need to Know to Protect Yourself, Your Family, and Our Planet* by Martin Teitel and Kimberly Wilson

(Rochester, VT: Inner Traditions International, 1999).

26. Editorial, "Fertility Rights," *The Economist,* 9 October 1999.

27. Cited in Barnaby J. Feder, "Plant Sterility Research Inflames Debate on Biotechnology's Role in Farming," *New York Times,* 19 April 1999, p. 18.

28. "Fertility Rights."

29. Laura Tangley, "Seed Savers Get a Break," *U.S. News and World Report,* 18 October 1999, p. 83.

30. Carol Kaesuk Yoon, "Altered Corn May Imperil Butterfly, Researchers Say," *New York Times,* 20 May 1999, pp. A1, A25; Editorial, *New York Times,* "A Warning From the Butterflies," 21 May 1999.

31. John Carey, "Imperiled Monarchs Alter the Biotech Landscape," *Business Week* (June 1999): 36.

32. Editorial, "Who's Afraid?" *The Economist,* 19 June 1999.

33. Diane Johnson, "France's Fickle Appetite," Op-Ed, *New York Times,* 2 August 1999. Warren Hoge, "Britons Skirmish Over Genetically Modified Crops," *New York Times,* 23 August 1999, p. A15.

34. Melody Petersen, "New Trade Threat for U.S. Farmers," *New York Times,* 29 August 1999, pp. 1, 28.

35. Charles C. Mann, "Biotech Goes Wild," *Technology Review,* July–August 1999, p. 36ff. Solid coverage of the whole issue, beginning with the concerns that engineered crops might spontaneously breed with wild relatives, creating super-weeds. See also Carol Kaesuk Yoon, "Squash with Altered Genes Raises Fears of 'Superweeds'," *New York Times,* 3 November 1999, pp. A1, A18. See also comments in Letters to the Editor, *New York Times,* 8 November 1999.

36. Peter Rosset, "Why Genetically Altered Food Won't Conquer Hunger," Op-Ed, *New York Times,* 1 September 1999.

37. "Seeds of Change: In the U.S. and Elsewhere, the Food Supply is Being Genetically Altered. Here's Why You Should Care," *Consumer Reports* (September 1999): 41.

38. Marian Burros, "U.S. Plans Long–Term Studies on Safety of Genetically Altered Foods," *New York Times,* 14 July 1999, p. A 18; Jeffrey Kluger, "Food Fight," *Time,* 13 September 1999, pp. 42–44.

39. News Item, "Monsanto Denies Cancer Threat from Weedkiller," *Farmers Guardian,* 15 October 1999, p. 7.

40. Barry Came, "The Food Fight," *Maclean's,* 18 October 1999, p. 44.

41. Loc. cit.

42. Paul Magnusson, Ann Therese Palmer and Kerry Capell, "Furor over 'Frankenfood'," *Business Week,* 18 October, 1999, p. 50.

43. Editorial, "Udder Confusion," *The Economist,* 3 July 1999.

44. Ibid.

45. "Seeds of Change," p. 41.

46. "U.N. Rules on BST," *Chemical Week,* 25 August– 1 September 1999, p. 60.

47. Rebecca Goldburg, "Something Fishy," first published in *The Gene Exchange (Summer 1998),* updated May 2000, available online at various websites.

48. Loc. cit.

49. Carol Kaesuk Yoon, "Altered Salmon Leading Way to Dinner Plates, but Rules Lag," *New York Times,* 1 May 2000, pp. A1, A20.

50. Frederic Golden, "Make Way for Frankenfish!" *Time,* 6 March 2000, pp. 62–63.

51. Ray A. Goldberg, "Transforming Life, Transforming Business: The Life-Science Revolution," *Harvard Business Review* (March–April): 94.

52. Vandana Shiva, "Small Scale Farming: A Global Perspective (South)," *The Ecologist* 30(4): S37.

53. A fair amount of such thinking is found in "Facing the Farm Crisis," *The Ecologist* 30(4): S28ff.

54. J. Madeleine Nash, "Grains of Hope: Genetically Engineered Crops Could Revolutionize Farming. Protesters Fear

They Could Also Destroy the Ecosystem. You Decide," *Time,* 31 July 2000, pp. 38–46.

55. Including "Playing God," cited earlier (n. 23), "The Great Yellow Hype," *New York Times Magazine,* 4 March 2001, and the best-selling *Botany of Desire* (New York: Random House, 2002).

56. Bill McKibben, *Enough: Staying Human in an Engineered Age* (New York: Holt, 2003), pp. 137–38.

57. Pollan, "Hype."

58. Daniel Charles, "Corn That Clones Itself," *Technology Review* (March 2003): 32–41.

3

Skunked

Crisis in the New England Fisheries

INTRODUCTION

A grim article in *Nature,* in May 2003, documented the devastation of fisheries worldwide.[1] The article dispassionately reports cold facts, but the authors' despair shows through: in ocean after ocean, fishery after fishery, the "20th century juggernaut" of commercial fishing has reduced marine life to a small fraction of its natural abundance. They argue that there is such a thing as sustainable yield for a fishery, maximum sustainable yield being found when the stock is half what it would be naturally, if there were no fishing at all. But fish stocks now are well below that size. For a measurement, they propose a comparison of "the average number of fish caught per 100 hooks set by boats that spool out and then reel in miles of baited lines."

> At the advent of intensive commercial fishing, Myers and Worm found, most fleets caught 6 to 12 fish per 100 hooks. But in every fishery the researchers studied, the number of catches declined by about 16% per year. Within a decade, most fleets caught only about 1 fish per 100 hooks. "Industrialized fisheries typically reduced community biomass by 80% within less than 15 years of exploitation. . . . the global ocean has lost more than 90% of large predatory fishes." Those species include tuna, swordfish, and others traditionally favored by chefs and gourmets.[2]

Removing the top predators from an ecosystem has predictable effects: the system becomes "bottom-heavy," overpopulated with prey organisms which may, in larger numbers, be very damaging to the ecosystem (consider the effect of the removal of the wolf and cougar from our New England woods, in the damage that the white-tailed deer has wrought in the gardens); since the smaller organisms cannot survive fluctuations in the food supply, the whole system may become volatile, varying significantly from season to season; and in the case of the fish, "fishing down the marine food web" creates economic anomalies that magnify the effects of the overfishing. The bluefin tuna stocks are low to the point where extinction is an immediate possibility, but since it remains desirable, "a single fish can fetch $40,000 in Japan. . . . [Its] enormous price essentially dooms it," according to University of British Columbia Fisheries Scientist Daniel Pauly; "The fishery will be profitable to the last fish."[3]

What follows is the story of one fishery in particular, our own Georges Bank, a shallow place not far from Gloucester, Massachusetts, that used to be loaded with fish. It should be still; at the end of the chapter, we will consider ways to restore it and some of the political obstacles to the restoration. For your own research, the American Museum of Natural History keeps the full story of the Georges Bank fishery on a particularly well-maintained website. It is one of the saddest tales in the history of resource management of any kind and a particularly arresting moral tale for the United States. It starts with a resource of incredible bounty, huge delicious fish so thick in the water you could scoop them up in bushel baskets, which American industry, courage and ingenuity turn into bountiful products for export and for food for a young and growing land, which American arrogance and thoughtlessness then overexploit to the point of scarcity and endangerment of the entire resource, while American rugged individualism and antigovernment animus utterly reject the rational regulation which would preserve it for future generations. It is our best story and our worst. Be sure to visit the website, which has well-made videos.[4]

TOO MANY BOATS CHASING
TOO FEW FISH

Where do the fisheries stand today? In 1973, the Northwest Atlantic fisheries yielded 4.4. million tons of fish; in 1992, only 2.6 million tons, a decline of 42 percent.[5] The take of Atlantic cod, crucial to the New England economy, had peaked in 1968 at 3.9 million tons; by 1992, it was down to 1.2 million tons— a decline of a horrifying 69 percent.[6] 1993 saw further declines.[7] Worldwide, the marine catch had been stagnant since 1989, despite an increase in the number and capacity of all boats. From the New England fisherman's point of view, the monetary loss has been staggering, especially in most recent years: the Northeast catch of the most popular commercial species was worth over $150 million in 1991, not quite $130 million in 1992, and less than $116 million in 1993. The value of the annual catch of Atlantic cod fell from almost $75 million in 1991 to $45 million in 1993, down 40 percent.[8] In this situation, unprecedented in the human experience, the United Nations Food and Agriculture Organization (FAO) was led to suggest that the only way to increase the supply of fish was "by reducing or temporarily eliminating fishing in many fisheries."[9]

What went wrong? In *Net Loss,* a 1994 Worldwatch Paper, Peter Weber puts the problem very simply: there are too many fishers chasing too few fish.

> Today, world fisheries have on the order of twice the capacity necessary to fish the oceans. Between 1970 and 1990, FAO [United Nations Food and Agriculture Organization] recorded a doubling in the world fishing fleet, from 585,000 to 1.2 million large boats, and from 13.5 million to 25.5 million gross registered tons.[10]

Size alone creates difficulties: each of those boats represents a hefty investment for its owner, who can only pay off the loans by bringing in ever more fish. Since at least until very recently the sorts of boundaries that can limit human predation on land do not apply on the sea,[11] management options are limited to constricting the permissible time for catching fish:

> . . . open access allows fishers to enter a fishery at will. If regulators limit the total catch, they must calculate the potential take of the fishers and adjust the length of the open season accordingly. Fishers then race each other to get the most fish possible. As the number of fishers or their capacity increases, the season gets shorter. . . .[12]

tending to zero as a limit. Under these conditions, of course, the owner who fields the most or the largest boats brings in the greatest share of the prize; the incentive is to increase the capacity to catch and store fish, and the speed to get to the fishing grounds. So building to overcapacity is structured into the system.[13] The only limit on entry comes when the latest entrant, no matter how efficient, cannot meet his marginal costs. Then the catch may stabilize— but at too low a level to sustain the fishery.[14] The situation is made bad by the free-market system, which abhors limits on individual exploitation of the natural world, and then made worse by the tendency of developed nations to vote government subsidies for the financially distressed but politically popular fisherman, thus keeping boats active in the water that pure market forces would scuttle.

Clearly something has to be done. But it is not in the nature of the fishing industry, carried on by thousands of entrepreneurs who own their own boats, to cooperate in making and enforcing rules to limit the catch, even though such rules are necessary to keep the fishery going for the long run. For fishing, like farming, is not so much a business as a way of life—inherited, valued, and tied up with all other institutions in the regions that have been supported by it. The fishermen keep on doing what they have been doing all their lives, even as it destroys the resource from which they draw. "Indeed what is fascinating," one observer commented, "and also tragic . . . about the fishing industry is that it so actively participates in its own annihilation."[15] Any remedial action, then, must begin outside the industry. Once begun and accepted as reasonable, it has a chance of obtaining the support of the fishermen; it cannot succeed without their cooperation.

Before trying to crack the political nuts at the heart of this natural disaster, let us review some of the history of this craft, profession, and way of life. The analysis and conclusions of this chapter—diagnosis, prognosis, and prescription— will hold good for any fishery anywhere in the world. But each fishery has its own history, customs, economic policies, and social-support systems, without which the environmental problem (and the difficulties with the solutions) cannot be comprehended. Since we cannot cover them all, we will start with the nearest, the one made famous by Rudyard Kipling's novel *Captains Courageous*— the Gloucestermen of Georges Bank. The rest of the Northwest Atlantic fisheries will follow the same pattern, and the rest of the world, apparently, will follow in these doomed footsteps.

THE CAPTAINS COURAGEOUS:
FISHING IN NEW ENGLAND

The Natural History of Georges Bank

The curious features of the water on the massive shoal known as Georges Bank ("St. Georges' Shoal," on the earliest maps) account for the tremendous concentration of fish. A system of "banks," huge underwater plateaus in shallow water, stretches from southern New England to Newfoundland, before the continental shelf drops off. The northern banks, called the Grand Banks, historically supported an immense fishing industry in Newfoundland and Labrador. Georges Bank is further south, an oval 240 km long by 120 km wide, 120 km off the coast of New England. When the sea was lower, during the last ice age, Georges Bank was a peninsula of the North American continent; then it was an island, with giant sloth sharing the ground with walruses and mastodons. Then it sank, and the fish took over.

Now it is a prime fishing resource, a breeding and feeding area for all kinds of shellfish and fish, cod, haddock, herring, flounder, lobster, and scallops. Its strengths as nurturer of fish come from the source, and variety, of the currents that sweep across this shallow land. The Museum of Natural History description is quite clear:

> The cold, nutrient-rich Labrador current sweeps over most of the submarine plateau, and meets the warmer Gulf stream on its eastern edge. The mingling of the two currents, along with sunlight penetrating the shallow waters, creates an ideal environment for tiny sea creatures—phytoplankton (photosynthetic algae) and zooplankton (tiny free-floating creatures such as krill)—to flourish, attracting an entire ecosystem of marine animals. On Georges Bank, phytoplankton grow three times faster than on any other continental shelf. They feed the zooplankton, which are then eaten by the

larvae of vast numbers of fish such as cod, haddock, and yellowtail flounder. Georges Bank is home to more than 100 species of fish, as well as many species of marine birds, whales, dolphins and porpoises.[16]

Other physical features of Georges Bank contribute to its fecundity. Complex tidal currents add to the Labrador and the Gulf Stream to create a clockwise swirl around the edge of the Banks, carrying eggs and larvae, giving them access to food across the banks. Rough parts of the sea bottom (created by sediment left by the glaciers) give shelter to growing cod, while the clean oxygenated water of the southern gravel beds are ideal for herring. Yet another component of the water flow is storm driven. Storms are constant in the North Atlantic, and the currents that they produce add to the rapid, healthy, circulation of nutrients, phytoplankton and krill.[17] And then there are internal currents and eddies. The tidal currents are complex, since the water moves much faster over the shallow areas than the deep.

> Out of this swirl come hints, some of them quite strong, of what makes Georges Bank so productive. First, its waters are rich in nutrients like phosphorus and silicates, supplied in part by the cold oceanic water welling up from the depths onto the Bank and in part by planktonic organisms, whose excretions contain some of the nutrients they have ingested. Second, over much of the Bank, waters are sufficiently shallow so that sunlight—essential to the growth of phytoplankton, the tiny plants at the base of the food chain—penetrates all the way to the bottom. Third, tides and winds mix the shallows so that the surface waters, which otherwise would tend to lose their richness to grazing organisms, are constantly being replaced by richer waters from below. Fourth, the clockwise gyre, which appears at times to be a closed circuit, may act to keep nutrients and plankton—including fish eggs and larvae—captive in a productive environment far longer than is normally the case.[18]

The fish who thrive in this rich soup were first cataloged and described by Henry Bryant Bigelow, an early enthusiast of the Western Atlantic. He was the founder and first director of Woods Hole Oceanographic Institute and in that capacity did research for the U.S. Fish Commission (predecessor of the National Marine Fisheries Service) on their schooner, the *Grampus*. He studied the Gulf of Maine, out into Georges Bank, from 1912 to 1929, and the work that came from that study, *Fishes of the Gulf of Maine,* written with William Schroeder, is still the best starting place for understanding Georges Bank.[19]

Bigelow started with the haddock, then described all the other fish he found—the yellowtail flounder, hake, whiting, pollock, and above all the cod. The cod, as MacLeish describes it, "is the eponym of the gadoids, the family that includes the haddock, the dark handsome pollock, the whiting, and other hakes. It is the largest gadoid. One that must have gone 180 pounds live came in on a fishing schooner back in 1838, and another six feet long and 200 pounds was taken on a line off Massachusetts in 1895." The days of the giants are gone, he points out, "and that's an indication of a stock under pressure.

Thirty pounds is a fine fish these days."[20] The sad part of it is that there really is no good reason for a well-managed stock of cod to be under pressure; cod will eat anything, survive almost anything, and are enormously prolific. The mindless greed of the fisherman is overwhelming a potentially infinite natural resource.

The importance of the industry for the northeastern section of the continent cannot be overestimated. Harold A. Innis, in *The Cod Fisheries* (1978) argued that despite possibilities for the coastal population to branch out into other industry, both the United States and above all Canada remained dependent on it. It is one of the most stable and long-lasting industries in the Western Hemisphere.[21] There was, as far as anyone knew at the beginning, fish in overabundance: John Smith (the soldier and adventurer who brought Pocahontas back to England for a visit) urged England to embrace the industry as a source of unending prosperity. And indeed, the ready availability of inexpensive fish contributed enormously to Europe's prosperity before the Revolution. Cod could be shipped directly to Europe, pickled in brine, but was generally salted and dried on frames on the beaches. "Men killed and governments threatened war over which stretch of beach would be used by what ships.[22] By the same token, the newly constituted United States could not afford to lose the fish. Parceling out the fishing rights on Georges Bank between the United States and (British) Canada was an essential, and hotly contested, point in the Treaty of Paris in 1783 ending the American Revolution. (The same dispute surfaced again in the 1980s, leading to the drawing of the "Hague Line," separating U.S. from Canadian fishing rights.)

The Gloucester Fishing Industry

In *Down to the Sea: The Fishing Schooners of Gloucester,* Joseph Garland gives us an exciting history of the Gloucester enterprise, illustrated with an incredible wealth of contemporary photographs. His account is essentially a celebration, with qualifications, of the fishing way of life.

> Three pinkies first tried fishing for cod on the tricky shoals of Georges Bank, 125 miles to the southeast of Gloucester, in 1821. They anchored and were so whipped around by the riptides that nine years passed before Captain John Fletcher Wonson of East Gloucester and his crew screwed up the courage to tackle the Georges again. They found the great bank teeming with gigantic halibut, discovered they could anchor and fish without being dragged under by the current after all, and thus opened up the richest fishery in the North Atlantic.[23]

> By 1859 [Gloucester's] fleet stood at 301 schooners crewed by 3568 men and boys, augmented by another fleet of smaller craft. Together they brought in, that year alone, 60,000 barrels of mackerel, 11,400,000 pounds of codfish and 4,590,000 pounds of halibut, and a few million more of haddock, hake, pollock, herring, sole and other species, lobsters and clams, tongues, sounds and oil.[24]

The first codfishing on Georges, as Garland describes it, was "handlining," over
the rails along the side of an anchored boat. The "Georges gear," sinkered tarred
line with several hooks, was let down to just off the bottom. The lines of the fishermen were kept apart by "sojers," wooden pins every 4 feet or so, on the fishing
rails. When cod got on the lines, the fisherman hauled back, maybe taking half
an hour to wrestle a pair of big ones to the surface and gaff them aboard.

> The codfish were worked off the hooks, their tongues cut out for keeping
> tally, and the gangings replaced with a pair baited in the meanwhile, and
> back over with the lead. This way, a high-line fisherman (the best, or
> luckiest fisherman—the one with the highest catch) on his best day might
> boat nearly two hundred fish, and a lucky crew as much as thirty thousand
> pounds in the round, eviscerated. If he chanced upon a halibut, each man
> cut his own distinctive mark in it for counting in his favor.[25]

By 1879, new fish products were bringing prosperity to Gloucester and the
surrounding region. In that year Gloucester packed off 14 million pounds of its
widely advertised "boneless fish"—salt cod packed in boxes. By that time also
the "fish cake" was enormously popular. Potatoes would be brought down
from Aroostook County, Maine, by the carload, with a stove (and stovetender)
in the boxcar to keep them from freezing. They'd be shredded, mixed with
chopped salt cod, and the mixture tinned, ready to be scooped out, fried, and
served up with ketchup.[26] As may be expected, the factory owners got most of
that prosperity, with the fishermen still scrabbling for a living.

> The average Gloucester fisherman in 1879 made $175, although the
> Goode study estimated that if he worked like the devil for twelve months,
> including winter, he stood to earn as much as $300 to $500, the skipper
> usually double that.[27]

By 1900 the town and the entire region depended on that catch for their
livelihood.

Garland's celebration of fishing and its role in New England is sobered by
his grim reminders of the cost.

> The fish were there all right, but what a deadly game! The best fishing was
> in the worst place, naturally, the east and southeast rim of the shoals in two
> to twelve fathoms, where the waves broke in rough weather. This was one
> hell of a lee in an easterly storm. . . . [28]

Brave souls but damn fools, observers at the time agreed. They would not raise—
or more realistically, cut loose—the anchor, in a storm, for fear of losing fish, for
fear of losing face with their rivals, and for (a very Yankee) fear of expense: their
anchor cables, first to go in any rough weather, were not insurable.

Many were lost. Garland documents the loss and danger associated with
that way of life, and the callousness, even then, of the capitalist system that
underlay this example of American industry:

> . . . in the twenty-five years between 1866 and 1890 Gloucester lost 382
> schooners and 2454 fishermen. All of those men didn't go down with

their ships, nor did every ship let down its men. Dories capsized or went adrift. Men were washed overboard, fell out of the rigging, or were struck by booms. Schooners were lost through negligence or in storms and under conditions that no vessel could be expected to survive. All the same, as Chapelle has been quoted on an earlier generation of schooners, " . . . the men lost cost the shipowner nothing, and insurance could take care of the loss of vessel property."[29]

. . . No one knows how many men and boys—fishing vessels usually carried one or two youngsters as apprentices—were lost from the town. One estimate, which seems high, puts the figure at 30,000 since the beginning 350 years ago. Ten thousand seems more like it, and still appalling. A good many went down tumbling in the wildness of Georges Bank.[30]

There was, for instance, the storm of February 23, 1862, when a hundred or so boats, most of them from Gloucester, were fishing the Bank. Thirteen went down in collisions, all hands lost, while two more were abandoned. About 138 people drowned in 24 hours.[31] And on the night of February 20, 1879, a gale wiped out 13 Gloucester fishing boats, at a cost of 143 men. "Before the year 1879 was out, the count would be twenty-nine Gloucester schooners and 249 men, by far the most of them gone down with their vessels."[32]

How long could such an industry have continued? There is no sign that the Gloucestermen were willing to give up their fishing because of the danger. (It should be noted, the danger continues, if to a smaller degree: "Their jobs are among the most dangerous in America," noted the *Times,* in its report on the loss of the trawler *Arctic Roseon* on April 2, 2001.)[33] And had they continued in their old wooden schooners, as Garland points out, their simple ways of fishing could have gone on indefinitely: there was a nice balance between human need and technology and the natural supply of fish.[34] We need only compare the proud yield of 5.7 *thousand* tons of cod brought in by the huge fleet in 1859 with the 3.9 *million* tons brought in 1968. When the technology changed, starting with the diesel engines and ending with the huge factory trawler, the balance was destroyed.

THE RUSSIANS ARE COMING! AND THE
GERMANS, POLES, SPANISH . . .

The disaster began in the mid-1950s, when a new kind of fishing vessel began to sail the Atlantic waters. It was huge (the earliest were over 300 feet, and they ranged higher), it fished from the stern instead of over the side, and it swiftly processed and froze everything it caught. It was called a "factory-equipped freezer stern trawler," or factory trawler, for short, and it spelled doom to any fishery it visited.[35] For the most part, the factory trawlers were foreign.[36]

The Soviets showed up with their giants at the beginning of the sixties,
and then the Germans and the Poles and the Spaniards. . . . The new technology moved in floating cities, and it broke the back of the fisheries from
Labrador to Georges and on southwest.[37]

This was no extension of an existing industry; "in an hour, a factory ship hauls
in as much cod—around a hundred tons—as a typical 17th century boat could
catch in a season. At first the fleets fished for squid and red hake and the like,
species not customarily marketed in New England ports. But they were fishers
of opportunity, and then, in the middle sixties, there occurred one of those
periodic blooms of haddock, or, more precisely,

> haddock surviving to catchable size. The trawlers took most of them and
> came back for more. There were more Russians on Georges by then than
> there were Americans. The foreigners swept the bottoms and the midwa-
> ters. To them, Georges was just one of many shoalings in the high seas,
> places with names like Whale Deep and Flemish Cap off Atlantic Canada,
> No Name Bank off Greenland, Bill Bailey's Bank off Iceland, Viking Bank
> and Tiddly off Scandinavia, Skolpen and Parson's Nose off the Soviet
> Union. Processors and trawlers moved along the chain pulse-fishing,
> setting their nets for one species until the catch became too small to
> bother with, and then moving on or setting their nets for another. The
> system worked so well that shortly it failed.[38]

It is not clear whether it was concern for the preservation of the fishery or
concern for national sovereignty that prompted the U.S. Congress to move,
but move it did. For the

> intolerable had happened: the Russians were now the highliners. . . . In
> 1960, just before the foreigners arrived on Georges, American boats were
> taking 90 percent of the harvest there, and most of the remainder went to
> the Canadians. Twelve years later the Yankees were taking 10 percent and
> the foreigners the rest. It wasn't just the long-distance fleets. New
> England's total catch had been dropping, with some surges here and there,
> ever since 1950. But you couldn't tell that to the captains. From Rhode
> Island to Maine, they sat in their small, wood-hulled, fifteen-year-old boats
> and roared.
>
> The response from Washington was the Fisheries Conservation and
> Management Act of 1976, known as the Magnuson Act. . . . [which]
> extended United States fishery jurisdiction out to two hundred miles.[39]

Other countries claimed 200-mile limits too, of course; the "exclusive economic zones" (EEZs) of 122 coastal states totaled 10 percent of the ocean's surface in 1992. (That area included all the good fishing.)[40] Ten percent of the total
EEZs belonged to the United States. Even after the World Court required the
United States to shave off the eastern corner of the Georges Banks for Canada,
the fishermen thought that now there'd be plenty of fish for all of them, and
no limits.

In 1980, fishermen caught about 294 million pounds of fish and shellfish from Georges Bank, worth a little under $200 million dockside and considerably more when processing and marketing are thrown in. The Americans, fishing all over the Bank, took three quarters of that poundage and two-thirds of the value. The Canadians, restricted by joint agreement to the eastern third, took almost all the rest, mostly scallops.[41]

But the fishery continued to decline. The fishermen were wrong: by this time our own fishing capacity was sufficient to overwhelm the capacity of the Georges. The act gave the government power to set quotas to conserve threatened species, and shortly these became necessary.[42] For the fishery did not recover; New England had "replaced overfishing by foreign fleets with overfishing by their own," and the catch continued to decline.[43] By 1993, cod and yellowtail flounder were at record lows off New England; after the haddock catch plunged 63 percent in one year, the federal government shut down part of the Georges Bank completely.[44]

The days of mass production fishing are essentially over. According to William Warner (in *Distant Water: The Fate of the North Atlantic Fisherman*) the factory trawlers were on their way out by the late 1970s. There were no more of the "floating cities—the massive concentrations of one hundred or more distant water vessels once so common on prime grounds."[45] Now they seemed, not the wave of the future, but dinosaurs of the past. With a daily operating cost of about $13,000 each, and operations scaled to a very high catch of single species at one time, they could not possibly make a living on the quotas they had been assigned by coastal states. The 200-mile limit had made the difference.

By 1980, when the last German ships were recalled from New Zealand, the industry had about folded in Germany. England had perhaps a dozen distant water ships in 1982; the Hull Fishing Vessel Owners Association (the port authority that ran the fishing docks in that city) went bankrupt in 1980, and Hull itself took on the aspect of a maritime ghost town. The Spanish boats continued to fish; less controlled by government or central agencies than the others, they simply went on doing what they knew how to do, catching fewer fish each trip.[46] Spanish and Portuguese fishing boats, flying flags of convenience to evade international treaties to which their nations are signatory, have been seized by Canada as recently as 1994, for predatory overfishing, with equipment that has been banned, in grounds where, according to the Canadians, they have no right to be.[47] We are looking at the tail end of an industry; the Grand Banks, like the Georges, are overfished, and large-scale fishing can no longer survive there. The question now, is whether any fishing can survive.

A Short History of a Short Controversy: Oil versus Fish

In the late 1970s and early 1980s, when oil prices were high, several American oil companies undertook to extend their offshore drilling operations from the friendly shores of the Gulf of Mexico to the decidedly less congenial shores of rocky New England. This controversy is treated at length in a highly readable account by William MacLeish, *Oil And Water: The Struggle for Georges Bank,* published in 1985.[48] In a sense, the controversy is of only historical interest, since not enough oil was discovered in the drillings that were made to make the enterprise commercially worthwhile. But at the time, there was strong interest in drilling, and controversy over sale of the leases for drilling gave the nation an opportunity to weigh the value of the fishery over against the value of a new source of petroleum. For the first time, the nation came to grips in the public forums of Congress and courtroom with the importance of the Georges Bank fishery.

One of the first legal actions, for example, came about over the sale of Lease Sale Forty-Two—roughly translated, the government's sale to an oil company of the right to lease a particular patch of ocean for the purpose of drilling for oil. It was in January 1978, that the Commonwealth of Massachusetts brought suit to delay that sale, and Judge W. Arthur Garrity—the same judge who ordered the busing to integrate Boston's schools—granted a preliminary injunction against it. Excerpts from his decision:

> This is no ordinary fishing ground. It is as important a resource as the people of this state will ever have to rely upon. . . . The plaintiffs are looking for a delay of a relatively few months to preserve a resource that has taken millions of years to accrue, and which will be with us, for better or for worse, for untold centuries to come. . . . The opposing considerations here are use for a period of about twenty years as a source for gas and oil, as against the preservation of the natural resource . . . for the indefinite future. . . . If there ever was a public interest case, this is it.[49]

The U.S. Government and the oil companies promptly sued to stay the injunction, in the United States Court of Appeals for the First Circuit (Boston). Judge Levin H. Campbell said absolutely not; the decision of the "judge below" was quite correct. There may be issues more serious than ones involving the future of the oceans of our planet and the life within them, but surely they are few.[50]

Five years later, for another example, in March 1983, a part of the controversy came to a head in a suit by the Conservation Law Foundation and several other environmental organizations (including Greenpeace and the Massachusetts branch of the Audubon Society) to obtain an injunction against another of the lease sales. In granting the injunction, federal judge A. David Mazzone emphasized the importance of preserving the fishery. "In short," he wrote, Georges Bank

> represents a renewable, self-sustaining resource for the entire nation. . . . in light of the significance of the Georges Bank fishery resource that may be jeopardized by that sale, I find that the plaintiffs have adequately demonstrated that they will suffer irreparable harm if this injunction does not issue.[51]

We will never know what would have happened, in the event that oil had been found in abundance beneath the Georges. At the least, the dialogue on its value had—after two centuries!—begun, and a foundation laid for a discussion of what we lose when we thoughtlessly destroy a major national resource.

PRESENT AND FUTURE

Taking Stock

Peter Weber, in *Net Loss,* a 1994 WorldWatch book, points out that overfishing has long-term environmental consequences. The chief cause

> of the decline of the Atlantic cod and haddock fisheries off North America. . . . appears to be long-term overfishing, which has reduced the average size of the cod and haddock, as well as their overall numbers. By removing such a large number of these predators, fishers may have also caused a long-term transformation of the North Atlantic ecosystem. Populations of dogfish and skate—types of shark—have boomed and are now filling the niche left by the cod and haddock. Because dogfish and skate prey on young cod and haddock as well, they are reinforcing this ecological shift. Although the ecosystem is still producing fish, the fishers lose out because there is little demand in North America for dogfish and skate, which do not store well.[52]

Demand can be changed. The dogfish, now marketed as a "cape shark," has picked up an audience, and the skate has been fished until its survival, too, is in question.

If fish become scarce, how to reduce pressure on the fisheries? Weber points out that the first reaction of fishing nations tends to be to adopt programs (consolidation, licensing, quotas etc.) that put fewer fishing boats on the water. These surviving boats tend to be the most "efficient," in terms of operating cost per unit of fish processed, and these, of course, turn out to be the biggest and the newest, and they employ the least crew. Weber, who is at least as concerned for worldwide employment as he is for the fish, finds that solution perverse: what is needed is a proliferation of small local fishers, who tend to employ many more persons in the process of taking many fewer fish, and whose simple fishing methods can never damage a large fishery.[53]

The employment issue on the Georges is addressed directly in documents prepared for the East Coast Fisheries Federation, by its executive director, James O'Malley. He cites the estimate by the New England Fishery Management Council, that "50% effort reduction"—cutting back the amount of fishing by one half—will be needed to replenish the stock of fish on the Georges.[54] The fishing fleet in the Northeast will shrink. How will it do this? Let us count the ways:

> The contraction of the fleet may take place through bankruptcy, attrition by age, consolidation of fishing power into fewer hands, or through a buyout of existing vessels.
>
> Each of these alternatives has a cost. Widespread bankruptcy is socially unacceptable. Furthermore, the economic failure of any vessel does not mean that its fishing power is removed from the fleet; only that it will be resurrected at a lower price by the next purchaser, leaving the same level of fishing pressure on the resource.[55]

Shades of the arrival of the Spanish and the Portuguese. There is no sign that attrition will have any significant effects soon; consolidation may mean fewer boats, but working at higher efficiency to bring in more fish per boat. As long as the marginal costs of the low-end producer are met, the fishing will continue; the market, unaided by government, does not hold a solution for the Georges.

The major obstacle to any rational plan is the entrenched opposition of fishermen to any restrictions *at all;* this industry has never had them. For the families who are invested in the industry, as Michael Parfit has observed, all such measures are anathema,

> as I learned one evening in New England at a hearing on bluefin fisheries. All it took was a speaker to gingerly suggest limiting numbers of fishermen. A gray-haired man leaped to his feet, furious.
>
> "Don't go to limited access!" he shouted across the room. "I don't want to be limited! That's not American!"[56]

Is It Possible to Strike a Balance?

From a variety of sources, a pattern emerges of suggested solutions in order of priority:

1. Immediately: reduce the fishing, allow the fishery to recover. That means taking boats off the water—temporarily, for periods, or permanently. The Grand Banks has already been temporarily closed to fishing, to allow time for the fish to breed and grow. But programs are needed to help in the transition. Weber identifies

> a $30 million package for New England fishers and their communities. Twelve million dollars of this is earmarked to help individual fishers move into other fisheries and other industries.[57]

That solution, a typical "bail out" designed to keep present fishers in business somehow, while directing others to "other fisheries" (which? all fisheries are depleted), meanwhile pretending to tempt others to "retire early," somehow fails in conviction. And just what "other industries" did the government have in mind? New England would like to know. (Computer operators are unemployed, too.)

2. We surely need international agreements to prevent the kind of flag-of-convenience raiding that the Spanish boats were caught at by the outraged Canadians. On August 8, 1995, the *New York Times* applauded the first international agreement that might do some good:

> The United Nations Food and Agriculture Organization, once an ardent booster of highly mechanized fleets that sweep up fish by the ton, now says that virtually every commercial fish species is either declining or at serious risk. . . . Last Friday, after two years of protracted and bitter negotiations, delegates from 100 countries meeting under the auspices of the United

Nations approved the first international treaty to regulate fishing on the high seas.[58]

The agreement only regulates "straddling" fish, which migrate from coastal waters to high seas. Still, the *Times* believes, it will reduce the appalling waste of "bycatch," undesirable fish caught in indiscriminate nets, rejected, and dumped dead back into the sea. The agreement at least regulates the nets, prohibiting the kind that catch everything, and provides for some international inspection. It is also time, the editorial concludes, that we stop "bailing out" the fishing fleets through subsidies that allow inefficient fishermen to continue in business.

3. "Individually transferable quotas (ITQs)" (also known as individual fishing quotas, or IFCs) assign quotas of certain numbers of certain fish to present fishermen; no one is then allowed to take fish at all without owning such a quota. The fishermen may use, give, bequeath, assign, sell, or otherwise treat that quota as personal property—thus, "individually transferable." For those presently in business, the ITQ is pure bonus, unbought value, a windfall, with no reason given for bestowing it. For the purchaser, it is a barrier to entry into the industry, which is the point.[59] (It has been suggested that the initial batch of ITQs be auctioned off instead of just given, so that the public can get some of the benefit of the resource that is, after all, public.) As the ITQs can be regulated—their number increased or decreased as the fishery waxes or wanes—there is a theoretical possibility of controlling the amount of fishing effort. But then, of course, there is the problem of enforcement—someone has to inspect every boat coming in off those foggy and storm-tossed waters, and there is no way short of having a permanent inspector on every boat to make sure that the boats don't simply catch everything they can, select and keep the most valuable part of their catch to the extent of their quota (as they come home to port), throw all the rest of the fish over the side dead, and tie up at the dock a perfect model of compliance. That will never save the fishery. A worse problem, from the point of view of justice, is the high likelihood that three weeks after the issuance of the quotas, it would be discovered that a consortium of large-boat operators and fish processors now own all the quotas in existence, having bought them from, and leased them back to, the picturesque but poor independent fishers whose image has protected the industry for so long. It doesn't seem to be a good idea generally, and such quotas have not been tried. They still have their defenders, among those who stand to profit most from the concentration of fishing rights in the hands of the few. One Frederick Meeker, for instance, a New York attorney who represents commercial fishers, addressing the Property Rights Foundation of America, Inc. on the occasion of their annual meeting in 1999, characterized the fishers' situation in classic terms:

> . . . in my lifetime we have gone from total freedom of the seas to a situation now where commercial fishermen are probably the most regulated people on earth, an occupation that was once characterized as total

freedom. . . . Now you've got a situation where the bureaucrats are telling you when you can fish, where you can fish, how much you can catch, and they have got to approve it before you leave.[60]

He goes on to recommend ITQs, for making it possible for fishermen to get "rich," which is "totally unacceptable to the bureaucrats." It is likely that here as elsewhere, the rhetoric of "freedom" (let alone "getting rich") conceals the extent to which such a distribution of private property rights in a public resource will rapidly enable the concentration of that ownership in a few, very wealthy, private hands. People will, indeed, get rich, just not the fishers.

4. A frank buyout might be a more adequate solution. A buyout would require that fishers turn in their licenses once for all and scrap their boats, in return for some federally funded retirement or retraining package. Such plans have worked in the United Kingdom, and are currently proposed for New England.[61]

5. That buyout might work better if put in combination with severe limits on the hunting seasons; the less efficient boats would have the hardest time making a living in a short season, which would give their operators an incentive to retire.

6. What about limiting the technology? Theoretically, limits on boats and methods should work—the Gloucestermen could have fished indefinitely. But such measures are very difficult to implement. Recall the cry of Parfit's fisherman: "Limits are not American!" Also, sailing boats insult the machismo of the machine-oriented American male. Besides, American ingenuity would sabotage the effect.

7. For long-term supply of fish for the world, we must encourage fish farming. It could be argued that the state of the art of the fish industry is at this time about where the state of the art in the beef cattle industry was at the time of Buffalo Bill—we find the wild species in their largest concentrations, then use our best technology to slaughter them. No wonder the fisheries are crashing. What could be accomplished if we put our technology to work breeding fish, experimenting with new breeds of fish, studying their diseases, and finding what combinations of food would produce the best flesh for the table?

There are disadvantages to fish farming, aquaculture, as it is now practiced. First, only fish for the rich man's table, the most expensive species, are raised; they bring in the highest profit. More important, we are currently dependent on coastline locations for the farms, since we dare not try to raise marine fish without their native waters. But the coastline is the most valuable land we have, in demand for industrial, recreational, and residential purposes. Worse, the coastal salt marshes, what are left of them, are the essential nurseries for the life of the sea; if we convert them to fish farms, we condemn all wild life in the ocean to death.

The objections can be answered: Let the state farms sponsor experimentation in feeding materials, diseases, and environment, in aquaculture as they do in animal husbandry. Let new nutrient broths be discovered and tried. There is no reason why aquaculture could not take place in the middle of the country or in any place where real estate is more available than on the coasts or, for that matter, in large pens in the shallow ocean.

The Sadness of It All

We have spoken, in the course of this chapter, of the attitudes of the fishermen and their families in this crisis. They are concerned; they are intelligent; they understand precisely the nature of the problem, the catastrophe that attends inaction, and the probable direction of any effective action. Yet they resist it to the core: they are against limits, against collectivization and consolidation, against being regulated, reformed, and brought in line with the common good for the long run. They view themselves as the last leaders of a heroic life, the last independents in a corporate country, the last real entrepreneurs, mustering intelligence, tradition, and courage to wrest a living from the merciless sea. All of this will be lost: whether we do nothing, and allow the fish, fisheries, fishermen, fishing towns, and regions to perish together, or whether we do what has to be done to save the resource by, essentially, telling fishers where and when and for what they may fish, their way of life will be gone. The collapse of the New England fisheries has been compared well to the Dust Bowl in the Midwest; as went the family farm, so goes the Gloucesterman. In the course of a community celebration of the "fishing way of life" in St. John's, Newfoundland, after the closing of the Grand Banks, Michael Parfit found himself meditating on that comparison:

> The Grand Banks disaster has been called the Dust Bowl of fishing. The Dust Bowl did not kill American agriculture, just changed it. It became big industry: highly regulated, tidy. Thus it may be with fishing. Fish farming, the only piece of world fisheries to show a real gain in recent years, will continue to grow. So will regulation of the sea itself. We will still have fish but not the fishermen we knew. In that auditorium in St. John's, the old life was turning from reality to myth before my eyes.[62]

Finally, the frontier is closed, and the government will have to come in and regulate. The old fisherman's protest against being "limited" hits home in its genuinely American character and in its futility. As Parfit comments,

> His words struck me as a cry of loss, and I imagined them rolling out across this world of inevitable limits, to the very edge of the sea.[63]

QUESTIONS FOR REFLECTION

1. What persuades us of the value of preserving the New England fisheries? Consider the following answers: (a) To preserve the New England Aquatic ecosystem; (b) To ensure the future of the food supply; (c) To protect the way of life of the New England fishermen; (d) Nothing: let it die and resort to fish farming. What say you?

2. How does it happen that it is in no one's interest to preserve the fishery, but it is in everyone's interest to preserve the fishery?

NOTES

1. Ransom A. Myers and Boris Worm, "Rapid Worldwide Depletion of Predatory Fish Communities," *Nature* 423 (May 2003): 280–83.

2. Ben Harder, "Catch Zero: What Can Be Done as Marine Ecosystems Face a Deepening Crisis?" *Science News Online* 164(4), accessed 26 July 2003.

3. Ibid.

4. "Will the Fish Return? How Greed and Gear Emptied Georges Bank," http://sciencebulletins.amnh.org/biobulletin/biobulletin/story1208.html.

5. Peter Weber, *Net Loss: Fish, Jobs, and the Marine Environment,* Worldwatch Paper 120 (Washington, DC: Worldwatch Institute, July 1994, p. 14, table 1.

6. *Ibid.,* p. 15, table 2.

7. Northeast Fisheries Science Center, *Status of the Fishery Resources off the Northeastern United States for 1994,* Woods Hole, MA: NOAA Technical Memorandum NMFS-NE-108, 1995.

8. James D. O'Malley, Draft Statement on Buyout Design, September 1994, p. 8; unpublished document, available from East Coast Fisheries Federation, PO Box 649, Narragansett, RI 02882, or call (401) 782-3440.

9. Food and Agriculture Organization of the United Nations (FAO), *Marine Fisheries and the Law of the Sea: A Decade of Change,* FAO Fisheries Circular No. 853 (Rome, 1993); cited in ibid., p. 16.

10. Weber, *Net Loss,* p. 28.

11. In theory, the use of global positioning systems should make it possible to put up electronic "fences" all along the 200-mile limits of the fishing nations and to patrol them by remote control. No one has yet suggested this practice.

12. Weber, *Net Loss,* p. 28.

13. Ibid., p. 28.

14. Ibid., p. 29.

15. James R. McGoodwin, *Crisis in the World's Fisheries* (Stanford, CA: Stanford University Press, 1990), note 14.

16. See note 4 above.

17. William H. MacLeish, *Oil and Water: The Struggle for Georges Bank* (Boston: Atlantic Monthly Press, 1985), pp. 16–164.

18. Ibid., p. 164.

19. Ibid., p.14.

20. Ibid., p.17.

21. Harold A. Innis, *The Cod Fisheries: The History of an International Economy* (Toronto: University of Toronto Press, 1978), cited in MacLeish, *Oil and Water,* p. 19.

22. MacLeish, *Oil and Water,* p. 21.

23. Joseph E. Garland, *Down to the Sea: The Fishing Schooners of Gloucester,* introduction by Sterling Hayden (Boston: Godine, 1983), p. 9.

24. Ibid., p. 15.

25. Ibid.

26. Ibid., p. 143.

27. Ibid.

28. Ibid., p. 101.

29. Ibid., p. 17.

30. Ibid. , p. 25.

31. Ibid., p. 26.

32. Ibid., p. 104.

33. Sam Howe Verhovek, "Accepting the Risk of the Sea Does Not Soften the Blow," *New York Times,* 5 April 2001, p. A18.

34. Garland, *Down to the Sea,* p. 18.

35. William W. Warner, *Distant Water: The Fate of the North Atlantic Fisherman* (Boston: Little, Brown, 1977), p. vii.

36. The United States has some of them, of course, but not for the New England

fishery. An excellent diagram of such a ship, with all its activities, is found on page 14 of Michael Parfit's "Diminishing Returns," an article on the state of fisheries worldwide in *National Geographic* (November 1995).

37. MacLeish, *Oil and Water,* p. 201.

38. Ibid., pp. 201–2.

39. MacLeish, *Oil and Water,* p. 203.

40. Weber, *Net Loss,* p. 47.

41. MacLeish, *Oil and Water,* pp. 28–29.

42. Ibid., p. 203.

43. Weber, *Net Loss,* p. 53.

44. Frank Graham, Jr., "Defender of the Fishes," *Audubon Magazine* (September–October 1994): 96–99.

45. Warner, *Distant Water,* p. 309.

46. Ibid., pp. 311–15.

47. Weber, *Net Loss,* p. 5 See also Clyde H. Farnsworth, "Canada Acts to Cut Fishing by Foreigners: Will Seize Boats Outside Its Waters," *New York Times,* 22 May 1994; Colin Nickerson, "Pirates Plunder Fisheries," *Boston Sunday Globe,* 17 April 1994.

48. MacLeish, *Oil And Water,* pp. 72–73.

49. Ibid.

50. Ibid., p. 74.

51. Ibid., p. 245.

52. Weber, *Net Loss,* p. 19. He cites as his authority on this change, Massachusetts Offshore Groundfish Task Force, *New England Groundfish in Crisis* (Boston, MA: Executive Office of Environmental Affairs, 1990).

53. Ibid.

54. O'Malley, Draft Statement.

55. Ibid., p. 19.

56. Parfit, "Diminishing Returns," p. 29.

57. Weber, *Net Loss,* p. 53.

58. Editorial, *New York Times,* "A Modest Step to Save the Fish," 8 August 1995.

59. Weber, *Net Loss,* p. 35.

59. Fisheries Conservation through Property Rights, http://www.prfamerica.org/FisheriesConservation.html.

61. O'Malley, "Draft Statement."

62. Parfit, "Diminishing Returns," p. 29.

63. Ibid., p. 29.

4

The Ingenuity
of the Bugs

Combating Resistance
to Antibiotics

INTRODUCTION: THINKING LIKE
AN ECOSYSTEM

How does an ecosystem think? Tyler Miller defines an ecosystem as "a community of different species interacting with one another and with their nonliving environment of matter and energy."[1] (He goes on to point out that the choice of what counts as an ecosystem for purposes of study is essentially arbitrary. An ecosystem can be as small as a child's aquarium or as large as the Earth. The ecosystem we will be studying in this chapter is the human body.) Each organism feeds on other organisms and is food to yet others. In their interaction, the species of a mature ecosystem are kept in balance by limiting factors in the system. Each species, we may assume with Thomas Malthus, will reproduce as often as it can and will overrun the earth unless it is kept in check by predation (other species eating it) or the natural limits of the food supply. (The food supply, plant or animal, reproducing as fast as it can, is limited in turn by the amount of water available. And so forth.) Within each species, there is fierce competition among individuals to reproduce. The biggest, prettiest, most sexually attractive members succeed in mating and having babies, while the less attractive ones often do not.

Imagine an ecosystem composed of open grassland dotted with deep swamps and thickets. Herds of wild deer roam the grasslands, preyed on by a few packs of small wolves. Deep in the thickets lives a species of small pigs, feasting on wild cabbage. There are no predators in the thickets, so periodically, if the cabbage has a really good year, the pigs become too numerous for the thickets, wander into the grasslands, and are promptly eaten by wolves. The system is in balance.

However, crises occur periodically. Every once in a while the pigs mutate into a huge species led by nasty tusked boars. They rapidly outstrip the food supply in the thickets and charge onto the grassland. Sometimes the wolves can kill enough of the pigs to save the grassland, and sometimes they cannot. Sometimes the wild pigs can crowd out and destroy all the other organisms of the ecosystem, including the wolves, and the ecosystem collapses.

Now introduce a park ranger and a few prides of lions into the ecosystem. When the ranger sees that the great big pigs are overwhelming the wolves, he turns loose about three dozen lions, who gobble up the pigs on the grassland and in most of the thickets too, and then go back to their cages. The wolves recover their numbers, and the system is again in balance.

Add a twist to the mix: the lions (although not the wolves) have distinct food preferences—they like dark-colored prey, and they won't eat light food. This characteristic works well for the ranger, because almost all the pigs, large or small, are dark, almost black. It seems that the dark pigs are much more sexually attractive to pigs of the opposite sex and experience proportionately more reproductive success. Some pigs are white; the lions won't eat those. But after the lions have finished with the dark-colored ones, the wolves can easily polish off the few white ones that are left.

The intelligent park ranger will only send out the lions if an eco-crisis is imminent, because the system generally works so well by itself. But now suppose some bureaucrat in the National Park System decides that it would be better to be proactive about protecting the ecosystem. He orders that a pride of lions should be deployed anytime a pig is seen anywhere near the grassland or anytime that wolves seem to be nervous about pigs *possibly* entering the grassland. Alternatively, he has a pride of lions introduced permanently into the system, to prevent the porcine community from overpopulating. Thanks to any one of these three measures, lions begin living full time in the ecosystem.

Remember, the lions differ from the wolves on two accounts: they are just as much at home in the thickets as in the grasslands, and they don't eat white pigs. So what's going to happen to the pig population? The lions will contentedly munch on the thicket-based native population of pigs and on minor outbreaks of pigs the wolves probably could have handled, but they will do so very selectively—they will eat only the dark-colored ones, which up to now have made up the vast majority of the pig population. With the pig population down, cabbage flourishes, and pigs that would not ordinarily be able to find mates and reproduce suddenly discover that they too can have families. White pigs begin to be seen in the thickets with far more frequency. After many generations of this happenstance, we have a new majority—most of the pigs are light.

What will happen the next time the pigs mutate into the large-tusked variety and begin to overrun the grasslands? The lions will leave most of the raging pigs alone, for most are of the color they won't eat. The balance of the ecosystem has depended on the wolves and the lions working together, but now the overwhelmed wolves and the finicky lions are simply unable to mount a defense. The ecosystem, therefore, is doomed.

Suppose we could interview the ecosystem on its preferences for its own survival. What would its priorities be? First of all, undoubtedly it would ask to be left alone. It doesn't need lions to munch on the pigs in the thickets. The pigs were contented there and kept the cabbage from getting out of hand. It doesn't need ranchers to shoot the wolves, gardeners to spruce up the grassland, or the introduction of cats, dogs, rabbits, zebra mussels, swans, bittersweet, or kudzu for any reason whatsoever. There is no telling what exotic things are going to do in an ecosystem, and the fewer of them the better. Second, the major defense against those wretched pig outbreaks is in fact the health of the wolf packs and of the system generally. If we want to protect the ecosystem, we should watch its general health, not just its pigs. And third, just to reinforce this point, please note that the introduction of lions to eat the pigs on a regular basis made it impossible to handle those foreseeable periodic outbreaks, thereby dooming the ecosystem. What can be done to restore its natural balance?

As mentioned earlier, the human body itself is an ecosystem. It lives ordinarily in a natural balance we know as "health," a condition that is compatible with several less-than-optimal conditions. That is, a person can be "healthy" although severely physically or mentally handicapped, deprived of limbs, brain-damaged, or even consigned to a persistent vegetative state. We are focusing here exclusively on the internal landscape of the body and the balance of its organisms. Among these organisms are colonies of microorganisms—bacteria, protozoa, fungus—that are doing no particular harm to the body and may be doing some good. (Years ago we found out that colonies of bacteria are essential to digesting our food.) To create a useful analogy, imagine these colonies as the pigs-in-the-thickets of our earlier discussion. Roaming through the ecosystem that is our body are the many phagocytes and other cells—the wolves—that make up the "immune system." Routinely eliminating the germs that we inhale with every breath and mobilizing to attack infectious outbreaks of alien microorganisms (the mutant pigs), phagocytes are the reason we don't die every time we cut a finger or catch a cold. The immune system is our first line of defense, and until the middle of the twentieth century, it was really our only line of defense. Before the introduction of antibiotics—species of fungus, usually, that like to eat bacteria—any outbreak of infection, even to scraped knees and sore throats, could easily be fatal to the whole ecosystem.

In keeping with our anaology, antibiotics are the lions. They attack germs anywhere in the body, as long as the germs are the kind they can eat. There are always a few germs of different kinds that are "resistant" to the antibiotics, germs that they just cannot get rid of. But the wolves are still around, and as long as they are not permanently put out of action by some other enemy, they can rally to destroy the germs that are left after the antibiotic has killed all that it can kill.

This chapter addresses the problem of the steady and alarming increase in "antibiotic resistance," whereby people are dying of infections that were thought to be licked—that is, the reliable lions are no longer eliminating the pigs. We need to ask, first, what practices are contributing to this very alarming turn of events, and second, are those practices justified on balance by the advantages they were instituted to secure? We will address them in that order.

THE SLOW DESTRUCTION
OF AN ECOSYSTEM

Antibiotics (the lions) were spectacularly successful when they were introduced, shortly after World War II. Penicillin, discovered in 1928 as a pollutant in imperfectly monitored bacterium cultures, had found its first major use during the war, knocking out infections in wounds and venereal disease with the same lethal thoroughness. After the war, it came into widespread use and rapidly developed a well-deserved reputation for magical effectiveness against diseases that had often been fatal. Every family has a "penicillin story" dating from those times, often several. My (the present author Newton's) husband's father, for instance, almost died of kidney disease in 1943, but because he was in the military, he received penicillin and lived. His older sister, however, died in the late 1930s of a skinned knee she suffered while roller skating—the infection got into the bone and killed her. I almost died in 1946 of a raging fever (probably due to a bacterial infection secondary to bronchitis), but since the hospital to which I was taken was an old army Air Corps facility, they had a supply of penicillin, so I got well. And so forth. There was nothing those lions couldn't do.

But beneath the surface of the "magic bullet" antibiotics, a selective process was at work. Antibiotics, like the lions in our hypothesized ecosystem, don't kill all the germs. They only kill the ones that are susceptible to their attack. Some germs (because they have thicker cell walls, or because they can expel the antibiotic through their waste disposal system, for instance) are not.[2] The immune system (the wolves) should get the rest of them and bring the outbreak (of pigs) to a close. There may be problems with the assumption that it can. First, if there's something really wrong with the system—if the wolves are badly compromised (see Plague Years section, below)—even a few of the resistant germs (the white pigs) may be too much for the weakened immune system to handle, and the disease will persist. At this point the resistant germs will multiply without opposition, possibly infecting many more people, before they finally kill the patient. "Through natural selection, a single mutant can pass such traits on to most of its offspring, which can amount to 16,777,216 in only 24 hours! Each time this strain of bacterium is exposed to penicillin or some other antibiotic, a larger proportion of its offspring are genetically resistant to the drug."[3]

Second, to change the order of our analogy, if the lions are called off too soon—if the patient is "noncompliant," and does not take the entire dose of the antibiotic as prescribed—too many pigs of all kinds may be left on the grassland, and the wolves may be unable to get rid of them. In that case, of course, the proportion of white to dark pigs will be higher than it was before the lions first attacked. When the wolves, the immune system, can't handle the problem, the symptoms of the disease will reappear, and the patient may begin to receive an antibiotic again. That amounts to letting loose a few more lions. They will happily eat dark pigs, but by now the white ones may have multiplied to the point where they alone can overwhelm the wolves. At some point in this process of inadequate medication, the tipping point will come, and there will simply be more germs, antibiotic resistant germs, than the body can handle, and the disease will become fatal.

Why are antibiotics a problem now? Because they were entirely too successful. We now have magic bullets to conquer the diseases that used to take our lives. Wonderful! If they can do that, then surely they can cure my cold and my child's cold—and earache and sore throat. To an unexpectedly large extent, it became, through the 1960s and 1970s, standard medical practice (especially pediatric practice) to treat hundreds of self-limited conditions with antibiotics. Parents insisted on it.

The practice of prescribing antibiotics liberally for self-limited medical conditions has two major consequences. First, an extraordinary number of antibiotics have been introduced into the ecosystem of the human community, where all those who have taken them have become discrete sources of antibiotic-resistant microbes. Second, antibiotic noncompliance becomes epidemic without anyone noticing it. It is normal human behavior, after all, to take a medicine when one is feeling sick and to stop taking the medicine when one is feeling better. If, in the scenario suggested above, the medical condition for which the antibiotic was prescribed is in fact a potentially lethal infection, then a decision to halt antibiotic treatment before the prescription is finished will be noticed quickly, as the disease returns. But if the antibiotic was prescribed for a cold (a viral condition), or any other self-limited medical condition, the condition will disappear on its own, and the patient can stop the antibiotic at any time without noticing new symptoms. Noncompliance, the patient will conclude, does no harm, saves money (the pills not taken can be sold, or saved for another sickness), and might as well become a habit.

Overprescribing of antibiotics, noncompliance, and the existence of diseases that impair or destroy the immune system's ability to mop up the resistant germs left over from antibiotic attack are factors that lead to the spread of antibiotic-resistant germs. To understand the full extent of the threat, however, we're going to have to leave the lions and pigs behind, for bacteria operate in strange and alarming ways. When a resistant and nonresistant bacterium come in contact with each other (in our bodies, for instance), resistance can pass from one to the other. Nonresistant bacteria can also pick up resistance from viruses that have invaded and expropriated DNA from resistant bacteria. "Indeed, the exchange of genes among different bacterial cells is so pervasive that the entire bacterial world can be thought of as a single huge multicellular organism."[4] An organism that feasts on human flesh—this is not a comforting thought.

Less comforting yet is the fact that the places where we would ordinarily seek treatment for disease can be the most fertile sites for bacterial proliferation. In 1998, officials at the Centers for Disease Control and Prevention estimated that about 2 million patients (most with a weakened immunity system) develop a hospital-acquired infection in the United States each year and about 90,000 of these patients die. In at least 70 percent of these hospital-acquired infections, the organism is resistant to at least one antibiotic. In 30–40 percent of infections, the organism is resistant to the best drug available for treatment. Currently, the risk of contracting an infection during a stay in a U.S. hospital is 1 in 15 and the rate of such infections increased by 36 percent between 1975 and 1995.[5]

Hospitals are not the only culprits. Any location that brings large numbers of human beings into close enough contact, under nonsterile conditions, for them to exchange germs, can be a similarly fertile focal point for the transfer of resistance to more strains of disease-causing organisms. The crowded urban areas of the developing world, without access to adequate supplies of pure water or the means to boil it, are a perfect medium. At the other end of the economic spectrum, jet-setting world travelers carry strains of bacteria out of their home areas (where the organisms on which they feed may have built up, by the mechanisms just described, some degree of resistance to them) into new parts of the world, where they may flourish unhindered. If a traveler carries antibiotic resistance in his bacteria, that resistance can be transferred to bacteria to the very ends of the earth, where people have never been exposed to any antibiotics at all.

How on earth can this be possible? The mechanisms of resistance transfer are complex. Bacteria genes do not stay quietly on the chromosome. Segments of genetic material called "transposons" can jump from the chromosome to free-floating loops of DNA called "plasmids," or from plasmid to chromosome. This jumping ability makes it possible for an exchange of genes that happens, in mammals, only among members of the same species and only at mating time—in the fertilization of egg by sperm; in bacteria this exchange happens through "conjugation," the transfer of a plasmid from one bacterium to any other with which it is in contact. The bacteria do not have to be of the same species. The recipient of the plasmid encodes its contents and can then pass on the genetic traits, including antibiotic resistance, to all of its offspring (numbering in the millions overnight, as explained earlier). "It is a process akin to a computer software program being copied from the hard drive of one computer onto a floppy disk, then passed on to other computers."[6] Gram-negative bacteria, responsible for many common infections of urinary tract and lung, often carry the genes for antibiotic resistance in their plasmids. (The mechanisms of "resistance" are themselves complex, varying from strain to strain of bacteria: some eat the antibiotic, some evade it by hiding the features by which the antibiotic recognizes it, some deceive it by making it bond to a site where it can do the bacterium no harm.)[7]

The implications of this ability are multitudinous and frightening. For instance, some strains of a bacterium called Enterococcus are resistant to the antibiotic vancomycin by virtue of a transposon that changes the composition of the cell wall so the vancomycin can't grab it and disable it. The number one cause of infections in the United States is the family of Staphylococcus bacteria, which can be brought under control only with vancomycin—all other antibiotics are ineffective against it. Now, what happens when an Enterococcus meets a Staphylococcus and shares a plasmid with the resistance transposon on it? It's happened in the laboratory, and in 1998, three real cases of vancomycin-resistant Staphylococcus infection turned up.[8] By now there may be many more.

The major hope for retaining the usefulness of the antibiotics is to persuade the bacteria to abandon their resistance. This may not be as difficult a task as it sounds. Antibiotic resistance is expensive for a cell to maintain, requiring mechanisms, triggers, and other materials that have to be fed, just as it is expensive, for instance, for an oil company to maintain the capability to contain and remedy an oil spill at sea. In a world without oil spills, the company that maintains, at its own expense, the capacity to contain a spill will be at a market disadvantage to those who do not maintain such a capacity. That's why many years without an oil spill can tempt a company, very strongly, to dismantle its spill-containment capability.[9] Given an environment free from antibiotics, bacteria will tend to release their resistance-carrying plasmids or lose out in the evolutionary competition to those who do (or who never had them).[10] Then why is resistance so prevalent, and why is it increasing at such a terrifying rate? Because sloppy practices maintain an antibiotic-rich environment in which resistance continues to pay off. Several factors have already been suggested: physicians overprescribe because their patients demand antibiotics; hospitals fail to maintain a sterile environment; crowded urban settings proliferate in the developing world; increased transportation carries the genes for resistance over the entire world. Nor are these conditions likely to get better by themselves; on the contrary, they are intensifying. The U.S. health care system's trends encourage antibiotic use and therefore antibiotic resistance. With the advent of "managed care," physicians find themselves with less time to talk to patients in the office and therefore tend to prescribe something that treats their obvious symptoms and sends them away happy. With less time to spend with each patient in the hospital, they have less time to carry out the time-consuming sterilization procedures (washing, changing gloves) between patients. With limited reimbursement for time and tests, they are less likely to order the careful cultures that identify specific germs and permit use of narrow-spectrum antibiotics, and they are more likely to order the broad-spectrum antibiotics that most contribute to resistance.[11]

Conditions fostering antibiotic resistance across the world are getting worse, not better. With the advent of agribusiness and the consequent dispersal of peasants from their ancestral villages in the rural areas of the developing world, more varied bacterial populations are crowding together in the urban slums. With the globalization of all economic activity, resistance-carrying plasmids hitchhiking on world travelers are more likely to show up in the remote areas of the world now favored for manufacturing. Clearing the bacteria of the world and the vast "multicellular organism" they compose of the antibiotic resistance received from our health care system is difficult and unlikely. But hang on—there is another source of antibiotic resistance, one that may be just as recalcitrant to change its ways.

DOWN ON THE PHARM

Another cause of antibiotic resistance is the use of antibiotics in agriculture, especially in the raising of livestock, hogs, and cattle. This application of "miracle drugs" stems from a chance discovery. In 1949 an American Cyanamid plant on the Pearl River, just north of New York City, made tetracycline, a powerful antibiotic. Downstream from the plant, the fish were bigger than you'd expect. Curious, chemist Thomas Jukes found out that Cyanamid extracted the drug from mold grown on a grain mash in enormous vats, then discarded the rest of the mash—into the river, of course. Jukes tried feeding some of the mash to lab animals and found they grew 10–20 percent faster than average. Delighted, Cyanamid promptly started marketing the leftover mash as a feed booster. Eventually, Jukes discovered that it was the drug, all by itself, that was doing the boosting. Animals fed low doses of antibiotics grow faster, larger, with less feed, probably because their bodies are not constantly fighting bacterial infections. That, according to Shannon Brownlee, "helped America become the agricultural powerhouse it is today. But," she continues, "there is no free hamburger, . . . and Jukes's discovery has turned out to have a potentially deadly downside: the more we use antibiotics, the more bacteria evolve into forms that resist them."[12] The concerns are not new. Twenty-five years ago, Lester Crawford, a scientist who worked with Jukes on the super-growing feed, recognized the danger and was among the first to try to get the FDA to end the use of antibiotics. They lost that battle in 1980. Maybe it's time to try again.

With enough time, bacteria will grow resistant to any drug. We've already established that. But for that very reason, all who use drugs for any purpose want the newest drug. In 1986, for instance, a new class of antibiotics, the fluoroquinolones, was approved for human use, because the old drugs were not working. "Only nine years later, in 1995, the FDA gave the go-ahead for veterinarians to begin dosing sick chickens with fluoroquinolones for the same reason: The old drugs no longer worked."[13]

The percentage of antibiotics used just to promote growth is not large—about 6.1 percent of the drugs sold for animal use. The rest of the farm drugs are used to treat sick animals or, significantly, to keep animals crammed into pens for long periods of time from getting sick from each other. Still, the number of animals affected is enormous. "That is because growers give antibiotics, in low but daily doses, to entire herds or flocks. . . . 75 percent of the 92 million pigs in this country routinely chow down on feed laced with antibiotics. So do about 6 percent of cattle, 25 percent of chickens and half the turkeys."[14] Low doses of antibiotics in animals have exactly the effect predicted from noncompliance and overprescribing described earlier: slowly but very effectively, the susceptible bacteria are overcome by the resistant bacteria until the latter is the only kind left.[15]

What kind of clinical evidence exists that the overuse of antibiotics in animals can cause human disease? It is very difficult to prove that any particular case of bacterial infection came from animals, let alone any particular case of antibiotic resistant infection. But in 1999, the *New England Journal of Medicine* published a case that demonstrated the connection. *Campylobacter jejuni* is a microbe that lives readily in livestock but causes acute gastroenteritis in people—somewhere between 2 and 8 million cases a year in the United States. Tracking only the "invasive" cases, when the germs escape from the intestines and enter the bloodstream, and only in Minnesota, a farming state that kept particularly good records, the *Journal* investigators found a pattern of increase in antibiotic resistance that could only have come from the local chicken farms.

> In 1992. . . . only 1.3 percent of the Minnesota cases were caused by strains of Campylobacter that were resistant to fluoroquinolones. By 1998, the number had risen to 10.2 percent. That's a pretty steep rise, and the researchers determined it was almost certainly because of antibiotic use on farms. Only a small fraction of the patients had ever taken fluoroquinolones themselves; and the genetic strain of resistant bacteria found in a significant number of the samples matched the genetic strain found on a variety of chicken products purchased at local grocery stores. Out of 91 chicken products, 80 were contaminated with Campylobacter. Twenty percent of those bacteria were resistant to ciprofloxacin, a fluoroquinolone that is needed to treat invasive gastroenteritis in humans.[16]

The National Chicken Council insists that "properly handled and cooked chicken product would be free of Campylobacter," and no doubt, in an ideal world, it would be. But that leaves us with the world that is, where there are each year 78 million cases of food-borne illness, 5000 of which are fatal.[17] *Salmonella* bacteria, which have been around even longer, have developed a new strain, DT104, that is resistant to most common antibiotics; a recent victim contracted the bug almost certainly from working around antibiotic-laced animals. Another source of infection is the local water supply, recipient of antibiotic and bacteria-rich runoff from the enormous factory farms on which hogs, chickens, and beef cattle are raised. Bacteria can travel freely from the farm to the supermarket to the home and hospital, exchanging resistance genes every step of the way.[18]

Farmers started using antibiotics on livestock to help them reach market size quicker, healthier, and with less food, all adding up to a better product less costly to produce. The free market surely justifies the practice of dosing the animals with antibiotics. But the consequence of the practice is that we are running out of medicines that work on us, when we are very sick. "It's time," Shannon Brownlee concludes, "to stop squandering drugs as precious as antibiotics to reduce the price of meat by a few cents a pound," and she calls on the Food and Drug Administration to do something to restrict their use.[19]

The first time any international body voted to do anything about antibiotics was on December 14, 1998, when the European Union's agriculture ministers met in Brussels. Despite apparently intense lobbying by the drug manufacturers, 12 of the EU's 15 farm ministers voted to prohibit the use of virginiamycin, spiramycin, tysolin phosphate and bacitracin zinc, as growth promoters for livestock.[20] All these drugs, or their close relatives, are used to treat human diseases. The debate leading up to the meeting was vigorous. Against the ban, farmers feared for their income,[21] and the antibiotic manufacturers claimed that the digestion-enhancing antibiotics reduced waste products and feed use, and therefore helped the environment. Meanwhile, the Soil Association (an organic farming association) claimed that antibiotic use was out of control and threatened human health.[22] Both sides claimed that "the safety of the food supply" depended on adoption of its view. Three of the ministers abstained. The immediate consequence of the vote was the announcement by the affected drug manufacturers—Pfizer, Rhone-Poulenc, Elanco, and Alpharma—that they would sue the European Commission for withdrawal of the ban or monetary damages. (The damages could be serious; sales of the four antibiotics, much of that for farm use, was estimated to be about 211 million pounds sterling, or about $150 million.)[23]

Six months later, in April 1999, just before the bans were to go into effect, a plan to monitor antibiotic use in farm animals, to find out if resistance genes were resulting from the practice, was recommended by a pan-European scientific conference meeting in Paris.[24] Thereafter, and through the summer, the discussion on the use of antibiotics continued in the agricultural literature. The topics covered are much the same as those that came up before the ban was voted, and in some the same trading of accusations reappears: the Soil Association accuses the farmers of overusing antibiotics, and the National Office of Animal Health (associated with the animal-raising industry) accuses the Soil Association of scaremongering.[25] But in others the tone is different. The articles now emphasize that farmers are well aware of the dangers of breeding antibiotic-resistant germs but strongly oppose the withdrawal of all antibiotic use, on grounds that it would raise the price of meat in the market and might endanger public safety. (It also might badly compromise their ability to make a living). They agree that monitoring for resistance is a good idea and are particularly emphatic that the same rules should apply to all. In any free-market setting, antibiotic-dosed meat, by their calculations, will be able to undersell antibiotic-free meat, and they would be very resentful if their adherence to healthful rules should render them noncompetitive with other growers who do not obey such rules. One segment of the industry, the Grampian Country Food Group, which produces a third of all U.K.-reared chickens, claimed that the antibiotic-growth promoters were not necessary in raising chickens "if high quality management systems and the right environment are in place."[26]

What are the alternatives to massive use of antibiotics in agriculture? The Grampian group speak of very careful sterile procedures, which they can be sure of because they raise all their own eggs and chicks. Occasionally in the literature certain current "factory farm" practices that require a very high density of animals to make their operations profitable, have come under direct attack. Many farmers, for many reasons, would like to see their livestock spread over more space, with room to move around and less chance to spread germs. These "free range" practices are a few steps away from what the Soil Association and its equivalents in the United States favor, which is a strict interpretation of "organic farming." Already the organic farmers have come down firmly on the side of simple ban of all antibiotics. To be "Certified Organic" by the U.S. Department of Agriculture, food must not have been produced using sewage sludge, pesticides, hormones, or antibiotics; irradiation and genetic modification are prohibited; and livestock must be given organic feed. Is "organic" a viable alternative to the usual sorts of farming? The market for certified organic food is significant, and still rising; but it has never been large, and we do not know if it could feed the world or any significant part of it.[27]

Plants, too, can contain antibiotics. In 1993, John Seabrook, writing in the *New Yorker,* introduced Calgene's controversial tomato, Flavr Savr, designed to resist pests and not get all squishy on the way to market.[28] Despite investor enthusiasm (or because of it), environmental activists led by Jeremy Rifkin, president of the Foundation on Economic Trends and an anti-technology activist of long standing, had already organized a boycott against it. One of the problems of the Flavr Savr, besides just being a genetically modified organism generally, was that it contained an antibiotic to cut down on bacterial attack. Rifkin and his followers fully understood the dangers of antibiotic resistance, viewing the Flavr Savr and its genre as very dangerous to human health.[29] Six years after the tomato, Marie Woolf documented the arrival in Britain of a type of genetically modified corn that seemed to threaten the usefulness of antibiotics.[30]

What is the place of antibiotics in agriculture? First, antibiotics are used to treat sick animals, just as they are used to treat sick humans. No one seems to oppose this practice. Second, they are used as routine prophylactics for animals crowded into pens for fattening, or raised in huge mobs for economy of land and manpower. There is strong sentiment, especially among the organic farmers, that those economies are too dearly bought. For the moment we cannot do anything about them and have the farmers stay in business, but an agriculture of the future will not need antibiotics for such purposes. Third, they are used lifelong, in low doses, as growth promoters. This is the use that seems to be most under attack; it is likely that the current ban by the European Union will be extended to other antibiotics and the whole practice phased out.

PLAGUE YEARS: AIDS, TUBERCULOSIS, AND THE FUTURE OF DISEASE

Where else can antibiotic resistance come from? Let us begin with an account of AIDS in South Africa.

By now, everyone knows what AIDS (acquired immune deficiency syndrome) is. It is a syndrome, not a disease in itself. It is caused by the human immunodeficiency virus (HIV), which may take several forms and which attacks and destroys the immune system of the victim. As the immune system collapses, the sufferer falls victim to one after another of "opportunistic infections," bacterial or fungal attacks that would be dispatched immediately by any healthy immune system but that the compromised immune system of the AIDS patient cannot handle. Increasing amounts of antibiotics are required to fight the increasingly frequent infections. Eventually they all fail, and the victim is simply eaten alive by the incurable infestations. When AIDS first showed up in the United States, in the gay community of San Francisco and the intravenous (IV) drug subculture in New York and other large cities, no one knew how it was transmitted. (Ethics classes used to be given on the obligation to give routine medical and nursing care for AIDS patients, for doctors and nurses who were terrified of catching it.) What we found out was that the conditions of transfer are very demanding. There must be direct contact of bodily fluids, blood to blood. The virus is carried in blood (and on the needle withdrawn from the vein after IV drug injection), in semen, and in mother's milk. It can be transmitted from sexual partner to partner in sexual relations unless blocked by a condom, it can be transmitted from one drug user to another in sharing needles during IV drug use, and it can be transmitted from mother to child in childbirth and in breastfeeding a baby. Before we knew to screen the blood supply, some people got HIV from blood transfusions; it can also (rarely) be transmitted by accidental needlesticks in hospitals, or by getting the blood from an HIV positive patient in any open cut or sore.

We cannot cure AIDS or remove HIV from the blood. However, the infection is not, in the developed nations, the death sentence it once was. There are "cocktails," or combinations, of retroviral drugs that have shown a great deal of promise in slowing the destruction of the immune system once HIV is found. It is possible that a seropositive patient of the future will be able to live for a long time on these drugs, without developing full-blown AIDS. The drugs are not easy to manage. They must be taken at precise times in precise order, and they have nasty side effects. Life with HIV is not easy for anyone. (Worse news yet: glowing reports of the effectiveness of these cocktails seems to have diminished caution among certain susceptible communities. The gay community of San Francisco had seen HIV infection rates plummet with the adoption of "safe sex," but HIV is now again on the rise.)[31] Retroviral drugs or no, the best course will always be prevention.

By now everyone knows how to prevent the transmission of HIV. Use a condom in any and all sexual relations; use clean needles only while injecting IV drugs; use universal precautions (fresh gloves, face masks, repeatedly sterilized tools and surfaces) in all dealings with patients in hospitals. And by now everyone knows why these measures are so difficult to implement. There are strong cultural resistances to the use of condoms (using a condom is "like wearing a raincoat when you take a shower," or "like eating a candy bar with the wrapper on"), and ironically, the influence of the Roman Catholic Church has made them more difficult to obtain. The free distribution of bleach kits for needles, or a needle exchange to provide sterile needles for unsterile, meets vigorous resistance from those who see these measures as condoning illegal drug use by taking away one of the natural penalties. Universal precautions take a lot of time, and when hospital staff are overworked, they may be easily forgotten. There is no such resistance in dealing with the transmission of HIV from a seropositive mother to newborn child, which occurs during the process of childbirth itself. To prevent mother–child transmission, successful trials (many in Africa) have shown that short-course administration of anti-viral drugs like ziduvidine (AZT) or nevirapine, given to a mother shortly before she gives birth, will reduce dramatically the rate of transmission of HIV during childbirth. Unfortunately, if the mother then goes on to breastfeed the child, the advantage is lost. Of course, if the mother acknowledges in time that she is HIV positive and asks for infant formula to feed her child, transmission can be avoided. But this is when we run most squarely into the cultural peculiarities of Africa.

With a large underemployed native population, rampant poverty and disease, and a cultural inheritance of centuries of tribal life, South Africa is in some ways a microcosm of sub-Saharan Africa. But in some ways it is not. Bearing the imprint of several centuries of British rule, it has a working governmental bureaucracy that makes earnest attempts to keep good records, and it gives access to journalists. South Africa is yet one country of the Dark Continent on which we can shine a flashlight.

And yet what we see is not reassuring. South Africa offered to host the thirteenth International AIDS Conference in Durban in part because the delegates would be meeting in "the most-infected province of the most-infected country on the most-infected continent," and would have no trouble relating to the terrible reality of the epidemic.[32] In this setting, South African president Thabo Mbeki outraged the delegates in his opening speech, in which he suggested that the link between HIV and AIDS was not as clear as had been thought and that the major cause of AIDS was poverty.[33] The delegates were aware that Mbeki had been pursuing "dissident" opinions in the AIDS debate, including those of Berkeley professor Peter Duesberg, as alternatives to the orthodox scientific view that HIV causes AIDS. (The dissidents, characterized by Helen Epstein in the *New York Review* as "a murky group of California scientists and activists," believe that AIDS is caused by "a vague collection of factors, including malnutrition, chemical pollution, recreational drugs, and by the very pharmaceutical drugs that are used to treat the disease." They think the HIV-AIDS link to be "part of a vast conspiracy cooked up by the pharmaceutical industry to justify the market in anti-AIDS drugs, such as AZT, worth billions of dollars a year.")[34] Why did Mbeki, a well-educated and dedicated public servant, elect to go this kooky route? Attending other remarks he has made is the strong feeling that he rejects "western-imposed" science and wishes to find a "purely African" explanation of this disease—and an African remedy. He had intervened, to a degree very unusual for any politician, in the AIDS research in his country, openly supporting (for instance) trials of "virodene," a substance developed at the University of Pretoria, whose developers claimed that it would cure

AIDS. The nature of the stuff (which includes dry-cleaning fluid) suggested that it would do AIDS sufferers much more harm than good, and Mbeki was severely criticized by the South African medical establishment for his open support of it. The controversy lasted for months; it became clear that the drug's supporters saw the matter as a conflict of Africa versus the West, even as it became ever clearer that the politicians' involvement with virodene was financial as well as intellectual. (A court battle brought to the surface documents that showed that the African National Congress [ANC] was to share in the profits of its company.)[35]

It is easy to see Mbeki's speech as symptomatic of the worst ills of the AIDS fight in South Africa. The major battle concerning AIDS in Africa has always been the battle for honesty. We were able to make the progress that we did in the United States—the isolation of the virus, the discovery of ways to prevent transmission, eventually the development of the retroviral drug cocktails that keep people alive—because the first U.S. citizens who suffered from it, the gay communities on both coasts, insisted that the nation must face the disease squarely and deal with it. Even so, as soon as apparently reassuring news came from the drug companies, the AIDS infection rate started rising again in the United States. Although some hopeful advances have been made in Uganda and Zimbabwe[36] in particular, sub-Saharan Africans in general cannot yet acknowledge the problem, face it in their own bodies and their own families, and set out to prevent its transmission by all the unpleasant ways that are required.[37] Death certificates are falsified to conceal the death from AIDS, women are beaten senseless if they tell their husbands that they are HIV positive (the men refuse to be tested, so the assumption is that the woman must have got it from someone else), and a decision not to breast-feed a child is taken as an admission, by the woman, that she is HIV positive. That is why the short-course doses of antiviral drugs to prevent mother-child transmission are ultimately not very useful.

Meanwhile, the traditional position of women in southern African society makes it very difficult to control the spread of the disease by teaching women to refuse unwanted or unsafe sex. Even the right of the woman to refuse gang rape, or to report it, is not yet established in South Africa.[38] Teaching "safe sex" to males has not proved effective.

> . . . these and other efforts. . . . have so far proved no match for custom, cultural confusion and peer pressure. "They say, 'We are going to die anyway, so what's the use of using a condom,'" says Sheila Mathemba, 20, of the Viros, a township rap group. "They say, 'Unless it's flesh on flesh, it's not real sex.' They don't want to take responsibility."[39]

The result of this culturally compelled inattention to the spread of AIDS has had predictable results. According to the Centers for Disease Control, about 4.8 million South Africans are HIV infected. In 1999 250,000 people died of AIDS; 420,000 children orphaned by the disease, and that number is expected to grow to 1.6 million by 2008. By 2015, population loss to AIDS-related deaths will be 4.4 million. The HIV-infection rate is now 11 percent; by 2010 adult HIV prevalence could reach 25 percent. In a grim note on the subject of antibiotic resistance, an estimated 50 percent of all tuberculosis patients are co-infected with HIV. This population is the largest repository of multi-drug-resistant tuberculosis (MDRTB), one of the biggest killers in the developing world.[40] The problem reaches beyond the borders of South Africa proper. The most vulnerable class of among all southern Africans is young women. The percentage of 15- to 25-year-old women with HIV (whether or not AIDS has yet developed) tops 15 percent in Namibia, Zambia, Malawi, and Mozambique; it tops 25 percent in Zimbabwe, South Africa, and Lesotho; and it hits an incredible 34 percent in Botswana.[41] And in most of that area, there are too many cultural barriers to discussing AIDS to make any significant progress. The situation can only get worse. The United Nations estimates that about half of all 15-year-olds in these countries will die of AIDS.

That, of course, is why the Durban conference was called "Break the Silence." The delegates arrived in Durban expecting a clarion call for action from the president of South Africa. Instead they got one more evasion, one more attempt to blame AIDS on absolutely anything except the behavior of South Africans. No wonder they were furious.[42] In retrospect, analysts have at least sympathized with his position—AIDS drugs are terribly expensive for a poor country, accepting free drugs from generous drug companies only increases the nation's dependency, since the victims must be supported for the rest of their lives, and all the expensive drugs in the world won't attack the underlying problem of ill health in southern Africa—the extreme poverty of the area.[43] In an ominous appraisal of the condition of AIDS-infested Africa, Lawrence Goldyn focused on the role of "pharmaceutical-based" medicine in the country of South Africa. It is not simply on account of the average allotment of $40 per person for health care that the $10,000–$15,000 per AIDS patient for the retroviral cocktails is beyond the country's means. It is also that the country simply does not have the infrastructure to support drug treatment.

South Africans' battle with tuberculosis (TB) is instructive. They have cheap, easy-to-take drugs but infection rates continue to rise because the TB patients known to the state are not taking them. Widely sold on the black market to those who have reason not to come in contact with the health care system or any public system, TB drugs are largely obtained from patients enrolled in treatment plans who are concealing their drugs instead of taking them. Prices for the drugs are high, higher for "dry" (untouched) pills than for "wet" pills (concealed under the tongue while the public health worker watches the patient swallow the water, spat out later for sale.) Imagine, Goldyn suggests, the black market price that could be commanded for HIV drugs.[44]

What role is played by South Africa in cultivating antibiotic resistance across the globe? It may just be the ultimate incubator. As antibiotics overused in inadequate doses in my body may make me more susceptible to resistant germs, as antibiotics overused in inadequate doses in the livestock may expose an entire population to antibiotic-resistant bacteria, so antibiotic resistant germs grown with the help of Western medicine in the AIDS regions of Africa may attack the entire globe. Consider what a fine incubator of antibiotic-resistant bacteria is an AIDS population. All sufferers from AIDS are repeatedly attacked by opportunistic infections, such as *Pneumocystis carinii,* a nasty lung infection that leaves alone those of us with intact immune systems. We Americans fight it with antibiotics (bring on the lions). South Africa has access to all antibiotics, but the patient is noncompliant, keeping some of the antibiotics for later sale (the lions are called off too soon), or the patient's immune system has become so weakened that it cannot deal with the bacteria remaining after the antibiotics have run their course (the wolves have just left). In either case, the patient is now one huge petri dish for the cultivation of antibiotic-resistant disease.

The important point is that the diseases so cultivated are not confined to Africa. There is no way they could possibly be confined to Africa, given the huge traffic across the oceans occasioned by the globalization of all business, especially agribusiness. And once a disease gets a passport, everybody's equally at risk. Antibiotic-resistant tuberculosis will kill any of us wealthy middle-class folks, all with access to good medicine, with the same inevitability that it killed our great-grandfathers before there were antibiotics at all. It is certain that much of the tuberculosis that the underdeveloped public-health system of South Africa is unable to treat, is by now resistant to the usual antibiotics. As AIDS spreads, it is certain that any disease treated with standard antibiotics will rapidly mutate into one resistant strain, since the antibiotics do not have a working immune system to back them up. We are, as the *New York Times* put it, "losing ground against microbes," and we may soon be back at the battle lines of the early twentieth century.[45]

A NUCLEAR SOLUTION?

Where do we go from here? The best bet is that all existing antibiotics will be useless for most serious diseases within the next few decades, as the African-born disease organisms join those emerging independently in the overfed and overprescribed West. What other approaches to bacterial disease control are possible?

As the first word in alternative-energy development must always be Conservation, so the first word in the treatment of bacterial disease is Prevention. We know how to prevent the spread of bacteria, through scrupulous attention to washing (hands, tools, foods, and surfaces) through the use of disinfectants in any context at risk of carrying bacteria, through thorough cooking of all food, and through avoidance of situations involving close contact with strangers. All of this is true, and in hospitals and other major sources of microbial infection, preventive scrubbing is the most important first line of defense. But the standard list of precautions just doesn't seem to fit the situation of the urban worker on the subway eating his fast-food lunch with one hand while he sorts through his calendar for the next appointment with the other. Punctilious sterilization of everything, everywhere, is not in the cards.

The addition of a few lions would provide some stop-gap help. A new drug, for instance, Synercid, developed by Rhone-Poulenc, has shown signs of success where others have failed. But its days, too, are numbered: virginiamycin, one of the four antibiotics banned by the European Union in 1999, is very similar in structure to Synercid and has been around since 1974 as a supplement to cattle feed. Germs that are immune to virginamycin seem to be immune to Synercid as well.[46]

Are there other ways to make our food safer? One suggestion is to lower the incidence of harmful bacteria through systematic irradiation of the food supply. Food irradiation is done by passing food through an irradiator, a closed chamber, in which it is exposed to an ionizing energy source. In the United States, the source tends to be gamma rays from cobalt 60, contained in stainless steel rods. That kind of radiation does not break down other atoms (no chance of "chain reaction" or meltdown), and makes nothing radioactive. But it does kill germs. Irradiation has been carried on for more than 40 years in small applications. There seems to be no downside to the process. There were initial claims that vitamins or other nutrients might be destroyed or that the food would contain new "radiolytic" (radiation-produced) substances that would be harmful. After exhaustive research, it seems that at the worst, the inactivation of vitamins caused by radiation amounts to 1.5 percent of nutrients lost (of B and C vitamins only, and only in some foods)—less than the percentage lost in cooking. The "radiolytic" substances irradiation produces in meats turn out to be the same produced in cooking. After examining the issue at some length, the American Dietetic Association (ADA) endorsed food irradiation as "an important approach in protecting the safety and quality of the food supply."[47] John Henkel, writing for the Food and Drug Administration, presented an extended defense of the effectiveness and safety of the procedure in the spring 1998 issue of the *FDA Consumer:*

> ...as long as radiation is applied to foods in approved doses, it's safe, says FDA's Pauli [Dr. George Pauli, FDA food irradiation safety coordinator]. Similar to sending luggage through an airport scanner, the process passes food quickly through a radiation field—typically gamma rays produced from radioactive cobalt-60. That amount of energy is not strong enough to add any radioactive material to the food. The same irradiation process is used to sterilize medical products such as bandages, contact lens solutions, and hospital supplies such as gloves, sutures and gowns. Many spices sold in this country also are irradiated, which eliminates the need for chemical fumigation to control pests. American astronauts have eaten irradiated foods since 1972.[48]

There is general agreement among researchers and scientists with the FDA and the ADA's position, especially in the light of recent bacterial infections: the DT104 salmonella, and especially the lethal *E. coli* O157:H7, both recent mutated arrivals on the infectious scene, both presenting problems of diagnosis and treatment. Irradiation of food prior to sale, especially of food (like seafood) that may be served only partially cooked, will prevent these infections. It should also eliminate *campylobacter* from the chicken supply. More speeches to food handlers about sterile precautions, and more inspections, may help, but ultimately, Minnesota Health Department's chief epidemiologist argued, the only way to ensure that food is free from infectious microorganisms is to irradiate it.[49] The World Health Organization, the American Medical Association, and most trade groups in food handling also agree that the process is safe and effective. In a recent note, the *Tufts University Health & Nutrition Letter* announced that the larger food processors (Cargill, Tyson Foods, IBP Incorporated) planned to use a new kind of irradiation that dispenses with radioactive compounds and uses electricity as the energy source instead (electron beams rather than gamma rays). The note adds that irradiation is already in use in nursing homes, for patients with compromised immune systems.[50]

As in other recent developments in food merchandising, the proposal to irradiate the food supply has drawn fire from some groups. The Washington DC–based Nuclear Information and Resource Service (NIRS) warns "that zapping food with the same radioactive materials used at Chernobyl and Three Mile Island is inviting disaster—particularly because these substances are being used in industrial buildings that do not use the same precautions that nuclear reactors do. 'The opportunity for unplanned exposure of workers and nearby businesses or residences is quite real,' NIRS executive director Michael Mariotte says."[51] Greenpeace also is opposed to radiation. In a secondary campaign, some groups have asked for "labels" to identify irradiated food—essentially, the three-segment "radiation danger" sign from the days of the fallout shelters.[52] (Not surprisingly, the food-packaging industry is opposed to conspicuous labeling of that sort.) It is difficult to find any factual basis for the anti-irradiation campaign.[53] That difficulty does not seem to be slowing it down. (Incidentally, the Tufts publication mentioned above addresses the three most common fears about irradiated foods—that the food is radioactive, that the irradiation creates radiolytic compounds that can cause cancer, and that irradiated food is of diminished nutritional quality—and examines them in depth.)[54]

THE SEARCH FOR BEARS

Irradiation may help kill off some of the worst of the microbes in some of the more dangerous places they live, but you can't irradiate the whole world. In the end, we will continue to get bacterial infections, just as we always have. If our lions are no good anymore, are there bears to keep the raging pigs under control? The surprising answer is that yes, there may very well be, and the source of the bears is the Soviet Bear itself: a decrepit laboratory in Tbilisi, Georgia, of the former Union of Soviet Socialist Republic. For 70 years, the bacteriologists of the Eliava Institute in Tbilisi have been perfecting Felix d'Herelle's work with "bacteriophages," tiny viruses that eat germs for lunch.[55] "Viral predators only one-fortieth the size of the average bacteria cell, they swarm unseen around us, busily searching and destroying their favorite food:

germs. . . . They are so tiny that a single drop of tap water may contain a billion of them."[56] Like all viruses, they kill by attaching to a microbe, inserting their own genetic material into the cell, and proceeding, over the next hours, to commandeer the entire cell to the production of new versions of the phage. Then all the little new phages go hunting. They work very well. Further, they mutate as rapidly as the bacteria on which they feed, so they are not likely to suffer the same obsolescence as the antibiotics.

Why don't we use them? Thereupon hangs a political tale. When d'Herelle discovered them in Paris in 1917, he was convinced they would revolutionize the treatment of disease. But the laboratory science of the time was nowhere near exact enough to isolate and store the phages. (There are hundreds of types of phages, and each one kills only one type of bacteria. "Predator and prey must be perfectly matched, a daunting process.") Nor were the researchers of the time able to purify the solution of phages. So although Eli Lilly actually manufactured phage-based medicines in the 1930s, they were not perfected by the time penicillin came along and drove everything else from the field. D'Herelle took his work to the Soviet Union in 1934 and, with Stalin's support, helped George Eliava develop precisely targeted phages for the Red Army during World War II. Eventually the Eliava Institute had over 300 clones of known bacteriophages in their library.

Why didn't we hear about this? First, because we had antibiotics, and needed no more. Second, because, well, what good could come out of the Soviet Union? Bacteriophage research was widely ignored all over the West. While Stalin lived, the institute was protected, for the most part (Eliava himself was shot by Lavrenti Beria, Stalin's chief of secret police—not over science, but over a woman). While the Soviet Union prospered, the institute prospered. When the Soviet Union imploded, support collapsed; poverty-stricken Georgia had no way of funding the exotic laboratory. Facilities fell into disrepair; brief flashes of Western interest had a tendency to be counterproductive. In 1996, for instance, a venture capitalist named Calsey Harlington formed a company linking a Seattle facility in "partnership" to the Eliava Institute, to be known as Phage Therapeutics. After the Soviet scientists showed the Seattle folks how the technology worked, the Americans went back to Seattle, announced that the Tbilisi facility was unworkable, and prepared to market phages all by themselves. "We gave the Americans access to all this background research," said Nina Chanishvili, senior researcher at the Institute, "and they simply walked away with it. They told us we were stupid at business. Well, that at least was true."[57]

Business in the 1990s was enthusiastically high-tech; the Georgian scientist who had brought phage technology to the United States, Alexander Sulakvelidze, promptly severed connections with Harlington and had no trouble locating some venture capitalists on his own, forming Intralytix, Inc. in 1998. By that time he had two competitors: Phage Therapeutics and Exponential Biotherapies, based on the work of NIH researcher Carl Merrill.[58]

Getting therapies approved for use in the United States is a grueling and expensive process of animal tests, clinical trials, and petitioning the FDA for accelerated acceptance. It would take years. By 2002, Phage Therapeutics was out of business, Exponential Biotherapies was faltering, and Intralytix came up with a new strategy—aimed at livestock, not people. Veterinary drug development has two advantages: first, the route to acceptance is much faster, going through the Environmental Protection Agency (EPA) rather than the Food and Drug Administration (FDA), and second, at the moment they started considering it, regulators across Europe and the United States were considering forbidding the use of antibiotics for livestock, for all the reasons outlined in previous sections. The first phage-based drug that Intralytix developed was designed to combat a common infection, *Listeria monocytogenes,* in poultry. It was granted an experimental use permit by the EPA in June 2002. Three other phage development projects are presently funded at the Eliava Institute in Tbilisi by Intralytix.[59] Researchers there have high hopes for the future.

Does this show that phages are ready for use in the West? Will they replace Vancomycin and all the other exhausted legions of miracle drugs? We are surely at the end of a 50-year run of magic bullets from the mold-based antibiotics. Maybe phages will be the Magic Assassin's Knives of the future. If the epidemic of resistant diseases, now brewing all over the world with its epicenter in Africa, proceeds the way it seems it will, we will need all the Magic Assassin's Knives we can get.

QUESTIONS FOR REFLECTION

1. Have people relied too much on antibiotics? How so?

2. What's wrong with Western medical practices, that they have produced antibiotic resistance? How might they be improved?

3. What's wrong with Western agricultural practices, that they have produced antibiotic resistance? How might they be restructured?

NOTES

1. G. Tyler Miller, *Living in the Environment,* 11th ed. (Pacific Grove, CA: Brooks/Cole, 2000), p. 89.

2. Ibid., p. 452.

3. Ibid., p. 413.

4. Miller, *Living,* loc. cit.

5. Miller, *Living,* loc. cit.

6. Paul F. Kamitsuka, "The Current Peril of Antibiotic Resistance," Guest Essay in Miller, *Living,* pp. 466–67.

7. Ibid., p. 468.

8. Ibid.

9. See Chapter 4 of this text.

10. Ibid.

11. Ibid.

12. Shannon Brownlee, "Antibiotics in the Food Chain: Farmers Who Give Animals Drugs to Make Them Grow to Market Weight Faster Unwittingly Contribute to Antibiotic-Resistant Diseases in Humans," *Washington Post,* 21 May 2000, p. B3.

13. Ibid.

14. Ibid.

15. Ibid. As Lester Crawford put it, "Low doses don't kill off bacteria—they just make them mad." We all know that's not

what's happening, but isn't it a cute way of putting it?

16. K. E. Smith, J. M. Besser, C. W. Hedberg et al., "Quinolone–Resistant Campylobacter Jejuni Infections in Minnesota, 1992–1998," *New England Journal of Medicine* 340, no. 20 (1999): 1525, cited in Brownlee, "Antiobiotics." See also report by Amanda Spake, "Do Livestock Breed Drug-Resistant Bugs?" *U.S. News and World Report,* 31 May 1999, p. 65, commenting on the same *NEJM* article.

17. Brownlee, "Antibiotics." Nicols Fox asserts that "Official estimates are that the cases in the United States run as high as 81 million cases a year, but recently the CDC's Dr. Morris Potter pushed that number up even higher," even as high as 266 million cases a year. See Nicols Fox, *Spoiled: The Dangerous Truth about a Food Chain Gone Haywire* (New York: Basic Books, 1997), pp. 13–14.

18. Brownlee, "Antibiotics," p. 83.

19. Ibid.

20. Katherine Butler, "European Ministers Ban Four Antibiotics from Animal Feed," *The Independent,* 15 December 1998, p. 4. Michael Smith, "Brussels Bans Antibiotics in Animal Feed: Food Safety Legal Action Threatened," *Financial Times,* 15 December 1998, p. 3.

21. Michael Hornsby, "Farmers Fear Pounds 160m Cost of Antibiotic Ban," *The Times,* December 4, 1998.

22. Charles Arthur, "Ban Antibiotics in All Farming," *The Independent,* 7 December 1998; Cathy Comerford, "Soaring Use of Farm Antibiotics Presents Threat to Humans," *The Independent,* 8 December 1998.

23. Susie Whalley, "Bacteria Threat of Mass-Farmed Meat," *Supermarketing,* 11 December 1998, p. 12; Jonathan Riley, "Antibiotic Restrictions Are Urged," *Farmers Weekly,* 11 December 1998, p. 6; "Organic Farming Campaigner Calls for Ban on Animal Antibiotics," *Chemist and Druggist,* 12 December 1998, p. 28; Charles Arthur and Cathy Comerford, "Europe Set to Curb Farm Antibiotics," *The Independent,* 14 December 1998, p. 6.

24. "Closer Watch on Resistance Signs," *Farmers Guardian,* 9 April 1999, p. 7.

25. Patricia Lieberman, "Antibiotic Resistance High-Priority Cattle Issue," *USA Today,* 25 June 1999, p. 14A; Charles Arthur, "Farmers 'Failing' to Limit Drug Use," *The Independent,* 29 June 1999, p. 9; Robin Young, "Health Risk as Farms Overuse Antibiotics," *The Times,* 9 August 1999; "Industry Rubbishes Threat of Drug–Resistant Disease," *Farming News,* 20 August 1999," Home News section, p. 2; "Antibiotics Claims Alarmist, say NOAH," *Farmers Guardian,* 27 August 1999.

26. Alistair Driver, "Antibiotics 'No Advantage' in Boosting Poultry Growth," *Farmers Guardian,* 10 September 1999, p. 17.

27. Deborah L. Shelton, "Going Organic," *Essence* (July 2000), Mind Body report, p. 81; Anita Manning, "Certified Organic" to Reflect Consumer Demands," *USA Today,* 8 March 2000, p. 6D.

28. See Chapter 2 of this text.

29. John Seabrook, "Tremors in the Hothouse: The Battle Lines are Being Drawn for the Soul of the American Consumer as Agribusiness Launches the First Genetically Altered Supermarket Tomato," *New Yorker,* 19 July 1993, Brave New World department, pp. 32–41 (quote at 38–39).

30. Marie Woolf, "Modified Corn on Sale in UK 'Kills' Life-Saving Antibiotics," *The Independent,* 6 June 1999, p. 13. Granted, the article is passing strange, alleging that the corn itself has an "antibiotic resistance gene," deliberately inserted apparently to protect the corn from antibiotics, which could render useless any antibiotic being taken by someone eating the corn—that can "degrade an antibiotic in the human gut in 30 minutes." I don't think that's true. I think I know what the original problem was, and I don't think that's it.

31. Scott Gottlieb, "The Limits of the AIDS Miracle," Op-Ed, *New York Times,* 9 July 2000.

32. Lawrence K. Altman, "Africa's AIDS Crisis: Finding Common Ground," *New York Times,* 16 July 2000, International section, p. 6.

33. David Brown and Jon Jeter, "Hundreds Walk Out On Mbeki: S. African's Speech on AIDS Protested," *Washington Post,* 10 July 2000, p. A1.

34. Helen Epstein, "The Mystery of AIDS in South Africa," *New York Review,* 20 July 2000, p. 50.

35. Ibid., pp. 53–54. Epstein cites, in support of her statements on virodene, S. J. Klebanoff et al., "Activation of the HIV Type 1 Long Terminal Repeat and Viral Replication by Dimethylsulfoxide and Related Solvents," *AIDS Research and Human Retroviruses* 13 (September 1997): 1221–1227; "Virodene Is Still Being Sold: SAPS," *The Citizen,* 6 March 1998; and many letters to the *South African Medical Journal* by physicians in South Africa. She suggests, without quite saying so, that some clinical trials that were supposed to be of AZT and nevirapine were actually using virodene, making the patients very sick or killing them.

36. More recently, AIDS treatment in Zimbabwe has failed because the corrupt dictatorship has lost the confidence of donor nations that AIDS funds will be spent properly. See Sharon LaFraniere, "Donor Mistrust Worsens AIDS in Zimbabwe," *New York Times,* 12 August 2004, pp. A1, A6.

37. Ibid.; see also Tom Masland, *Newsweek,* 17 July 2000, pp. 30–32.

38. Masland, "Breaking the Silence," p. 32.

39. Ibid.

40. Data from the CDC: http://www.cdc.gov/nchstp/od/gap/countries/south_africa.htm.

41. See table in Masland, "Breaking the Silence," p. 32.

42. Editorial, *New York Times* "AIDS in South Africa," 12 July 2000; Brown and Jeter, "Hundreds Walk Out."

43. Rachel L. Swarns, "Dissent on AIDS by South Africa's President, Thoughtfulness or Folly?" *New York Times,* 8 July 2000, p. 5; Brown and Jeter, "Hundreds Walk Out," Rachel Swarns, "South Africa Faults Critics of Its President on AIDS Stance," *New York Times,* 11 July 2000, p. 3.

44. Lawrence Goldyn, "Africa Can't Just Take a Pill For AIDS," Op-Ed, *New York Times,* 6 July 2000.

45. Editorial, "Losing Ground against Microbes," *New York Times,* 18 June 18 2000.

46. Brownlee, "Antiobiotics"; Spake, "Do Livestock."

47. American Dietetic Association, "Position of the American Dietetic Association: Food Irradiation," *Journal of the American Dietetic Association* 96, no. 1 (January 1996): 69–73. See extensive references attached to this article for a history of research on irradiated food. See also "Red Meat Irradiation Approved," *FDA Consumer* (March–April 1998): 2.

48. John Henkel, "Irradiation: A Safe Measure for Safer Food," *FDA Consumer* (March–June 1998): 12.

49. Michael T. Osterholm, "No Magic Bullet: More Inspectors Is Fine and Dandy, but Don't Kid Yourself: Government Can't 'Solve' the Problem of Food Safety," *Newsweek,* 1 September 1997, p. 33.

50. Editorial note, "Irradiation Back on the Front Burner," *Tufts University Health & Nutrition Letter,* 4 March 2000, p. 4.

51. Cristin Marandino, "Is Zapping Food the Answer?" *Vegetarian Times* (December 1997): 12.

52. Katherine Gallia, "Food Irradiators 1, Public 0," *Natural Health* (January 1999): 23.

53. The website of the Public Citizen (www.citizen.org) has a bibliography on the "unwholesomeness of irradiated food." It cites 23 articles in reasonably prestigious journals, all considering the effects of radiation damage on foods. The articles generally date from the mid-1960s through the early 1980s; there are none dated later than 1986.

54. "Irradiation," *Tufts University Health & Nutrition Letter* (n. 47 above).

55. Lawrence Osborne, "A Stalinist Antibiotic Alternative," *New York Times Magazine,* 6 February 2000, pp. 50–55.

56. Ibid., pp. 51–52.

57. Ibid., p. 54. The issue was underscored on the evening following the conversation recorded here, when Osborne visited the head of the institute and found him

watching an American documentary on cable TV. The documentary, concerning bacteriophages, used images that had simply been lifted, without compensation, from the uncopyrighted files of the institute. The head of the institute was not happy.

58. Richard Martin, "How Ravenous Soviet Viruses Will Save the World," *Wired* 11 (October 2003): 10.

59. Intralytix website, http://www .intralytix.com.

5

Oil on the Rocks

The Wreck of the
Exxon Valdez

INTRODUCTION

On April 27, 2003, a Bouchard Transportation Company barge struck a ledge and spilled as much as 98,000 gallons of oil into Buzzard's Bay, Massachusetts. The spill killed hundreds of sea birds, polluted 100 miles of coast and closed 90,000 acres of shellfish beds.[1] Why haven't we solved this type of problem? What risk factors for oil spills, present in the story of the *Exxon Valdez,* make it so difficult to get spills under control?

The story of the *Exxon Valdez* is a story about technology, navigation, and profound environmental damage. But it is also about our laws and institutions generally. Fifteen years after it was determined that Exxon, Inc. was liable for damages, ten years after the damages were assessed, the matter is still in court. Why?

REFLECTIONS ON RESPONSIBILITY

In the aftermath of the wreck of the *Exxon Valdez,* it became crucial, if only to save our own sanity in the face of all that ugliness and environmental destruction, to place responsibility for the disaster somewhere, to hold someone to account for it. By the time the terms of the discussion had become clear, three levels of responsibility had surfaced: (1) at the first level and most obviously, Exxon's corporate responsibility for the negligent seamanship that spilled the oil and corporate responsibility on the part of Exxon and Alyeska Pipeline Service Company, for the lack of preparation ashore that failed to contain its spread within hours; (2) at the next level, Alaskan citizen complicity in what could be called the Alyeska syndrome—the willing participation, for money, in the exploitation of oil resources at the peril of the pristine Alaskan environment, against their better judgment; (3) and finally, the accountability of us all, given our cars and our heated houses, and our use of all that oil despite our knowledge that the environment would be better off if we cut out, or cut down on our use of fossil fuels and despite our willingness to forget about the environmental effects of an oil spill as soon as the crisis has passed.

This chapter examines responsibility—individual, corporate, national, and environmental—and at the end of the discussion raises the ultimate questions arising from the *Exxon Valdez* incident: Is it imperative that all our energy demands be filled? If they must be filled with fossil fuels, are there safer ways to extract and transport them? Are there better ways to protect the fragile environments in which oil is extracted and transported? What kind of society might we Americans have, that it would have room for a decent human life and sea otters too?

THE EVENT: SHIP MEETS REEF

From various accounts, including Art Davidson's book-length treatment of the incident (*In the Wake of the Exxon Valdez,* 1990),[2] it is possible to reconstruct the incidents of the late night of March 23 and the early morning of March 24, Good Friday, 1989. At 9:30 P.M., March 23, the *Exxon Valdez,* a 987-foot oil tanker owned by the Exxon Shipping Company (subsidiary of Exxon U.S.A., which is part of Exxon Corporation, now Exxon Mobil Corporation) left the dock at the port of Valdez with a cargo of 1.26 million barrels of North Slope oil, brought in from Prudhoe Bay to the terminal at Valdez through the Alaskan Pipeline, and headed out to sea through Valdez Harbor, under the command of Captain Ed Murphy, an independent harbor pilot. Captain Murphy took the ship safely through the Valdez Narrows, where the harbor ends, and into Prince William Sound. At 11:24 P.M. he left ship, returning control to the master of the vessel, Captain Joseph J. Hazelwood. One minute later Captain Hazelwood called the Coast Guard to tell them that he was leaving the outbound shipping lane and steering a course south (180 degrees) into the inbound lanes (empty at that time), to avoid ice floes broken from the Columbia Glacier to the north.

Then Hazelwood gave a series of unusual orders: he told the lookout, Maureen Jones, to stand her watch from the bridge instead of 800 feet in front of it; he told the helmsman Harry Claar to accelerate to sea speed, although they were about to start maneuvering around icebergs of unknown dimension, and to put the ship on automatic pilot, which would complicate any course changes. Then, in direct contradiction to company policy, Hazelwood went below, leaving command in the hands of Third Mate Gregory T. Cousins, with orders to continue southerly to the lighted buoy off Busby Island, then return to the shipping lanes. The first thing Cousins discovered was that the ship was on autopilot, and he put it back into manual mode. Then he turned to the radar to concentrate on missing the ice.

Why was Hazelton acting so strangely? Probably he was under the influence of alcohol. Within four days after the accident, both Coast Guard Lieutenant Thomas Falkenstein (the first to reach the *Exxon Valdez* after the grounding) and harbor pilot Captain Murphy had told a federal investigating team (headed by William Woody of the National Traffic Safety Board) that they had smelled alcohol on Hazelwood's breath just before and just after the accident.[3] He was still legally drunk (0.061 percent) when the blood tests were finally made, nine hours after the accident.[4] This was not some recent deviance, and the record was not difficult to find. By March 29, an unsigned article appeared in *The New York Times,* datelined Hauppauge, Long Island (Joseph Hazelwood's home town), tracking Hazelwood's drinking history. During the five years preceding the accident, he was twice convicted on charges involving drinking and driving; his license to drive a car had been suspended or revoked three times, and it was suspended at the time of the accident.[5] Exxon had known of Hazelwood's alcohol problems, had sent him through rehabilitation and reinstated him. Still he drank openly.[6] How far does the company's responsibility—and right to monitor behavior—extend in such cases? Meanwhile, the condition of those left on the bridge may not have been much better.

The crew was exhausted. To save money, the company had cut back the crews on their ships, and there were only 20 aboard the *Exxon Valdez.* That left the members of the crew with an average of 140 hours of overtime a month per person. Further, Third Mate Gregory Cousins was not licensed to navigate the ship in Prince William Sound. Did the Mate's inexperience cause the accident? On the one hand, the channel as marked and as normally traveled presents no difficulties for navigation. Paul Yost, commandant of the Coast Guard, commented on the accident a week after it happened: "Remember, we've got 10 miles of open water there, and for that vessel to have come over and hit a reef is almost unbelievable," he told reporters. "This was not a treacherous area, as you people in the press have called it. It is not treacherous in the area they went aground. It's 10 miles wide. Your children could drive a tanker up through it."[7]

On the other hand, Hazelwood had planned a course that would skirt the southern edge of that 10-mile opening in order to avoid the ice. "A well-timed right turn would be necessary to avoid Bligh Reef, which lay 6 miles ahead in the darkness. There would be little room for error. The vessel needed at least six-tenths of a mile to make the turn, and the gap between the ice and Bligh Reef was only nine-tenths of a mile wide. The tanker itself was nearly two-tenths of a mile long. The tanker would have to start its turn well before the gap between the ice and the reef if it was to make it through."[8] Absorbed in his computations, Cousins missed the Busby Island light, where he was supposed to have started his turn, and had no idea how far off course he was until lookout Jones called his attention to the flashing red light off Bligh Island off his *starboard* side, where it had no business being if he was headed out.

After the *Exxon Valdez* hit the first rock, Cousins tried very hard to make the turn back into the shipping lanes, but the ship's momentum kept her going south to the reef, where 15 minutes later, she grounded. The reef punched eight holes in her hull, spilling a quarter of a million barrels of oil (about 11 million gallons) into the clear waters of the Sound. Cousins called Captain Hazelwood to the bridge immediately, and Hazelwood spent 15–20 minutes trying to dislodge the ship from the reef, to no avail. At 12:27 A.M., Hazelwood radioed the Coast Guard and told them that he had fetched up north of Goose Island, at Bligh Reef. Coast Guard Commander Stephen McCall promptly warned off all ships, sent a pilot boat out to investigate (manned by Lieutenant Falkenstein and Dan Lawn of Alaska's Department of Environmental Conservation [DEC]), told incoming tankers to drop anchor, and closed the port of Valdez.

What had gone wrong? In many such cases—as we will see throughout this text—predisposing factors for the incident were in ample supply, and by foul chance they all converged on one hapless third mate and one beautiful ecosystem, sending death and destruction into the animal communities of the sound, and anger and confusion into the human communities affected by the spill. To understand the impact of the spill, we need to have an idea of the ecology of the sound and of the kind of damage done by oil in those waters.

PRINCE WILLIAM SOUND: THE END OF INNOCENCE

Every account of the monster spill includes reference to the "pristine" beauty of the sound before the accident: the wealth of birds, fish, wildlife, kelp, living things of all sorts; the complex web of interdependence that makes a threat to any of those species a threat to them all. "Pristine" is a word rarely heard, primarily because it designates a very rare condition: the original condition, according to the dictionary definition, pure, untouched, unspoiled, uncorrupted. Prince William Sound had never been fouled, polluted, cut over, industrialized, or settled by environmentally intrusive human groups. The home of Chugach Eskimos and Aleut Indians, its existence was recorded by Captain James Cook in 1778, who named it in honor of the British Crown; Spanish explorers had christened Valdez and the nearby town of Cordova, and Russian fur trappers had set up bases on Hinchinbrook Island, but neither of these occurrences had had any impact on the stunningly beautiful natural setting. Before construction of the Alaskan Pipeline, the sound had been immune to the normal depredations of the twentieth century.

The Sound

Prince William Sound is roughly 70 miles long and 30 miles wide, with many bays, inlets, and islands to break up its shoreline. It comprises approximately 2,500 square miles of open water, 1,800 miles of mainland shoreline, 1,200 shoreline miles on islands and rocks. Its depth, averaging 480 feet in the shipping channel, ranges from 2,850 feet to virtually nothing over Bligh Reef at low tide. It is bounded by rocky peninsulas and towering mountains, most prominently the glacier-covered Chugach Mountains to the north.

The wildlife is diverse and abundant: "ten species of marine mammals, including sea lions, whales, seals, porpoises, and 10,000–12,000 sea otters; more than 30 species of land mammals, . . . more than 200 species of birds, including swans, cormorants, more than 15 million shorebirds, and 3000 bald eagles."[9] All of these were at risk at the time of the oil spill.

> The sound is . . . the crossroads for huge migrations of fish and birds. . . . The Copper River delta at the east end of the sound, 75 miles from the *Exxon Valdez*, is home to an estimated 20 million migratory birds in late April and early May, including one-fifth of the world's trumpeter swans. . . . One bay in the sound is home to the largest concentrations of orcas, or killer whales, in the world; its sea otters make up perhaps one fourth of the total U.S. sea-otter population; marshes and estuaries near Cordova on the eastern side of the sound support the entire nesting U.S. population of the rare dusky Canada goose."[10]

The risk from the spilled oil was the greater because the sound was enclosed, and therefore the oil slick was continuous. The oil could not break up as it would in the open ocean, so the benzene and other volatile components of the spill, instead of evaporating, soon dissolved in the water to be consumed by zooplankton and other microorganisms at the beginning of the food chain, crucial for the life of the sound.[11] The enclosure of the oil made matters worse; it "delayed dissipation of the spill, exposing animals to oil for a long period of time and allowing oil to soak deeply into beaches and sediments."[12]

The Deadly Invasion of Oil

How does oil kill an animal? The diving birds and the sea otters are most at risk. The birds catch their food by plunging into the water, diving to catch their fish, coming to the surface and taking off to fly to their nests. Any weight on their feathers makes that flight impossible. If they get to shore, they try to clean the oil off their feathers with their beaks (preening), thereby ingesting the oil, which is fatal. Since oil makes their insulation (the inner layer of down feathers) matted and useless, most of them freeze to death before they have time to die of poisoning. Of particular concern are two rare birds, the yellow-billed loon and the merlet, which may be very badly affected. We will probably never know just how badly: to jump a bit ahead in our the story, when Exxon applied for permission "to dispose of oil-soaked wastes some weeks after the spill, its list of throwaway items included twenty *tons* of dead birds."[13] A wildlife photographer counted 650 dead birds on a half-mile of beach on Barren Island. But as David Cline (the National Audubon Society's regional vice president for Alaska) pointed out, "You see only the birds that have managed to struggle to shore, where they shiver to death. And you find only a fraction of them. The majority of the dead you never see. Their oil-sodden plumage weighs them down and they drown." Up to 90 percent of oiled birds sink to the bottom.[14]

The sea otters were equally at risk. Unlike the other marine mammals of the area, seals and sea lions, otters have no blubber to keep them warm, but insulate themselves with the air trapped in their thick soft undercoat. Oil destroys their insulation, so only a little on them will quickly freeze them to death in the frigid water. The oil also destroys their eyes, lungs and intestines (when they ingest it from attempting to lick their coats clean).

The fish were the most expensive victims. The fishing industry earns $100 million annually in Prince William Sound (out of $2 billion for all of Alaska). Herring and salmon are the mainstays, but those fish "are just the start of a rich web of major species, including crab, shrimp, Pacific cod, Alaska pollock, rock-fishes, halibut, flounder and sharks."[15] In 1988, Prince William Sound salmon fishermen earned $70 million from a harvest of 14.9 million salmon, 15 percent of the state harvest. King crabs (48,422 pounds in 1988) and shrimp (178,000 pounds) were the species most endangered by dissolved benzene.[16] The herring roe industry does $13 million of business annually. (Herring roe sells for up to $80 per pound in Japan.) The herring need clean kelp to lay their spawn; after the spill, the kelp was sure to be covered with oil. Most of the towns, and most of the independent businessmen on the sound, make their living one way or another on the fishing industry, which employs 6,000 people all by itself. It is a growth industry—the average American consumption of seafood has nearly doubled in the last 20 years—and the fishermen were looking forward to a good year.

Nor are the fish just a means to make a living; the fishermen are united in a love for their way of life (which is why they accept without protest the complex web of restrictions on fishing licenses, gear, and seasons, to preserve the fish runs for the future), and for their spectacularly beautiful home. If the spread of the oil could not be stopped soon, the fishing seasons would have to be canceled and a year's income lost, or at least they would be placed at the mercy of Exxon to make good; and homes might well be lost, or their value destroyed. The fishermen had a tremendous amount at stake in stopping the oil. Would the Alyeska plan for stopping the oil work well enough, and quickly enough, to save the fishing season?

THE RESPONSE: STUDIES
IN DYSFUNCTION

There is no way to characterize the Alyeska/Exxon response to the situation except as failure—dismal failure. The causes of the failure are instructive: the unpreparedness; the dysfunctionality of large size; the incentives for ineffectiveness that are built into the system, especially the clouding of the boundary between appearance and reality (between public relations and environmental remediation); and the distractions of the law. These failure factors, which recur in all such situations (by themselves or generously mixed with human villainy), are worth noting in the discouraging tale of the response to the spill.

One Very Unprepared Consortium

Alyeska Pipeline Service Company, the consortium of seven oil companies (including Exxon) that actually owns the oil pumped out of the North Slope, had promised, when they were seeking approval for the pipeline, that the operations in Prince William Sound would be "the safest in the world."[17] Alyeska's plan, approved by the Alaska DEC, had specified that containment booms and skimming equipment (machinery for mechanically lifting the thick oil off the top of the water into transfer barges, which would take the oil to shore and offload it) would be on the scene of any spill in five hours, with backup equipment (lasers for burning off patches of oil, chemical dispersants) available if the booms and skimmers were inadequate to the job. There was no doubt in anyone's mind that speed was of the essence to contain a big spill. From Alyeska's containment plan: "Speed in deploying booms is essential in order to contain the maximum amount spilled oil;" it promised that "the necessary equipment is available and operable to meet oil spill response needs."[18] That equipment was supposed to be available at the dock.

Unfortunately, Alyeska had estimated that a spill of the size of this one could happen only once every 241 years, which made it seem pointless to keep all that equipment around and all those experts on the payroll. "Alyeska fought steadily to cut back safety measures. The oil-spill contingency plan was trimmed and weakened. A twenty-man oil spill emergency squad was disbanded," in 1981. "Instead of the twelve miles of boom materials that the state wanted Alyeska to have on hand, Alyeska insisted that a fourth that much was sufficient."[19] The pattern of cost cutting and crew reduction that (perhaps) had contributed to the spill in the first place now crippled the response. Barges were supposed to be available for transporting oil and equipment: Alyeska's one barge, on the morning of the spill, was in dry dock. Skimmers and boom were in a local warehouse and had to be dug out.

So even at the outset, when Alyeska's obligations were well understood and the weather was calm—ideal for containing and skimming the oil—the Great Promise (as Art Davidson calls it in *Wake of the Exxon Valdez*) was simply broken. A barge carrying 25 tons of cleanup equipment did not arrive at the accident site until 14 hours after the spill, after agonizing effort to find, load, and operationalize the equipment that they were able to find, and even then there was not enough containment boom at that time to encircle the spill.

The Alaskans had been betrayed, because Alyeska's cleanup plan had been crucial for the authorization of the pipeline to begin with. When the right-of-way permit was in doubt, back in 1971, "British Petroleum's top pollution specialist, L. R. Beynon, testified at Department of Interior hearings that Alyeska's contingency plan will detail methods for dealing promptly and effectively with any oil spill which may occur, so that its effects on the environment will be minimal. We have adequate knowledge for dealing with oil spills. . . . The best equipment, materials and expertise—which will be made available as part of the oil spill contingency plan—will make operations in Port of Valdez and Prince William Sound the safest in the world.[20]

Dennis Kelso, DEC Commissioner, at one point labeled that plan "the biggest piece of maritime fiction since *Moby Dick,*" also stating, "Yet, it was Mr. Kelso's office that approved of the contingency documents. He said later he placed too much trust in industry to live up to its paper promises."[21] "Too much"? Should we not be able to rely on citizens to live up to promises this specific and detailed, promises leaving no room for the possibility that there might have been some misunderstanding? What grated with particular harshness in this sense of betrayal was the value of the quantity at risk—the incredibly fertile beauty of Prince William Sound—and the clear fact, that without such promises, there would have been no pipeline.

Where indeed, now that the spill spread across the sound, *was* Alyeska? As the DEC's Dan Lawn put it so succinctly, "The people of the United States didn't want 4,700 different oil companies coming in here with 47,000 different cleanup contractors. They wanted one. That was Alyeska. And Alyeska was going to take care of everything. We've got a plan that says that. Where the hell were they?"[22] Why was Exxon suddenly the responsible party, and Frank Iarossi of Exxon Shipping Company in charge? In all the discussion afterward and to this day, there has not been a good explanation for the sudden disappearance of Valdez-based Alyeska and the ascendance of the Houston-based Exxon Shipping Company as responsible for the accident and charged with the cleanup.

Cleanup Efforts

Meanwhile, the weather, which had been balmy for two days after the spill, turned rough after that, and skimming would have been very difficult. It might be possible to use dispersants (detergents that break up the oil spill), which are made more effective by wave action. Dispersants have problems of their own, however. They do not really remove the oil from the water. They just sink it a few feet below the surface in an emulsion of oil and detergent (killing all marine life in that area just below the surface); the emulsion ultimately diffuses in the ocean. It kills young fish, and there is no doubt that it would hurt the otters and birds even more (since the detergent would dissolve the natural oils that insulate fur and feathers); the only real good that dispersants do is make the oil spill disappear.

The problem was moot on the practical level. Exxon had only 69 barrels of dispersant on hand in Alaska.[23] At great expense, Iarossi flew in dispersant from around the world. But it would have taken nearly 10,000 barrels of dispersant to treat that spill, and there was not that much in the world.

The damage, at any rate, was done. A crucial 48–72 hours of calm weather had passed without the booms being deployed and the oil skimmed from the water to waiting barges. The transfer of the remaining million barrels from the stricken *Exxon Valdez* to the *Exxon Baton Rouge* had begun, and it continued through the winter storm that tore through the area on the fourth day after the spill and spread the oil from 100 square miles to 500 square miles. Now, forced to improvise, how would the agencies faced with this massive disaster respond?

The first major problem was one of authority. Davidson describes it:

> Alyeska, which the state had relied on for spill response, had disappeared. Exxon was trying to respond but needed authorization. Most of Exxon's people, having flown up from other parts of the country, had little knowledge of Alaska and virtually no connection to the land and to Prince William Sound. They didn't know Alaska's weather, Alaska's waters, Alaska's shorelines, or Alaska's people. But the state and the Coast Guard, which could have provided the needed direction, strained against the limits placed on their own authority.[24]

The fishermen of the fishing towns on the sound then mounted their own initiative. After all, they had very little to do. On April 3, 1989, Alaska officials canceled the herring fishing season. That was good news for the herring fishermen, for it meant that they would surely get restitution for the season from Exxon (although the impact on the future of the herring will not be known for years). It also left their boats free to work, and as the oil continued to advance, it became clear that the precious salmon hatcheries were in danger. Nothing was being done to protect them, so the fishermen decided to act.

The hatcheries had been built in the early 1970s, when overfishing had reduced the pink salmon run so low that the season had to be closed. The fishermen borrowed $18 million from the state to build the Sawmill Bay and Esther Island hatcheries. "By 1989, the Koernig Hatchery, once an abandoned cannery on Sawmill Bay, was producing more than $20 million worth of salmon each year. The Esther had become the world's largest salmon hatchery, releasing 200 million pinks, 100 million chum, 4 million kings, and 2 million silvers."[25] The fishermen were afraid that even a few gallons of that oil, sweeping through the rearing pens, could wipe out an entire generation of pink salmon. So they took their own boats and went to work, dipping oil and laying booms to protect their hatcheries. Difficulties attended every step of getting better supplies from Exxon: "There were so many people in the chain of command that if one link goofed, nothing got done. Some of the Exxon people were trying their damnedest, but there simply wasn't enough equipment available."[26]

Heroic efforts staved off the oil until more solid containment boom was available; the hatcheries were saved. But they were saved by people acting on their own, with no chain of command, no formal plan, cooperating with each other only informally. The proper authorities—the huge state, the corporation, and the Coast Guard, acting together—found themselves locked into one vast unworkable gridlock.

Much the same observation could be made on other phases of the cleanup. The animal rescue efforts, for instance, recruited some of the best people available to clean, cure, and release wild birds and sea otters (especially), and volunteers worked tirelessly to save the lives of the oil-slicked wild creatures. Yet this effort continually ran afoul of, of all agencies, the U.S. Fish and Wildlife Service (FWS), which ordinarily catches the oiled birds and animals and brings them to the veterinarians. In Alaska, the FWS instructed the experts brought up from the Berkeley-based International Bird Rescue Research Center (IBRRC) that they would have to find their own animals to rescue, and incidentally talk Exxon into paying for their efforts—the role of the FWS was to "monitor" the operations. Eventually the IBRRC decided, just as the fishermen had, that they would have to run the entire operation themselves without help from the corporate government giants that had, at least on paper, authority over such decisions.

Systemic Disincentives

There may have been more at work than simple bureaucratic bungling in Exxon's handling of the extended cleanup effort. In the complex job of managing human interaction with nature (and each other), legislators are challenged to make sure that the incentives are in the right place: that it is in the perceived best interest of any agent to do what it is that we want that agent to do. Where the territory is familiar, the incentive patterns are known, used, and generally reliable. One of the best analyses of such patterns, for instance, is the treatment of voluntary economic exchanges in Adam Smith's *The Wealth of Nations,* in which he proves that government management of the market is unnecessary to protect justice, and counterproductive in the accumulation of national wealth.

However, where the territory is unfamiliar, we grope, and sometimes we fail. In the case of oil spills, for example, European nations immediately assume public responsibility for the spill, clean it up, and then send the offending oil company the bill for the damage. That approach has problems, for the government workers have no incentive to be frugal and to minimize the cost of the cleanup. So with Alyeska, a different approach was adopted: Alyeska and the spiller would assume responsibility for the cleanup if they could and would. The federal government would not step in and start running the operation ("federalizing" the cleanup) unless the spiller disclaimed responsibility or admitted inability to continue dealing with it. Exxon never did that. At the beginning of operations, as above, there was no doubt that the Exxon officers, especially Frank Iarossi, were doing their best to help the cleanup. Only as the oil spread across the sound, to more and more remote islands, to the Katmai National Park, 400 miles southwest of Bligh Reef, did the faltering of the cleanup begin to seem systematic.

Support from Washington, by this time, was beginning to fade. Much of the fading seemed to be emanating from Vern Wiggins, a Reagan appointee at Interior (deputy undersecretary for Alaska), who honestly believed that oil development was essential to the state of Alaska, and that therefore it was essential to underplay the effect of this spill and the dangers of spills generally; and his influence was very broad, extending to the Coast Guard as well as to the entirety of the Park Service.[27]

Meanwhile strong signals came from Exxon that it was time to wind down the cleanup. There were never enough boats to transport the oily sludge that the volunteers had collected. When transport boats did show, the Exxon employees did not want to transport the oil because it contained oil-soaked sand, pebbles, and kelp; Exxon's position was that it was committed to transport *oil,* not all that the oil had penetrated. In some places, workers had to pick up oil with their hands because even the trowels picked up pebbles. "Oil's hard to pick up just in gloves," commented one of the volunteers. "It goes through your fingers."[28] After a while, workers began very sincerely to doubt Exxon's commitment to getting oil off the beaches. The doubt was reinforced by days of sitting on beaches with no assignments, and reinforced again by the observation that those who worked hardest, especially those who came up with better ways to remove oil from the beaches, tended to get fired.[29]

Appearance and Reality

What were the incentives? Clearly Exxon had a major incentive not to let the spill be federalized, for then they would lose control of the cleanup expenditures. So they wanted to keep up the appearance of cleaning, at all costs. For Secretary of the Interior Manuel Lujan, boatloads of reporters, Exxon officers, and members of Congress, therefore, trips were arranged to the beaches, where 40 Exxon employees could be found skimming oil, mopping rocks, and scrubbing pebbles.[30]

However, the incentive to keep up an appearance of doing something is not the same as the incentive to do it. The greatest incentive Exxon had, of course, was to erase all evidence of the spill—to make it seem less serious than people thought and to have the cleanup over and done with. To do this, it would be necessary not to appear to find very much oil damage. The best way to do that would be to make sure, one way or another, that not very much oil was recovered and brought back to town for the news media to see and measure. And so the citizens and volunteers began to detect a pattern in the way Exxon conducted the cleanup later—no vessels available to cart the spill back to Valdez; haggling reminiscent of Shylock and Portia over whether the oil may contain sand or other oiled debris; all initiatives and hard work punished by termination. Beaches were not to be "cleaned," they were to be "treated" and then left.

The chronicle of the *Exxon Valdez* did not solve the problem of oil spill cleanup, which remains as pressing as ever: How to allot the tasks of cleanup after a major oil spill if the objective is to get it cleaned up, as quickly and as frugally as possible? How to allot the tasks of cleanup and of authority to command persons and equipment so that the responsible parties will have an incentive to clean up and not to retreat to the appearance of a job?

A SLICK OF LAWYERS OVER ALASKA

Further disincentives to real remedy flowed from the operations of the law. By now we are familiar with the kind of legal wrangling that goes on when people are injured by the actions of a large corporation. Exxon was acutely aware of this wrangling and swiftly promised to recompense anyone injured by the spill (the fishermen, for instance). That did not stop the lawsuits. Exxon and Alaska competed for the best law firms; at a preliminary hearing on some 150 lawsuits (58 of them class-action suits) held in Anchorage, 65 law firms were represented. Calculating damages, even those Exxon promised to pay, was extremely difficult. No problem arises in paying a fisherman for a missed season, given solid figures for work done previously, but the damage to the ecosystem's species, especially genetic damage, and the damage to wildlife habitat and to microscopic life were incalculable.

Law and Oil

The legal actions that followed the *Amoco Cadiz* spill off France in 1978 suggested that the ultimate liability of the parties to disputes of this nature will depend on a judge's perceptions of the relative contributions of oil company and government action. Judge McGarr had found in that case that the French Government's refusal (on environmental grounds) to authorize the use of dispersants in water less than 50 meters deep was "without scientific justification," and "seriously interfered with the success of the dispersant method" and so had relieved Amoco of much of the financial liability for the damage to the victims of that spill. Accordingly, Exxon immediately claimed that authorization for use of dispersants had been refused by Alaska—and Reagan's secretary of the interior, Manual Lujan backed them up. There was no doubt that the wrangling drained energy from the cleanup, as the state and Exxon fought each other for moral high ground in the press and for billions of dollars in court.

> The protagonists, entrenched with their lawyers and press agents, became increasingly isolated from each other. The result in many instances was that the battles took precedence over the problem. Too often the oil cleanup effort appeared to be driven more by legal and public relations strategies than by scientific considerations. And the common goal of restoring the coastal environment frequently seemed to get lost in the shuffle.[31]

The Blame

While the state and the company remained locked in a death grip of public relations and financial liability, the citizens of Alaska had an opportunity to reflect on their own complicity in the spill. "We're not victims of Exxon," said Tom Copeland, the fisherman whose bucket brigade outskimmed Exxon's best, "we're reluctant participants. Basically, Alaskans are addicted to that oil money. We've got that needle in our arms. . . . We don't deserve another dollar from that pipeline."[32] The oil companies had paid enough oil royalties in 1988 so that each citizen of the state got a royalty check in excess of $800. There is no record that any sent back their checks. And when Exxon offered to hire the fishing boats to fight the spill, at the rate of $5000 per day, most fishermen took them up on the offer. Somehow, it seemed in the historic opportunistic spirit of Alaska to do it.[33]

Ray Bane of the Katmai Park Service summed up the feeling of many of the residents:

> Exxon caused this mess, but it had plenty of assistance. I think all of us who have benefited from that oil have a responsibility to bear. Alaskans take too much for granted. It's a big land—good fishing, lots of animals, wild rivers. We take it all so damn much for granted. The oil spill is only a symptom of all of us closing our minds to the fact that there is always a price to pay when you develop oil, or cut down some trees, or build a road.[34]

But that kind of complacency went beyond the Alaskans. Shortly after the spill, Greenpeace put an ad in newspapers nationwide, showing Joseph Hazelwood's face, with a caption: "It wasn't his driving that caused the Alaskan oil spill. It was yours." Because the truth is, it continued, "the spill was caused by a nation drunk on oil. And a government asleep at the wheel."[35] "And ultimately," Cordova fisherman Ed Monkiewicz concluded, "we're all at fault, every single one of us. We've got to have our cars. We use the fossil fuels. Maybe if we put more value on our environment, this wouldn't have happened."[36]

Aftermath in Court

Exxon offered to settle the whole case two years later, submitting guilty pleas in an agreement that would have taken care of both criminal charges and civil claims of federal and Alaska state governments arising from the spill. Under that agreement, Exxon would have paid $100 million in criminal fines and as much as $1 billion for civil claims. (That was not very much, an editorial in the *New York Times* pointed out: by mid-April, Exxon had already paid an estimated $2 billion for the cleanup.)[37] But on April 24, 1991, Judge Russel Holland ruled that the $100 million in fines was not sufficient, and the legislature of Alaska subsequently voted that the civil settlement also was not enough.[38] Eventually Exxon agreed to pay $900 million over 10 years for "restoring, replacing, enhancing, rehabilitating or acquiring the equivalent of natural resources" damaged by the spill. Like most large sums of money, it was immediately examined by the lawyers: Of the first $240 million spent, only $11.4 went to the environment. The rest went to "reimburse the expenses" of the governments involved.[39] And now the trustees of the fund, bitterly criticized by environmentalists for mismanaging the money, have to decide which of two environmental causes, marine research or purchase of forest land, should get the remainder of the money, for there is no agreement among the environmental organizations.[40]

After years of efforts on the part of Exxon's scientists to show that there really was no long-term damage to Prince William Sound,[41] the matter was complicated again in 1993, when a geochemist working for the United States Geological Survey discovered by analysis of the residue that much of the oil on Alaska's beaches comes from an unnoticed 1964 spill of oil from Monterey, not from the *Exxon Valdez*. Exxon's lawyers immediately drew the legal implications and began work to extricate itself from further blame.[42] They were not entirely successful. In September 1994, after a 20-week trial, a jury awarded $5 billion in punitive damages to 34,000 fisherman and other Alaskans. That is a great deal of money (even for Exxon), although *The New York Times* did not find it excessive,[43] and the matter was appealed, for quite some time. (Ten days later another jury awarded $9.7 million in land damages to six Alaska native corporations and a village that had sued for damages.[44]) In 2001, the Ninth Circuit Court of Appeals ruled that the $5 billion award was "excessive"; in December 2002 District Court Judge Russell Holland reinstated the award at $4 billion. Judge Holland was unsparing:

> Exxon officials knew that carrying huge volumes of crude oil through Prince William Sound was a dangerous business, yet they knowingly permitted a relapsed alcoholic to direct the operation of the *Exxon Valdez* through Prince William Sound.

Exxon took it back to the Ninth Circuit, which was still sympathetic; the Ninth Circuit sent it back again to Judge Holland to reconsider. They should have known better. On January 28, 2004, Judge Holland found that a damage award of $4.5 billion *plus $2.25 billion in interest* was perfectly consistent with the law. The interest award is particularly important: by January 2004, 15 years had passed since the grounding. Exxon, now ExxonMobil, is wealthy; there is no reason why they could not keep the case in court until 2089, as long as no penalties accrued. Now, it seems, there may be penalties. Undaunted, Exxon announced its intention to appeal; resolution of the case may not come in our generation.[45]

HAZELWOOD WAS NOT ALONE

As the *Exxon Valdez* had headed for the reef, Alyeska officials were holding a self-congratulatory victory dinner celebrating the cleanup of a spill days previously in Valdez harbor. As Frank Iarossi reached for the ringing telephone in the small hours of the morning of March 24, 1989, he was still winding down from the Hawaiian spill of March 2, when the *Exxon Houston* broke loose from her moorings in a storm off Barber's Point, about 15 miles from Waikiki Beach, and went aground on a coral reef about 2,000 feet off the west coast of the island of Oahu.[46] Three months later, the nation watched fascinated as three major spills happened in twelve hours: On June 23, 4:40 P.M. the World Prodigy struck a reef in Narragansett Bay, Rhode Island, apparently because the ship had blundered into unfamiliar waters without waiting for a pilot and repeated the error of the *Exxon Valdez*, straying to the wrong side of the red channel buoys; 420,000 gallons of Number 2 fuel oil flowed into the waters of the bay. At 6:20 P.M. the same day, an oil barge collided with a tanker in the Houston ship channel, spilling 250,000 gallons of crude oil, about half of which had been cleaned up four days later. At four o'clock the next morning, the Uruguayan tanker *Presidente Rivera* managed to stray from its channel in the Delaware River and hit a rock, spilling 800,000 gallons of Number 6 fuel, rather little of which was recovered.

> The three spills reopened many of the questions that maritime lawyers, environmentalists and lawmakers had debated after the *Exxon Valdez* spill. Some environmentalists were asking whether the spills were a coincidence or an indication that something was so wrong that long-established maritime rules need to be changed.[47]

A bit of investigation showed that these incidents were not at all unusual. Captain Gerard Barton, chief of the Coast Guard's investigations division, told a House subcommittee that in 1988 "there were 5000 to 6000 spills involving oil and other toxic substances along the coasts and in other navigable waters," 12 of them major (more than 100,000 gallons or more), but that that was "down sharply from about 13,000 a year a decade ago." The House was unimpressed by the improvement and called for change in the oil transport system.[48]

Change did not happen in time to prevent the next rash of dreadful spills, in the winter of 1992–1993. On December 3, 1992, the tanker *Aegean Sea* grounded off the coast of Spain; 23 million gallons of crude oil were lost, most in the fire that followed the explosion, the rest in the sea.[49] In the first week of January, the Liberian-registered tanker Braer lost power and went aground, eventually spilling all its 22 million gallons of oil, and severely damaging wildlife—and again, salmon hatcheries.[50] Then the Danish tanker *Maersk Navigator* collided with another tanker on January 21, and its 78 million gallon cargo began to spill into the sea. (Much of that, also, burned off.) Nor do any of these, including the wreck of the *Valdez*, claim the title of largest: 88 million gallons of crude was lost off Trinidad and Tobago in 1979 when two oil tankers collided; 79 million gallons went into the ocean off Cape Town, South Africa, in 1983.[51] As if to remind us that the safety problem continues unaffected by all our efforts, the spill in Buzzard's Bay, cited at the opening of this chapter, spilled 98,000 gallons before it was stopped.

Tanker and barge accidents account for only two-thirds of the oil that spills accidentally into the waterways each year (an estimated 91 million gallons, for instance, in the period 1980–1986). (By far the largest portion of oil that pollutes our waters comes from ordinary runoff, the non–point–source pollution that is so very difficult to stop.)[52] The rest comes from pipe ruptures, like the rupture of an Exxon pipe that filled the Arthur Kill, off Staten Island, with oil in January 1990. A detection system had failed: malfunctioning for a year without repairs, operators had simply ignored its warnings when the real spill came.[53] That spill was to cost Exxon up to $15 million, and there was no chance of restoring the environment.[54] Probably the worst spill of all was from the largest act of eco–sabotage known to history: the deliberate destruction of the oil wells of Kuwait by the retreating Iraqi army during the Gulf War in 1991, which released 250 million gallons into the desert and the Persian Gulf.[55]

Opinions on the ultimate significance of these spills will differ, of course. Part of the difference is disagreement on the facts, since the effect of oil on fragile environments is often completely unknown. And part is simply difference of perspective: in Philip Revzin's reassuring article, "Years Temper Damage of Worst Oil Spill [the sinking of the *Amoco Cadiz*, off the coast of France]" we are told that "For a year after the gooey oil washed up . . . business [fishing, oyster-growing, tourism] all but stopped. For five to eight years the aquatic food chain was disrupted, costing crab fishers three generations of their most prized catches." And oil remained, in pockets. "But generally, 'it's finished, all is back to normal,'" says Lucien Laubler, chief scientific adviser to a French oceanic research institute. Back to normal? The French were suing Amoco for $600 million—eleven years later.[56] *The New York Times* angrily editorialized that it was time to stop the self-deceptions and make rational plans for safety and cleanup for the next spill.[57]

SO IT WILL NEVER HAPPEN AGAIN

Ultimately, the big story is the story of oil and energy—not Hazelwood's driving, but ours. From the renewed public discussion that followed the spill, three sets of imperatives emerged, to set the agenda for the effort to avoid another *Exxon Valdez* (*Amoco Cadiz, Aegean Captain, Sea Empress. . .*).

Enforce the Law

First, there were the imperatives to enforce the law, monitor compliance to existing policies, and implement known technology for the safe transport of oil. There are sufficient laws on the books, and clauses in the contracts, to make the oil industry operate safely. Complacency, carelessness, and criminal negligence produce these spills. Tankers can be required to have double hulls; more effective containment booms can be developed (the ones in use in Prince William Sound kept breaking); and we may develop new technology for the containment of spills (one interesting suggestion involves using fly ash—a pollutant removed from the chimneys of many industrial plants—fused with titanium dioxide to form tiny glass beads, which will absorb a spill, permit burning it off, and incidentally get rid of the fly ash).[58] More important, if the penalties are sure enough, and severe enough, the industry will find it to its advantage to monitor the state of preparedness of its cleanup crews, not to mention the state of inebriation of its employees.

There has been little improvement: A spokeswoman for the Skomer island Dyfed Wildlife Trust, in the path of the 1996 *Sea Empress* spill, "blamed the Government, charging that it had 'failed to provide an adequate and rapid response' to what she called 'an ecological disaster.'"[59] But at least in theory, that set of imperatives is not controversial; if we pass a law or set a policy, we presumably have no objection to carrying it out. The others present more problems.

Preserve the Land

The second set of imperatives aims to protect forever the last remaining tracts of unspoiled land in the world, to the extent that it is in our power to do so. Whatever we thought we would gain by building the Alaskan Pipeline from Prudhoe Bay to Valdez—and we certainly had our doubts about it at the time (1973), when the vote of Spiro Agnew was required to break the tie in the Senate—the sight of the beaches mired with oil changed our minds, at least some of our minds. Everything else in this world—energy, money, production, recreation—is ultimately fungible; we can find some sort of substitute that will do just as well. The land alone is unique and, once polluted, can never be fully restored.

But protection of the land means setting it aside from human use and exploitation. It may mean leaving oil under the ground forever in the Arctic National Wildlife Refuge, the Bristol Bay fishery, the Florida Keys, and New England's Georges Bank fishery. It will surely mean protecting it from all mining, timbering, and other exploitation of resources. What other sources of oil are there? The major oil companies are prospecting for new oil all over the world and are drilling dry hole after dry hole.[60] In an increasingly crowded world, to what extent may we prefer the interests of the land—land that only a handful of people will ever see—to the material interests of people presently alive?

Discover Alternative Sources of Energy

Ultimately, we need liberation from oil. Oil is a very embarrassing addiction: we end up pandering to the desires of the most backward regimes on the face of the earth in Africa and the Middle East; we are forced into unlikely alliances with sworn enemies against our friends; we pay vast amounts of money to feed our cars; and should the unreliable sources dry up, we seem to have no alternative but to hire and send the rigs to Alaska, to finish the job started by the *Exxon Valdez*. We will have to do better. This topic deserves more than we will be able to devote to it here; in another chapter in this volume the topic of alternative energy sources will be given proper consideration.

QUESTIONS FOR REFLECTION

1. Until the citizens of the twenty-first century find a way to do without oil, we are going to have to transport it over long distances, sometimes through dangerous passages. How can we make that transport as safe as possible?

2. What kind of political balance should we seek, between the pursuit of energy sources and the preservation of wild land and other valuable real estate? What sorts of places should be off limits?

NOTES

1. Daniel E. Goren, "Lobbyists Cry Foul over Oil Spill Law," *Standard Times, SouthCoastToday,* http://www.southcoasttoday.com/daily/08-04/08-05-04/a011o071.html.

2. This account is taken from Art Davidson, *In the Wake of the Exxon Valdez* (San Francisco: Sierra Club Books, 1990), and from contemporary newspaper accounts, as noted.

3. Philip Shabecoff, "Captain of Tanker Had Been Drinking, Blood Tests Show; Illegal Alcohol Level; Coast Guard Opens Effort to Bring Charge of Operating Ship While Intoxicated," *New York Times,* 31 March 1989, pp. A1, A12.

4. Ibid.

5. "Captain Has History of Drinking and Driving," Special to the *New York Times,* 28 March 1989, p. B7; Timothy Egan, "Elements of Tanker Disaster: Drinking, Fatigue, Complacency," *New York Times,* 22 May 1989, p. B7.

6. Egan, "Elements of Tanker Disaster."

7. Shabecoff, "Captain of Tanker Had Been Drinking," p. A12.

8. Davidson, *In the Wake,* p. 16.

9. Catherine A. Dold and Gary Soucie, "Just the Facts: Prince William Sound," insert in George Laycock, "The Baptism of Prince William Sound," *Audubon* (September 1989): 74–111.

10. Ken Wells and Marilyn Chase, "Paradise Lost: Heartbreaking Scenes of Beauty Disfigured Follow Alaska Oil Spill," *Wall Street Journal,* 31 March 1989, pp. A1, A4.

11. Malcolm W. Browne, "Spill Could Pose a Threat for Years," *New York Times,* 31 March 1989, p. A12.

12. Malcolm W. Browne, "In Once-Pristine Sound, Wildlife Reels under Oil's Impact: Biologists Say Spill Could Set Records for Loss of Birds, Fish and Mammals," *New York Times,* Science Times section, 4 April 1989, pp. C1, C5.

13. George Laycock, "The Baptism of Prince William Sound," *Audubon* (September 1989): 81. Emphasis added.

14. Ibid., p. 81.

15. Ken Wells and Marilyn Chase, "Paradise Lost: Heartbreaking Scenes of Beauty Disfigured Follow Alaska Oil Spill," *Wall Street Journal,* 31 March 1989, pp. A1, A4. Other sources for this section include George Laycock, "Baptism," and Michael D. Lemonick, "The Two Alaskas," *Time,* 17 April 1989, pp. 56–66.

16. Browne, "Once Pristine Sound," p. C5.

17. George Laycock, "Baptism," p. 84.

18. Davidson, "In the Wake, pp. 24–25.

19. Laycock, "Baptism," p. 84.

20. Statement by L. R. Beynon for Alyeska Pipeline Service Company, Trans-Alaska Pipeline hearing, Department of Interior, Anchorage, 25 February 1971, exhibit 48, vol. 3, cited in Davidson, *In the Wake,* p. 81.

21. Timothy Egan, "Elements of Tanker Disaster: Drinking, Fatigue, Complacency," *New York Times,* 22 May 1989, p. B7.

22. Cited in Davidson, *In the Wake,* p. 81.

23. Egan, "Elements of Tanker Disaster." Iarossi claimed that Exxon had 365 barrels ready to use; Davidson, *In the Wake*, p. 53.

24. Davidson, *In the Wake*, p. 58.

25. Ibid., p. 103.

26. Ibid. p. 110.

27. Ibid., pp. 242–43.

28. Ibid., p. 261

29. Ibid., p. 262.

30. Matthew L. Wald, "Cleanup of Oily Beaches Moves Slowly," *The New York Times* April 23, 1989, p. 30.

31. Ibid., p. 199.

32. Ibid., p. 109.

33. Ibid., p. 147.

34. Davidson, *In the Wake*, p. 273.

35. Greenpeace USA; 1436 U Street NW; Washington, DC 20009.

36. Davidson, *In the Wake*, p. 277.

37. Editorial, "Dolphins and Double Hulls," *New York Times*, 14 April 1990.

38. Charles McCoy and Allanna Sullivan, "Exxon's Withdrawal of Valdez Pleas Will Maintain Pressure to Settle Case," *Wall Street Journal*, 28 May 1991, pp. A3, A6.

39. Keith Schneider, "Dispute Erupts on Settlement in Valdez Spill," *New York Times*, 16 October 1994, p. A22.

40. Ibid., p. A22.

41. Caleb Solomon, "Exxon Attacks Scientific Views of Valdez Spill," *Wall Street Journal*, 15 April 1993, p. B1.

42. Agis Salpukas, "Spilled Oil May Not Be from Exxon Valdez," *New York Times*, 1 December 1993, pp. A2, D7.

43. Editorial, "Long Shadow of the Exxon Valdez," *New York Times*, 21 September 1994.

44. "$9.7 Million Land Damages Won in Valdez Case," *New York Times*, 26 September 1994, p. A 12.

45. Website of Lieff Cabraser Heimann & Bernstein, LLP, attorneys for the plaintiffs, http://www.lieffcabraser.com/wbh_exxart. htm. That website also has a 1996 article by William B. Hirsch, describing the legal proceedings in the case (it is not clear where the article was originally published). Be forewarned: this is a law journal article,

38 pages long, 20 pages of which are footnotes.

46. "Tanker Spills Oil Off Hawaiian Coast," *New York Times*, 4 March 1989, p. 6.

47. Loc. cit..

48. Philip Shabecoff, "The Rash of Tanker Spills Is Part of a Pattern of Thousands a Year," *New York Times*, 29 June 1989, p. A20.

49. Wells, "Ship Spews Oil."

50. William E. Schmidt, "The Afflicted Shetlands Pray, For Man and Beast," *New York Times*, 11 January 1993; William E. Schmidt, "Storm Batters Wrecked Tanker, Worsening Oil Spill in Shetlands," *New York Times*, 12 January 1993, pp. A1, A9; Ken Wells, "Oil Spill Drifts; Salmon Farms Are Threatened: Shetland Fishing Operations Face Millions of Dollars in Immediate Damages," *Wall Street Journal*, 11 January 1993, p. A11; Ken Wells, "Volunteers Battle Storm, Pollution, But Oil Spill's Wildlife Toll Mounts," *Wall Street Journal*, 11 January 1993, p. A3.

51. Wells, "Ship Spews Oil."

52. From Smithsonian's "Ocean Planet," a 1995 traveling exhibit: Runoff accounts for 363 million gallons of oil in our waterways each year, bilge-cleaning and other routine maintenance work accounts for another 137 million gallons, hydrocarbons from air pollution enter the waters to the extent of 92 million gallons, eroding sedimentary rock accounts for another 62 million, and only then do accidental spills kick in with 37 million gallons.

53. Craig Wolff, "Exxon Admits a Year of Breakdowns in S.I. Oil Spill," *New York Times*, 10 January 1990, pp. A1, B3; Craig Wolff, "Leaking Exxon Pipe Ran Through Regulatory Limbo," *New York Times*, 11 January 1990, pp. B1, B7; Tim Golden, "Oil in Arthur Kill: Publicity and Peril for Urban Marsh," *New York Times*, 18 January 1990, pp. B1, B4.

54. Allan R. Gold, "Exxon to Pay Up to $15 Million for Spill," *New York Times*, 15 March 1991, p. B1.

55. Wells, "Ship Spews Oil."

56. Philip Revzin, "Years Temper Damage of Worst Oil Spill: Starkest Fears of 1978

Amoco Disaster Weren't Realized," *Wall Street Journal,* 4 April 1989, p. A10.

57. Editorial, "On Oil Spills: Trust Turns into Anger," *New York Times,* 28 June 1989.

58. Malcolm W. Browne, "Experts See Glass Beads as Low-Cost Tool for Oil-Spill Cleanup," *New York Times,* 11 April 1992, p. 12.

59. Sarah Lyall, "Oil Tanker Refloated Off Wales," *New York Times,* 22 February 1996, p. A8.

60. Caleb Solomon, "The Hunt for Oil: Petroleum Industry Pins Future on Finding Large Overseas Fields," *Wall Street Journal,* 25 August 1993, pp. A1, A4.

6

The Extended Family

The Saga of the Great Apes

INTRODUCTION

"**I**n a clearing in the jungle of the Congo river basin," Laura Spinney writes, "local hunters hold an illegal market twice a month with workers from a nearby logging concession to trade bushmeat for ammunition, clothes and medicine. Among the carcasses that change hands are chimpanzees, gorillas and bonobos (pygmy chimpanzees), all of which are protected species."[1] That is not the only market. All over the tropical forests of West and Central Africa, Latin America and Asia, increasing numbers of commercial hunters are slaughtering the primates, especially the great apes, for food and also for export. Conservationist Jane Goodall, the world's foremost expert on the chimpanzee, has stated that unless this hunting is stopped, "in 50 years there will be no viable populations of great apes left in the wild."[2]

THE TRADITIONAL FOOD OF THE
INDIGENOUS POPULATIONS

It is not easy to tell people in poverty not to hunt monkeys and apes. They are traditional food in Central Africa, and to the hunters, "They're just animals."[3] A hunter will get $60 for an adult gorilla, and a full-grown chimpanzee would bring almost as much. (Since gorillas bring a better price than chimpanzee,

chimpanzee meat is often sold as gorilla.) Concerned observers in the area often have reservations about the practice but end by defending the hunting. As David Brown of the British government's delegation to the Convention on Trade in Endangered Species put it, bushmeat is "a major component of the economies of much of equatorial Africa. It is a primary source of animal protein and the main export commodity for the inhabitants." He therefore thinks that the "industry" should be "managed, not stigmatised and criminalised."[4]

Hunting is now a greater threat than habitat loss to ape populations already strained to the breaking point. "The World Wide Fund for Nature estimates that there are no more than 200,000 chimps, 111,000 western lowland gorillas, 10,000 eastern lowland gorillas and 620 mountain gorillas left in the wild." With respect to bonobos, their "numbers are thought to have halved in the past 20 years."[5] Why has the hunting of primates increased so dramatically, especially in Africa? In all probability, the hunting has been triggered by the African population explosion of the last 20 years, which has increased the density of human population all through the forest and countryside and left a hungry population in the burgeoning cities. The pygmies, for instance, in Congo and Cameroon, used to eat anything that moved in the forest with no fear of impacting the species: there was one pygmy for every 10 square kilometres, and with their poisoned arrows, at that density, they could do no real harm. They would probably do no harm at ten times that density, at one person per one square kilometer.[6] But now there are many more people than that, not only pygmies but participants in the new extractive industries.

The mainspring for the crisis was clearly the logging industry. In efforts to pay off their debts and develop their nations, governments in West Africa have contracted with foreign companies to log the remaining rainforests. According to Jeff Dupain of Belgium's Royal Zoological Society in Antwerp, the companies usher hunters into previously inaccessible forest land when they make the logging roads; they "make it easier for hunters to get to the wildlife and transport carcasses back to towns, often using the loggers' lorries and boats."[7] Worse yet, as it happens, is their technique of driving roads deep into the bush to divide the forest into sectors to be worked. Where the forest is fragmented, the ability of a forest species to reconstitute itself after hunting is severely compromised, probably destroyed. As if to ensure the maximum destruction of wildlife, the companies issue the loggers rifles ("to protect themselves"), and don't send in enough food, expecting the workers to live off the land.[8] In one logging camp alone, in one year, according to a report released by the Wildlife Conservation Society (WCS), more than 1,100 animals were killed, totaling 29 metric tons, and the hunting of wild game is three to six times higher in communities adjacent to logging roads. The WCS estimates that the annual harvest of bushmeat in equatorial Africa exceeds 1 million metric tons.[9]

In 1998, a coalition of 34 conservation organizations and ape specialists called the Ape Alliance estimated that in the Congo, up to 600 lowland gorillas are killed each year for their meat. Although the initial exchanges of that meat take place in the bush, the bulk of the meat is sold in the cities. The railway station at Yaounde, the capital of Cameroon, houses a bushmeat market that does not close; one ton of smoked bushmeat, largely chimpanzees and gorilla, is unloaded there on a daily basis.[10] It is no secret. "It's a 500-foot stretch of sidewalk only a few blocks from the presidential offices and the $200-a-night Hilton Hotel. . . ." Behind the antelope stalls are "piles from which long arm bones protrude, obviously those of chimpanzees and gorillas. At the fetish stalls, you can buy chimpanzee hands, gorilla skulls, round slices of elephant trunk or the bright red tails of endangered gray parrots."[11] (If you boil the finger of a gorilla, the people believe, and add the water to the baby's bath, the baby will be strong like a gorilla.)[12] Thousands of chimpanzees are killed each year. Chimpanzees reproduce at the rate of one baby every four years, gorillas usually more slowly than that. The apes do not have the reproductive capacity to bounce back from this kind of assault.[13]

There can be no doubt of the reaction of the developed nations to the facts. A World Wide Web query on the subject of "bushmeat" yielded "about" (the search engine's word) 26,300 entries in 0.42 seconds, and all that were sampled were linked to organizations determined to stop the slaughter and protect the apes. In April 1999, the same month that the WCS report came out, 28 organizations and agencies, led by the Jane Goodall Institute, issued a major statement on the protection of the apes. It enumerated the measures that would have to be taken immediately if the apes were to survive, calling on educators, governments, corporations in general and above all the logging, mining, and other extractive industries to take immediate action to protect the apes.[14] A year later, the situation had not improved. Writing in the *Washington Post,* Jane Goodall estimated that the number of chimpanzees had declined to 150,000 from the million and more that roamed the wild when she began her chimpanzee research in 1960.[15] Six months later, the 2,500 delegates to an eight-day environment meeting in Amman, Jordan, ended with a request to IUCN–The World Conservation Union to put all possible pressure on governments to take steps to curtail the trade in bushmeat. By that time the hunting was "a commercialised industry where automatic weapons have replaced bows and arrows," an industry worth $350 million a year in Ghana, $121 million annually in the Ivory Coast.[16] The directors of the represented environment groups talked grimly of "strong conservation solutions" that had to be adopted immediately.[17]

Yet there is clearly no unanimity with the developing world. The sense of revulsion that attends the contemplation of the market in ape hands and fingers, shared by so many in the nations of Europe and North America, is obviously not shared by the hunters, by the loggers, or even by the African and Asian governments nominally in charge of the hunting grounds. How come we feel it? Before we go any further in examining this controversial subject, let us take a closer look at the great apes and see if we can discover, first, who these apes are, and second, based on that information, possibly, the source of the conviction that the bushmeat harvest is fundamentally wrong.

THE QUARRY IN THE GREAT
BUSHMEAT HUNT

Who are the great apes? At one point a variety of species of large tailless apes lived in large numbers in equatorial Africa and Southeast Asia, but those populations have been reduced to fragmented pockets. As noted earlier, we know that the individuals in the four remaining species number only in the hundreds and thousands and that a new virus could wipe them all out. In our generation, we may see the end of the wild apes. Let us find out who they are—quick, before they are gone.

First of all, as is commonly known, the apes are our relatives. Furthest from us on the family tree are the "lesser apes," the gibbons (*Hylobates*) of Southeast Asia, who show amazing dexterity and acrobatic skill but who are distinguished from monkeys only by their tendency to walk upright. The "great apes," our closest relatives, are the orangutan, the gorilla, and the chimpanzee. We will take a quick look at them before exploring the enormous ethical dilemma they pose for us.

The orangutans (*Pongo pygmaeus*), native to Borneo and Sumatra, live in solitary splendor in the canopy of the Asian rainforest, from which they rarely descend to the ground. They are not bipedal (disposed to walk on two feet) at all but rather bibrachial—their major mode of locomotion is swinging through the trees. About twice the size of females, males command overlapping territories of about 40 square kilometers. They do not tolerate each other, tending to harass and kill any males they meet in the course of a day's foraging.[18] Normally they have little use for humans. However, as their habitat withstood the impact of war, agriculture, and logging and their numbers fell to 20,000 in 1992 and ever further with the passage of time, they cannot survive now without human help. According to a *National Geographic* report on orangutans published in August 1998, the apes may reproduce only once in an eight-year interval; the mothers nurse their infants for about six years, and older siblings can hang around for several more years. As habitat shrinks, male violence increases, and the death rate of males rises. The prospects for the survival of the species in the wild are not good.[19]

The African apes are more closely related to us humans. The bonobos (*Pan paniscus*), native to central Congo, are simply smaller chimpanzees, recognized as a separate species only since the 1930s. The chimpanzee (*Pan troglodytes*) is probably our closest relative, sharing 98.5 percent of our DNA. (Does that make the consumer of bushmeat 98.5 percent cannibal? Karl Ammann would contend that indeed it does.[20]) The gorilla (*Gorilla gorilla,* as named by a biologist fresh out of imagination) is the largest of the apes, the male averaging 400 pounds. None of the apes is truly bipedal, suggesting to some anthropologists that bipedalism made the 1.5 percent difference between the ape and the human. The mechanisms by which the change occurred are still under scrutiny.

The extensive similarities between us and the apes raise serious moral questions about the great bushmeat hunt. The chimpanzees, for instance, use tools. They extract termites from their mounds with straws and sticks, and they crack nuts with hammers. They pick out "anvils," depressed knotholes of harder wood where a nut can be positioned securely; find "hammers," pieces of hard wood or stones for the tougher cases; bring their piles of nuts to the anvils; and start hammering.[21] The behavior is in no way instinctive. It is learned, taught to each new generation by the last. Further, it is cultural; in different areas, different groups of chimpanzees have learned different ways of cracking nuts and use different sets of tools to catch termites. In contrast to the gorillas, who live in foraging tribes much like those of our own hunting-gathering forebears, in which dominant males protect and lead the troop and gentle females painstakingly rear their infants, widely spaced by birth, chimpanzees hunt in groups. They communicate complex messages, we know not how. Spoken language as we know it is impossible for chimpanzees because of the placement of the structures of their throat—they cannot guide air over a voicebox as we can—but they can learn language: chimps have been taught American sign language, lexigrams, and token languages. They can communicate with us when we are willing to use these languages, not at any high intellectual level, but at least at the level of a young child.[22]

How do we know what we know about the apes? Because of their similarities to us, they have attracted many of the best students to observe and inform us of their ways. Louis Leakey, the great anthropologist of early humanoids, sent three of his best students into the wild to study the apes.

The careers of those students—all women (Leakey thought that women would develop better rapport with wild apes)—are instructive. "Leakey's Angels," as they were called, followed identical paths. They each studied the apes on site, seeking to advance the science of zoology by collecting and publishing data on these fascinating animals. Later, graduate students came to join them, also to study. Then, as they became alarmed at the pressures on the habitat and on the shrinking numbers of their "subject matter," the researchers turned their emphasis to public education, hoping to effect more enlightened policies that would be to the longterm benefit of both animals and humans. Then, no doubt as a consequence of that 98.5 percent identity with their subjects, inevitably they became advocates for them, setting up orphanages and hospitals for the surviving victims of the bushmeat and black-market rare-animals trade. By this time, they had dropped all pretense of seeing the apes as mere beasts. Having originally taken up their posts in Africa simply to study the apes, they stayed on to protect them.

Dian Fossey, who chose the mountain gorillas, achieved the dubious and quite unexpected fame of martyrdom. She arrived in Africa in 1963 determined to study the mountain gorillas of Rwanda. With the support of Louis Leakey and financial help from the National Geographic Society, she set up permanent residence in the Karisoke Research Center in Rwanda in 1967. During her 18 years of studying the mountain gorillas at Karisoke, she became, effectively, part of a gorilla group. She was able to watch youngsters be born, mature, and become responsible adults in the group. Proudly she observed as one of her favorites, Digit, became the head of a family. When Digit was killed by poachers (his head taken as a totem, his hands cut off to be made into ashtrays), Fossey was galvanized into action. She wrote a book, *Gorillas in the Mist,* to popularize her cause, and turned her research center into a refuge. As a crusader for the protection of the gorillas she eventually made herself suffi-ciently bothersome to become a murder victim—killed (in 1985) by the poachers whose prey she was trying to protect. Two years later a movie was made of her highly readable book to recount her career and (not incidentally) to publicize the cause of protection of the animals who had become her friends. It is through that movie that most of us know of her.

Biruté Galdikas, possibly the least known of the Angels, chose the most remote setting for her work—Borneo, one of the last habitats of the orangutan. She met Leakey in 1968, and with his support and that of the National Geographic Society she set up a research camp in Borneo (Camp Leakey, of course). She has been there ever since. In 1995 she published her autobiography, *Reflections of Eden: My Years with the Orangutans of Borneo,*[23] which describes her education, scientific career, and the establishment of Camp Leakey. By then the camp had become not so much a research center as a refuge, where wild orangutans, rescued from the poachers, are rehabilitated and integrated eventually back into the wild. With a co-author, she published another book in 1999, rich with photographs of the orangutans, for the sole purpose of raising money for her center.[24]

But for the dramatic movie about Dian Fossey, Jane Goodall, who has spent 40 years studying the chimpanzees in Gombe National Park in Tanzania, would surely be the best known. Goodall spent the first 30 years following a mid-size group of chimpanzees as they hunted, socialized, and squabbled on a mountain within the park. Eventually they got used to the zoologist following them around, and she was able to document their lives in some detail. As she studied she wrote, presenting to the world a picture of omnivorous and versatile per-sonalities of animals very like ourselves; it was she who first documented the use of tools and the possibility of culture among the chimpanzees.[25] She went through the same mutations as the other Angels: once spending time in Africa to study the chimpanzees, she now spends most of her time on the lecture cir-cuit trying to raise money for them.

Goodall also brought us the most startling and disturbing revelations about the lives of the great apes. She had studied the chimps for years, raised her child among them, learned their social structures, customs, and laws and the distinct and quirky personalities of the troop she chose to follow, when she sent in new and alarming reports, this time of psychosis among the chimpanzees. A female who had no infants of her own had started to steal infants from weaker females. Since she could not care for the infants, she ate them. Other females started accompanying her on her kidnapping raids and begged infant flesh for them-selves. A terrible pattern of psychotic murder and cannibalism, hitherto unseen in the animal world, played itself out before Goodall's eyes. Apparently the behavior had a physical origin, for it stopped when the female perpetrator her-self became pregnant.

Worse yet were the implications of vicious intergroup violence among Goodall's chimpanzees. After many years of group living, her troop split up, a small band of them taking up residence on the other side of the mountain.

Then mysteriously the smaller group began to die off, one by one. Troubled, Goodall began closer observations to see what was killing them. To her surprise and horror she found that the killers were bands of raiders from the other half of the group. Chimpanzees were attacking other chimpanzees in a way that she had never seen before. Violence was not unusual among the chimpanzees: males often fought each other for dominance in the group. But in those ordinary conflicts no one died or got seriously hurt. In these new conflicts, the victim always died or was left for dead. The attacks were planned, organized, and directed for maximal effectiveness, isolating a single member of the victim group and ambushing him. The strongest chimps led the attack; youngsters followed along and gleefully pounced on the victim when he was almost dead.

No reason for the attacks could be determined. There was no rivalry over food—in plentiful supply for all on both sides of the mountain. There was no rivalry over land, females, or any other resource. There was no discernable environmental threat (except to the victims after the raids started). And finally, there was no question that the hunt and the killing were deliberate: the night before a raid, the raiding party would take up their positions in a tree near the normal territory of the other group and spend the night in very untypical silence; then the hunt itself would be carried out in dead silence so that the victim might not have warning to get away. It was deliberate killing by the chimpanzees of another of their own species and acquaintance for no reason but that he belonged to a different group. It was, in the words of one observer, a clear case of genocide. And the killers clearly enjoyed it, very much.

Far from challenging the notion of human–ape relatedness, the psychotic and genocidal behavior witnessed by Goodall reinforces it. The great apes are alarmingly human. Their lives are much like ours in the foraging period. Their families are much like ours. They sin. They have rituals of forgiveness for individual sin and are totally unconscious of group sin. *They are just like us.* When we look into the eyes of the ape, we look at our own not-so-distant past.

Is it that fact primarily that grounds our conviction that we must somehow protect the apes from slaughter? As of October 2000, even the tightfisted U.S. Congress had voted $5 million for the Department of the Interior, "to use for grants to organizations involved in efforts to protect the great apes."[26] On what is this conviction based? Where, ethically speaking, do the apes stand? Apologists advance different, and occasionally incompatible, arguments for their protection. We will examine these arguments in the following sections.

APES IN THE WILD: THE PRESERVATION OF ENDANGERED ECOSYSTEMS

In the objections to the uses of apes for meat, one of the first points always noted is that apes, as species, are "protected." What is this "protection"? What is the rationale for "protecting" species?

First, let us be clear that it is not the "species," in the sense of a certain pattern of DNA, that is being protected—in that sense, we could freeze a few tissue samples and preserve the species forever. Nor is it the separate individuals that we propose to save, except perhaps in desperation. The entire ecosystem in which the species operates is and must be the object of conservation activity (in the case of the apes the ecosystem is the tropical rainforest). We may think of every species as a unique tract, a text from nature, a storehouse of information, infinitely valuable, and each species as a chapter in the book of its own ecosystem. The species and the ecosystem evolved together and must be preserved together.

We should bear in mind that in the worldwide initiative to preserve the environment the great apes play two roles, roles in tension with each other. The first role is as a keystone of the ecosystem, the animal near the top of the food chain without whose presence the balance would not be kept. The New England ecosystem was for all intents and purposes destroyed, for instance, when for good and sufficient reason the cougars and wolves were killed or driven out. By now accustomed to the overpopulation of white-tailed deer and rabbits and to the impoverishment of the woods and fields caused by overgrazing, we will never know how that ecosystem functioned when it was in balance. Similarly, the tropical forest cannot be saved unless we can preserve it with all of its species flourishing. And the danger is real: with the slow rate of reproduction of the great apes, these species are under significant threat.

The second role played by the apes is as a symbol of the ecosystem, much as the northern spotted owl symbolizes the redwood forest in the battle to save the giant sequoias of California's northern coast. Because they are so like us, the apes garner sympathy on their own. Portraying them as endangered wins sympathy for the effort to preserve the ecosystem as a whole. .The first role is described as part of ecology, the second is frankly part of preservation strategy. This second role can be viewed as strategic (as part of a preservation strategy), the first as ecological. When environmentalists confuse the two roles, the result can be ethically ambivalent.

Consider a case in point. When the forest fires broke out over the West and Central Kalimantan provinces of Indonesia some four years ago, primatologist Barita Manullang, head of the World Wide Fund for Nature's Orangutan Conservation Project in Jakarta, went to Central Kalimantan to see how the orangutans were faring. The result horrified him.

> In each [village] he found a baby orangutan held in a crude cage. He knew immediately that the animals' mothers were dead: a mother orangutan would never abandon her young. When pressed, the farmers in each village told Manullang the same gruesome tale. A mother with the baby clinging to its long reddish hair had fled from the nearby smoking forest into the village's gardens in search of food. Barking dogs had alerted the villagers to the presence of the animals. As the dogs attacked, farmers wielding machetes and sharpened sticks hacked and stabbed the mothers to death. The babies were taken captive—to be sold for up to $100 apiece as pets or to illicit wildlife traders. The dead mothers were skinned and eaten.[27]

The habitat problem is particularly severe for the orangutans, who are found only in the wilderness of Sumatra and Borneo. The rich tropical forest in which they make their homes provides abundantly if left alone. But agribusiness is making constant inroads on the forest, and the 1997 fires made their situation much worse. There is strong suspicion that the fires were not accidental. International proposals (including an environmental impact study in 1996) had recommended conserving 70 percent of the Central Kalimantan orangutan habitat as environmental reserve. But Jakarta (including President Suharto's powerful family) saw more profit in a mega–rice project that would require massive deforestation of that habitat. Deforestation went forward regardless of environmental impact, and the burning finished the job. The fires drove the animals out of the woods, making life easier for the poachers, and simultaneously made those areas not worth preserving as forest habitat. Agribusiness and poachers alike profited from the fires.[28]

Yet Manullang found it difficult to condemn the small farmers who had killed the orangutans, even as contemporary observers find it difficult to condemn all killing of gorillas for bushmeat. The farmers have no choice in their approach to the orangutans. They live by subsistence farming, close to the edge of survival, and cannot afford to let the hungry apes, driven out of the forest, demolish their gardens. Indeed, the meat of the adult orangutans killed in this latest slaughter probably added significantly to the annual protein intake of the farmers.

Ethical ambivalence also attends the situation of the Karisoke gorillas. Rwanda, neighboring Burundi, and several other nations of Central Africa have been involved in terrible civil wars, genocide (especially between the Tutsi, or Watusi, tribe and the Hutu, ancient rivals), revolutions, and military coups. The planting cycles have been disrupted, and often the people do not have enough to eat. The wars and the genocide have severely compromised the ability of Rwandans to preserve their gorillas. Their occupations wiped out, the people occupy the land wherever they can, demolishing the forest for food, fuel wood, and building materials. They have no choice.[29] How can we tell them, that the gorilla's life is more valuable than their own—even if, in the grand sweep of history, that's true?

APES IN THE LABORATORY:
UTILITARIAN BENEFITS AND TROUBLING
CLAIMS OF RIGHT

The chimpanzee shares 98.5 percent of our genetic endowment. Then why does the chimpanzee not get asthma, rheumatoid arthritis, acne—or AIDS, even when the virus is clearly present in the bloodstream? Especially HIV and AIDS. How can the apes harbor a similar virus harmlessly? What can we learn about human diseases, now and in the future, from experimentation with these animals? Scientists are calling for sequencing of the chimpanzee genome and for study of the chimps' resistance to diseases.[30] But even now, the poachers have lowered the number of wild chimpanzees available, to the point of hindering research. With all the human benefits at stake from a multiyear study of the immune system of chimpanzees, is there no way we can keep them out of the cooking pots?

Beyond the uses of chimpanzees' bodies for medical research, what else may we learn from that overwhelmingly similar genome? Since the great apes can learn language and seem to experience all emotions that we know, they may provide an irreplaceable subject for the study of language acquisition and human psychology. As noted earlier, we also find (or rather, Jane Goodall found) the same psychopathologies in the chimpanzee, even the tendency to genocide.[31] Is that subject amenable to study? We cannot do research at all on sophisticated human criminal behavior, because it becomes impossible to conceal from the subject what is being studied. Yet chimpanzees, who exhibit all the psychopathological behavior that we do, are not able to understand the hypotheses of the research. Perpetually naïve subjects, they may well be able to give us pure results about very impure behavior. Maybe we could even learn to control it ourselves.

What limitations affect the use of the apes in the laboratory? A growing movement is afoot to end all animal research or at least regulate it much more strictly. In the past, animals of all kinds have been beaten, tortured (not as part of the research but for the amusement of the staff), abused, neglected, caged without fresh air or exercise, starved, and left to die of infection in uncleaned cages. Clearly such treatment is wrong, and wrong for reasons that have nothing to do with the special qualities of the apes. Civilized people generally acknowledge an obligation to treat all animals humanely—not humanly, but gently, so as not to cause them pain or distress. That general obligation entails at least that animals be fed and watered properly, allowed adequate exercise and companionship, and kept in clean and well-lighted quarters. The obligation applies to pets, dogs, and cats, and to farm animals, as well as to the monkeys and apes kept in captivity for research or for the amusement of our children. (The imperative for the "humane" treatment of animals actually first applied to horses and was much encouraged by nineteenth-century English books for girls, like Anna Sewell's *Black Beauty*.) The humane perspective asks only that we show mercy and consideration to creatures who share with us the capacity for pain.

Because of the history of, and propensity for, abuse, scientific research that uses animals for its subjects requires enforcement of specific protocols by federal regulation. Such regulation, however, has not prevented studies of unimaginable cruelty—one of which, Thomas Gennarelli's University of Pennsylvania study on head injuries, came to national attention when the Animal Liberation Front "liberated" a particularly damaging set of videotapes from the laboratory and gave them national exposure.[32]

Some of the rules developed in the name of humane treatment undermine the scientific purposes for which certain studies are done. When higher mammals are to be used for experimental surgery, for instance, and there is a strong likelihood that the animal will be in pain should it be allowed to regain consciousness, the rules call for the animal to be humanely killed before it wakes up. However, unless the animal is kept alive, it might not be possible to ascertain whether surgery is a success.

But in using apes as subjects of experimentation, humane treatment is not the only issue. With regard to chimpanzees in particular, their very similarity to us raises questions about the way research is conducted. In the major studies of chimpanzee research, especially Roger Fouts's semi-autobiographical account of his life with the chimpanzees,[33] questions of right and humane treatment tend to overlap. He abhors the "prison-like" setting of most experimental labs, roundly condemns the scientists who do research for their own professional purposes, and ends up suggesting that no matter how useful it is, we ought to abandon animal research altogether.[34]

APES IN COURT: SHOULD THEY HAVE THE RIGHTS OF PERSONS?

We may grant that it is important to preserve ecosystems, for environmental reasons. We may also grant that it is important to preserve animals that are useful for research and to treat those animals humanely. But there seems to be more to the apes question than those provisos. As seen in our earlier discussion, in many respects, they are human: they have culture, they react to suffering as humans do, they display a multitude of similar behavioral traits. Should apes be treated as humans? This is the final and great question.

Stories always propel the argument. Anecdotes of ape behavior continually grab us where our human sympathy lives. Eugene Linden tells us one of them:

> Twenty years ago I met a chimpanzee named Bruno. He was one of a group of chimps being taught American Sign Language to determine if apes could communicate with humans. Last year I went to see him again. The experiment is long past, and Bruno was moved in 1982 to a medical laboratory, *but he is still using the signs. . . .* [35]

Bruno had learned how to talk in the community in which he found himself. Then, the experiment over, his ability to talk was of no further use to the members of that community, so researchers shipped him off to someplace where he could be used as an oversized lab rat to test vaccines or new drugs. But he still wants to talk, to communicate. He is not content with the secure and well-fed life. He is like us humans, and he wants to reach out to humans as they once reached out to him. What right have we to impose isolation on such an animal?

Given Bruno's humanness, should we extend to him, and to his species, the rights of humans? John Blatchford, a British zoologist, suggested as much in 1997.[36] David Pearson, of the Great Ape Project (a systematic international campaign for rights for the great apes, founded in 1993) took up Blatchford's suggestion in January 1998, calling attention to a "paradigm shift over the past 20 years or so in our understanding of the complex emotional and mental lives of the great apes—a complexity that demands we confer the basic rights of life, individual liberty and freedom from torture on all great apes."[37] By 1999, the Great Ape Project joined the New Zealand campaign for full "human rights" to apes: to ensure that New Zealand's Animal Welfare bill contained a "clause making nonhuman great apes the first animals in the world with individual, fundamental rights that will stand up in a court of law: the right to life, the right not to suffer cruel or degrading treatment, and the right not to take part in all but the most benign experiments."[38] The campaign failed, voted down in the New Zealand parliament in May of that year.[39] Parliament did, however, recommend an end to all experiments involving apes except for the benefit of the apes themselves.

The campaign continues, calling for a United Nations Declaration of the Rights of Great Apes. This declaration would include all the above rights as well as the right not to be "imprisoned" without due process. Due process? The language necessarily causes nervousness, not only among the zookeepers but also among those who carry on research designed to protect the welfare of apes. Must they obtain informed consent in the future?

Primatologist Frans de Waal of the Yerkes Regional Primate Research Center in Atlanta argues that according rights to the apes puts us on a "slippery slope" toward the absurd. "[I]f you argue for rights on the basis of continuity between us and the great apes, then you have to argue continuity between apes and monkeys," and so on down to the laboratory rats.[40] Philosopher Peter Singer, author of *Animal Liberation,* is less worried about rats obtaining legal rights and wonders whether the slippery slope can't be tilted the other way: "[I]f you deny chimps certain rights, then logically you have to deny intellectually disabled children too."[41] Do we?

Insight magazine decided that the topic was worth a debate and just prior to the New Zealand vote, asked Steven Wise, author of *Rattling the Cage: Toward Legal Rights for Animals,* to defend the affirmative, and David Wagner, professor of constitutional law at Regent University, to defend the negative, on the question, "Should great apes have some of the legal rights of persons?" Wagner's opposition rests flatly on the assertion that

> Humans are nonarbitrarily different. There is a remarkable consensus of both religion and philosophy on this uniqueness. . . . Judaism was the first to proclaim that god made man in His image and that He revealed Himself to mankind. Later on, Christianity proclaimed a radical redemption for all humankind, rooted in the claim that God Himself had taken on human nature . . . Kant . . . taught that the capacity of human beings to give and demand reasons for their actions was the basis of their rights and duties. And finally, our Founding Fathers declared that the American experiment was based on certain self-evident truths, beginning with the truth that all men are created equal, that they are endowed by their Creator with certain unalienable rights. Notice the constant copackaging

of certain ideas: human uniqueness, capacity for reason-giving and special divine creation.[42]

The claim is reinforced with abundant quotation from Scripture and Shakespeare.

Steven Wise rests his position on the extensive similarities between humans and great apes and on the appropriateness of including rights for apes in the wave of rights-consciousness that has come into being across the world in the last half century. The scope of these rights has expanded inexorably and irreversibly. At one point we (of Western civilization) were willing to confine political rights to a small circle of propertied white men—the "men," by the way, of the quote from Jefferson in Wagner's piece. The natural expansion now includes the whole human race, including those who have no capacity whatsoever for reason-giving. There is no inconsistency, Wise insists, between arguing that the great apes should be accorded certain rights of persons now and claiming that not every life form need be given the same rights. The ultimate limits of equal justice will have to be determined by the legal and political process as the common law and constitutional interpretation evolve. Our inability to know or foresee the ultimate outcome of that process does not force us to tolerate the manifest injustice of denying basic rights to beings for whom we know they are appropriate.[43]

What does it take to make a person? Note that rightful treatment does not presuppose or require "rationality," in any usual sense. Retarded persons, after all, are not "rational," and are not extended all the rights of citizenship, such as the right to vote. But they still have rights, in fact, they are offered even more protections than average citizens because they cannot protect themselves as the able-bodied can.

The jury is still out on the question. We should note that the question of animal rights in this sense—the question of whether the higher mammals, especially the great apes, should be accorded the rights of humans—is rarely debated unemotionally. The people who believe that apes should enjoy the rights of humans tend to get irrational in the presence of people who don't. They come on like John Brown pleading for the African Americans, like Lawrence of Arabia pleading for the Arabs, and very like the "pro-life" faction, the foes of abortion, pleading for the lives of the unborn children. Animal rights proponents honestly believe that they are pleading not for some special interest or loony sentimental indulgence but for the extension in our law of rights to creatures who are fully entitled to them. They will not give up, and there is a strong possibility that this conflict will become violent in the years to come.

ECOTOURISM AND RESPECT

Suppose we decide that apes are, indeed, sufficiently like ourselves to deserve human rights. What follows? Should we treat them the way we treat human beings with limited mental capacities—lock them in homes or institutions, with staff to make sure they dress in the morning, use the bathroom properly, and eat healthful food until they die? God forbid. The central right for any creature with rights is to live according to its own laws with members of its own community, which right the apes surely will never enjoy if we dragoon them into becoming members of human society. (Whether or not they would survive such "care" is another question, one that need not be answered.) That central right alone entails that the apes be left in the wild and left alone, their habitat protected from infringement and their communities respected as we would respect any human community. In short, the implications of full rights for apes are the same as the conclusions of the conservationists. We must work to preserve the forests where the apes live, we must end all poaching of "bush-meat" immediately, and we must structure our encounters with all the apes to reflect the respect owed persons with rights, living according to their own customs and laws.

Meanwhile, such respect will carry out the environmentalist agenda of preservation of an endangered species. For the species is complex. We do not really preserve the species by capturing sufficient numbers of the apes and putting them in safe cages to eat and breed. For the apes, like ourselves, do not exist merely as biological organisms but as social animals under evolved systems of governance. We don't want the only apes left to be those in captivity. We want them to be wild, to continue to evolve, to anchor their ecosystems, and to show us a unique way of living.

An agenda of leaving the apes in the forest, protecting the forest by law, and enforcing that law against poachers, satisfies two criteria for sound public policy: it is environmentally beneficial and it is ethically correct. But for such policies to be truly sustainable, they need to be economically viable too. The best way to set up an industry to sustain the apes is through enabling "ecotourism," entertaining tourists who want to visit the apes in the wild. After all, tourists have been traveling to Africa and Asia to see the animals for several centuries. Ecotourists do not come to shoot, but to enjoy and to learn. When ecotourism is established and running well, the tourist dollars support the local economy. For this reason it is in everyone's interest to make sure that the animals are not harmed or frightened, so that the tourists will enjoy themselves and will come back, bringing more dollars. Local officials will also ensure that the habitat is protected for that reason; as noted earlier, the presence of the apes is becoming the best protection a forest could have.

There is some interest now in promoting international policies (debt relief is foremost among them) to encourage nations in the developing world to protect the remnants of the forest where apes may live. Even those who promote such policies acknowledge that under the present system of global sovereignty, it would be up to every nation to decide for itself whether funds allocated to development should be designated to the protection of the forests.[44] The attitude displayed by governments of developing nations is not encouraging on the matter. But there is some hope.

Local experiments have worked well, on occasion. Richard Ruggiero, a wildlife biologist in the Office of International Affairs of the U.S. Fish and Wildlife Service, recounts a tale of a lowland gorilla in a village in the Congo that contains many of the elements of hope and caution that attend the effort to create ecotourism. Named "Ebobo" (gorilla; pronounced "ay-bobo") by the Bon Coin villagers, this solitary male had adopted the custom of frequenting the village, especially on the trail where the children went to school. His apparent motive was curiosity, nothing more. (He was too young to challenge the older males of the area for the right to a territory and a family.) The villagers immediately called for a gun to shoot him. Since they considered gorillas to be at once very dangerous and very good to eat, shooting him seemed the best course of action. Ruggiero, assigned to that village for the purpose of studying the wildlife in a local pond, spent hours—months—talking to various groups of the villagers, trying to keep Ebobo off the menu and out of the gunsights. (The gorilla had survived his first visit only because no one could find a gun.) In the end, the most persuasive protectors were the shamans, who pointed out that since Ebobo was not acting like normal gorillas (who avoid human habitation as much as they can), he might well be a returned spirit of the dead and should be treated with respect. As the villagers got used to him, however, problems arose of a different sort; they started wandering very close to him, teasing him, while the children threw stones at him to see what he would do. As before and with equally patient urgency, Ruggiero had to persuade the villagers at length that although Ebobo was not dangerous unless provoked, he was an accident waiting to happen if teased, and they should leave him alone. At the writing of the article, the villagers had learned to let Ebobo wander where he would, and he was doing no harm—even making his way through cornfields in a way that did not damage the crop. And the village was becoming someplace special because of the resident gorilla—a place worth going to, which it seems, is the minimum precondition for the success of ecotourism. In the case of Ebobo, it took a bit of education, but it worked.[45]

Zoologist John Blatchford points out that without the help of the local communities, no protection will work, but thinks the enterprise possible. A recent experiment in the Bwindi Impenetrable Forest of Uganda—home to 300 of the 650 mountain gorillas alive in 1995—has already shown how this might work. Local subsistence farmers were given limited access to the forest perimeter and allowed to harvest some sustainable resources. They were also permitted to keep their bees there and use the mineral springs. . . . In the experiment, an estimated $30,000 per year, 10% of the revenue generated by tourists visiting the park, was given to the communities living around the forest. Given that a Ugandan family of six must manage on $526 per year, the extra income to the farming community represented a great sum of money, and gave the community an incentive to protect the revenue-earning gorillas. *These people were, in effect, being paid by the gorillas for their help in maintaining the park.*[46]

Such efforts should be conjoined, Blatchford argued, with efforts to establish protections for apes based on their rights as persons, as discussed in the last section.

Ecotourism will allow apes to stay in their wild habitats and preserve the ecosystem. It will allow, possibly, selective recruitment of individuals from prospering groups for research and possibly (see Concluding Questions, below) for exhibit. The respect engendered by wide experience with apes in their native communities will ensure that to the extent that they are removed from those communities, kept for display, or used in research, they will be treated well. And their fundamental right—the ability to run their own communities according to their own laws—will be honored.

QUESTIONS FOR REFLECTION

Ecotourism notwithstanding, questions will remain. Let us pose a few of them.

1. As far as we can observe, chimpanzees recruited into traveling shows thoroughly enjoy the experience. Apes regularly associating with humans have no objections to them and seem to enjoy the attention and company. They don't even mind being dressed up in tutus. May such practices continue?

2. As discussed earlier, it would be tremendously useful to be able to continue research with chimpanzees. But how can we do this? If we must treat them as humans, they cannot give consent, so we cannot use them. We can treat them as animals, very humanely, no doubt, but they will still be forced to live in cages and suffer blood draws and strange diets and possibly odd surgeries. Is this justifiable?

3. When an infant (now known to the world as Baby Fae) was born with hypoplastic left heart syndrome some years ago, a baboon (Goobers) was killed so that her heart could be transplanted to the infant. The transplant didn't work, and no one

has tried the same thing since—but what if we could make it work? Would it be justifiable to kill an ape to get its heart for a child?

4. Are we under any duty to enhance the lives of the apes? If they find themselves in an environment that is not totally to their liking, what is the extent of our duty to go beyond protection of their community to ensuring that it flourishes?

5. The next time the chimpanzees get genocidal, do we have an obligation (1) to intervene, in order to stop the slaughter, or (2) not to intervene, in order to let chimpanzees live and die by their own laws?

These are all one question, of course: Are the apes essentially human, and how much are we invested in treating them as human? This is a question unlikely to be solved within the lifetime of either of the remaining Leakey's Angels.

NOTES

1. Laura Spinney, "Monkey Business," *New Scientist,* 2 May 1998, p. 18.

2. Cited in ibid.

3. Donald G. McNeil Jr., "The Great Ape Massacre," *New York Times Magazine,* 9 May 1999, pp. 54–57.

4. Cited in Fred Pearce, "Eating Our Relatives," *New Scientist,* 29 April 2000.

5. Spinney, Monkey Business," p. 18.

6. Ibid.

7. Ibid.

8. Ibid.

9. "Bushmeat: Logging's Deadly 2nd Harvest (Wildlife Harvest in Logged Tropical Forests)," *Science* (23 April 1999).

10. Ibid.

11. McNeil, "Great Ape Massacre," p. 56.

12. Eugene Linden and Michael Nichols, "A Curious Kinship: Apes and Humans," *National Geographic* (March 1992): 1–45.

13. Ibid.

14. Jane Goodall Institute Press Release of April 1999.

15. Jane Goodall, "At-Risk Primates," *Washington Post,* 8 April 2000, p. A17.

16. Patricia Reaney, "Growing Demand for Bushmeat Endangers Wild Animals," *news.excite.com,* October 10, 2000.

17. Ibid.

18. Cheryl Knott and Tim Laman, "Orangutans in the Wild," *National Geographic* (August 1998): 30–55.

19. Ibid., p. 36.

20. Joseph B. Verrengia, "Bushmeat Hunters Push Primates to Extinction," Associated Press , 23 July 2000.

21. Linden and Nichols, "Curious Kinship," p. 22.

22. Ibid., pp. 32–33.

23. Boston: Little, Brown, 1995.

24. Biruté M. F. Galdikas, Nancy Briggs, and Jane Goodall, *Orangutan Odyssey* (New York: Abrams, 1999).

25. See her account of her work, *Jane Goodall: 40 Years at Gombe: A Tribute to Four Decades of Wildlife Research, Education, and Conservation* (Ridgefield, CT: Jane Goodall Institute, 1999).

26. "$5m voted to save apes. . . . " *Connecticut Post,* 21 October 2000, p. A8.

27. Ron Moreau, "A Shove toward Extinction," *Newsweek,* 8 December 1997, p. 33.

28. Loc. cit.

29. John Toon, "Gorillas in the Bits: Remote Sensing Technology Boosts Efforts to Protect Endangered Mountain Gorillas and Rebuild Rwanda's Economy," *Research Horizons,* Georgia Institute of Technology, Spring 2000.

30. John Travis, "Human, Mouse, Rat . . . What's Next? Scientists Lobby for a Chimpanzee Genome Project," *Science News* 158 (October 2000): 236–39.

31. Eugene Linden and Michael Nichols, "A Curious Kinship: Apes and Humans," *National Geographic* (March 1992): 10–45, esp. pp. 33ff.

32. A good account of these studies and the controversy they caused, may be found in Gregory E. Pence, *Classic Cases in Medical Ethics,* 3d ed. (Boston: McGraw Hill, 2000), pp. 225ff.

33. Roger Fouts, with Stephen Tukel Mills, *Next of Kin: What Chimpanzees Have Taught Me About Who We Are* (New York: William Morrow, 1997).

34. He pointedly ignores the efforts of other research centers, especially the Yerkes Regional Primate Research Center in Atlanta, to improve the treatment of apes in captivity. See Deborah Blum's review of the book, *New York Times Book Review,* 12 October 1997, pp. 11–12. Interestingly, Fouts's career tracks those of Fossey, Galdikas, and Goodall, from research scientist to activist on behalf of the apes.

35. Eugene Linden and Michael Nichols, "A Curious Kinship: Apes and Humans," *National Geographic* (March 1992): 10, emphasis added.

36. John Blatchford, "Apes and Gorillas Are People Too," *New Scientist,* 9 November 1997, p. 56.

37. David Pearson, "Justice for Apes," *New Scientist,* 3 January 1998, Letters section, p. 46.

38. Rachel Nowak, "Almost Human," *New Scientist,* 13 February 1999, p. 20.

39. News item without byline, *New Scientist,* 29 May 1999.

40. Cited in Rachel Nowak, "Almost Human," p. 20.

41. Ibid.

42. David Wagner, "Should Great Apes Have Some of the Legal Rights of Persons? No: At Stake Is a Valuable Philosophical Consensus on the Uniqueness of Human Beings," *Insight,* 1 November 1999, p. 41.

43. Steven M. Wise, "Should Great Apes Have Some of the Legal Rights of Persons? Yes: Chimpanzees Have Mental Abilities Similar to Young Children and Deserve Some of the Same Legal Rights," *Insight,* 1 November 1999, p. 40.

44. John Blatchford, "Apes and Gorillas," p. 56; Tam Dalyell, "Thistle Diary," *New Scientist,* 24 January 1998.

45. Richard Ruggiero, "Phantom of the Forest," *Wildlife Conservation* (September–October 2000), pp. 51ff.

46. John Blatchford, "Apes and Gorillas," emphasis added.

7

Chlorine Sunrise

The Beneficent Possibilities of a Known Poison

WILLIAM F. CARROLL AND
LISA H. NEWTON

BETTER LIVING THROUGH CHEMISTRY,
OR MAYBE NOT

Early in the now–classic movie "It's a Wonderful Life," George Bailey is offered the "chance of a lifetime" to join his friend Sam Wainwright in the plastics business. "I may have a job for you, that is, unless you're still married to that broken–down building and loan. Ha, ha, ha. It's the biggest thing since radio and I'm lettin' you in on the ground floor." Sam had already made a fortune in plastic hoods for airplanes in World War II and would eventually help bail out that broken–down building and loan. We suspect he made prodigious amounts of money as the plastics industry grew. Of course, George has a higher calling at the building and loan and turns Sam down. The audience in 1946 had no more idea than George that plastics would eventually become a 100 billion-pound-per-year product less than 60 years later. The meteoric growth of plastics, and in fact the growth of industrial chemistry in the twentieth century, paralleled an unimagined growth in standard of living, particularly for those in the developed world.

The age of plastics—and that of the limitless usefulness of industrial chlorine—began right after World War II. Despite outraged opposition (mostly on aesthetic grounds), it has shown few signs of retreat. The plastics we use in all areas of our lives are part of a mighty postwar transformation of American (and global) society. Just as pesticides had introduced a new era of agriculture, and antibiotics (many of them based on chlorine chemistry) a new era of medicine, chlorinated compounds like polychlorinated biphenyls (PCBs), widely used as dielectrics (insulators in electrical devices) and chlorinated plastics like polyvinyl chloride (PVC) transformed our lives and the American landscape. That light, bright, inexpensive, practically indestructible material—America (as well as the rest of the world) loves plastics.

Into this love affair crept some bad news: the chlorinated compounds of which many of these miracle products were made could be very dangerous to our health. In 1992, and again in 1994 and 1996, the International Joint Commission (IJC), the body that regulates the waterways that border the United States and Canada, published in its biennial report to its sponsoring governments a survey of persistent toxic substances in the Great Lakes, noting that most of them contained chlorine in some form. It recommended a "chlorine sunset," a gradual phasing out of all chlorinated compounds. Specifically, the governments of Canada and the United States should

> consult with industry and other interests to develop timetables to sunset the use of chlorine and chlorine-containing compounds as industrial feedstocks and examine the means of reducing and eliminating other uses, recognizing that socio-economic considerations must be taken into account in developing the strategies and timetables.[1]

This approach was not without precedent. The example that the IJC followed was the phasing out of lead from the manufacturing feedstocks of paint and gasoline that had occurred some years earlier. When the evidence became overwhelming that environmental lead was causing nerve damage, especially in children, the decision was made by the Environmental Protection Agency to remove lead from these manufacturing processes. With the implementation of this measure, the amount of ambient lead in the atmosphere, in our food, and in our water rapidly decreased to negligible levels.

Although the chlorine phase-out recommendations may have come as a surprise to industry, the recognition of environmental problems was not new. Evidence of the problematic nature of "organochlorines," products formed when chlorine reacts with organic compounds, had begun to enter the public consciousness in 1962, when Rachel Carson's *Silent Spring*[2] showed the potential for harm of DDT (dichloro-diphenyl-trichloro-ethane), a highly effective broad-spectrum pesticide. Apparently harmless to higher forms of life, it had been accumulating in the fat of the fish and small birds that lived on the insects it had struck and had been slowly, subtly, disrupting their reproductive systems. Organochlorines, it turns out, mimic estrogen in the bodies of some fish and birds, displacing the natural hormones and confusing the entire endocrine system. Insoluble in water, they cannot be metabolized and excreted by the body. Any predator that ate the fish gathered and condensed the stored organochlorines into their own fat, in a process known as *bioconcentration*. As the predator continues to eat the contaminated fish, the burden of organochlorines grows, in a process known as *bioaccumulation*. Eventually the organochlorines reach a concentration that interferes with the normal hormonal processes of the body, and reproduction begins to fail. Raptors—eagles and hawks—that had eaten the fish stopped laying viable eggs. As Carson noted in her book, many of the most beautiful raptors, most notably the peregrine falcon, were in danger of extinction.

In many ways, *Silent Spring* headlined the urgent issue of chlorine chemistry. It wasn't just that most pesticides are organochlorines. It was that a substance that had become part of our lives was suddenly seen to carry risks that no one had suspected, opening the possibility that many other substances carried unsuspected risks. Consider the American idols (of the 1950s variety) that fell from grace when *Silent Spring* appeared.

1. Science: Scientists had proclaimed the safety of DDT, and in the short term, indeed, it did appear to be safe—children munched picnics in the midst of clouds of the stuff, just to prove that. You could eat it, they said. Yet the scientists had turned out to be wrong after all, and the risk had come from an angle (problems with the eggs of hawks, of all things) that few had suspected.

2. Government: Government regulators were supposed to protect us from such risks, and government had failed. Indeed, government had been among the biggest promoters of the pesticides, especially among the farmers.

3. American business: Industry, in the form of the chemicals manufacturers, had joined science and government in proclaiming the safety of the pesticides. It had developed a sense of invulnerability—after all, hadn't the inventors of DDT won the Nobel Prize? Business profited; chemicals were a growth industry. That success and the need to defend and maintain it generated arrogance. In the aftermath of *Silent Spring*'s publication, industry representatives not only demonstrated appalling taste but, arguably, a complete disregard for public safety: uttering not a word of remorse or even concern for the fate of the raptors, they inflicted a barrage of unjustified (not to mention undignified) attacks on Rachel Carson's science (which was unimpeachable), character, emotional stability, and gender. Instead of attacking the problem, they attacked the messenger. It wasn't pretty.

Who was covering up? When Carson's voluminous sources are examined, we see that suspicions about the pesticides had been raised in professional journals for years; all Carson did was connect the dots. Lobbyists, primarily from the chemicals industry, had deflected the many suggestions made for firmer government regulation. Carson's attack, in short, did not come as a bolt from the blue. Why, then, had a whole line of inquiry been stifled for so many years? Conspiracy theories and suspicions of cover-ups do little to improve the political atmosphere, and the seeds of paranoia had already been sown when *Silent Spring* came out. They are now well grown and available for inclusion in all present and future controversies.

Whom do we trust now? Carson's book precipitated the first of many crises of faith in our triple guardians—beneficent industry, rational science, and vigilant government. (Ralph Nader's *Unsafe at Any Speed* caused a similar crisis, and the "mad cow" scare in Europe of recent years falls into the same category.) By the time the International Joint Commission reports came along, a skeptical world was willing to listen.

THE CLASSIC ENVIRONMENTAL DEBATE

The chlorine issue, complex in its technologic, economic, and political aspects, displays (in part because of these very complexities, as we shall see) a refreshing logical simplicity. The indictment of chlorine, based on the hazard it poses to health and the environment, is reducible to the following proposition for debate: "Resolved: That chlorine should be banned as an industrial feedstock for all purposes worldwide." There happens to be a large and articulate industry at the receiving end of that resolution, so there is a strong defense of chlorine chemistry mounted in the literature. For clarity and convenience, let us present the controversy in debate format, as outlined below:

A. The *Pro exposition* for the resolution is based on the argument that chlorine chemistry is hazardous to your health and that chlorine should be phased out, "sunsetted." Since Joe Thornton has made that argument in comprehensive form in his highly influential book *Pandora's Poison,*[3] the pro exposition section will simply trace his position. (Elaborations on Thornton's position will be noted; otherwise, the argument is all Thornton's and in his "voice.")

B. The *Con exposition* (essentially in the voice of the Chlorine Chemistry Council, unless otherwise noted), against the resolution, is based on the argument that chlorine chemistry contributes significantly to our lives in ways that cannot be duplicated in its absence.

C. The *Con rebuttal* then argues that the Pro exposition is misleading and inadequate and does not stand up to reasonable scrutiny.

D. The *Pro rebuttal* follows, in which the conclusions of the Pro exposition are defended against the arguments of the opposition (sections B and C).

At the end of the "debate," we will pause to sum up, and then present, in the Construction of a Sustainable Industry section, the case that might be made for a chlorine industry that avoids most of the criticisms leveled at it—the case, in other words, for a sustainable "chlorine sunrise."

Resolved: It's Time for a Chlorine Sunset

The first comprehensive indictment of the organochlorines (and of the chlorine industry as a whole) appeared in 2000, in Joe Thornton's densely documented and carefully reasoned work, *Pandora's Poison: Chlorine, Health, and a New Environmental Strategy* (MIT Press, 2000). Thornton's argument is unsparing, clear, and short, summed up in the first 20 pages of the 600-page book (past which, it would seem, several reviewers did not read). He begins with a litany of fears and catastrophes, starting with worries about his unborn child and the toxic burden present now in all human and animal tissue—toxic chemicals present in his semen and his wife's milk, PCBs in polar bear fat, dioxin in fish. Remember the sickness and abandoned houses of Love Canal, and the evacuation of Times Beach? Remember the hole in the ozone layer, threatening us with skin cancer? Remember DDT and the dying eagles of *Silent Spring?* Remember Agent Orange in Vietnam? The list is very long—but every villain on the list is an organic compound with the same middle name, Chlorine.

> Not all pollution is due to organochlorines; some metals and nonchlori-
> nated synthetic organic chemicals . . . also pose public health threats. But
> organochlorines dominate virtually all official and unofficial lists of haz-
> ardous pollutants in the environment, wildlife, and human tissues.[4]

Chlorine is born of brine, that is, salt water. Salt is not a problem; sodium chloride, ordinary table salt, is very stable, and circulates through our bodies (performing many useful tasks along the way) without combining with anything. But electrolysis of brine separates it into sodium hydroxide (caustic soda, with its own multiple uses) and chlorine gas, the heavy greenish gas once used as a battlefield weapon.

Chlorine is deadly because it reacts readily with much of the organic matter it encounters, invading the cell membranes of microbes in water purification systems and effectively destroying them, eradicating molds on buildings being prepared for painting, and combining in predictable ways with certain organic compounds to make the organochlorines for pesticides, solvents, plastics, and bleaches. In the process of making useful substances, of course, it makes many other substances, less predictable and possibly harmful.

Chlorination also affects the stability of organic compounds, making some of them so stable that they live for centuries (the chlorofluorocarbons that depleted the stratospheric ozone layer, for instance), making others so reactive that even in trace amounts, they can attack cells in the body and cause cancer.

A third effect of chlorination is to make organic compounds more soluble in oil, again adding to their industrial usefulness as solvents, but ensuring that when they enter the system of any animal, they will seek out and stay in the animal's fat—indefinitely. The toxicity of the organochlorines comes from their similarity to organic molecules generally, meaning the body will not expel them, and from their one difference, their chlorine molecules, ensuring that wherever they go in the body they will disrupt natural processes. That is why they are good pesticides and good antibiotics. But anything that will kill unwanted life forms may very likely injure wanted ones.

Organochlorines therefore figure prominently among the materials designated persistent bioaccumulative toxics, or PBTs. (A practical synonym for

PBTs is POPs—persistent organic pollutants. See later discussion.) The problems caused by chlorine compounds are multiplied by the enormous size of the industry. The world produces 40 million tons of chlorine annually, funnels it into organochlorines, and puts them into the environment—some of them directly, like pesticides, others only later, when they end up in landfills or, worse yet, incinerators. One way or another, they are now present in every environment on the planet, from the depths of the oceans to the stratosphere, from the recesses of the equatorial rainforests to the polar ice cap, where the polar bears (the top of a long food chain) have enormous bioaccumulations of organochlorines in their thick layer of insulating fat.

Organochlorines are all potentially harmful; virtually all those that have been tested with any thoroughness (except for pharmaceuticals) have turned out to be very harmful in fact, some of them in concentrations as low as parts per trillion.[5] Some of the dangers have been known, or strongly suspected, since the 1950s, but advances in environmental testing since then have shown the enormous extent of the contamination, and advances in physiology allow us to characterize precisely the damage that the 1950s could only guess at.

> . . . molecular biology has made possible the study of mechanisms of toxicity, revealing that organochlorines disrupt biological processes at the most fundamental levels. Some are potent mutagens, undermining the integrity of the genetic messages in our DNA, while others block communication between cells or interfere with the control of gene expression, turning genes on and off at inappropriate times and altering the natural course of development and physiology. A large number of organochlorines have been found to mimic or otherwise interfere with the body's natural hormones, the potent chemical signals by which multicellular organisms regulate their development and coordinate the unified function of their parts.[6]

These physiological effects—carcinogenesis, endocrine disruption, immunosuppression—occurring essentially at random wherever organisms are exposed to organochlorines, are now universal, since the entire globe has been laced with these compounds. We have no way to get rid of them, internally or externally. Already we are seeing the effects of this global pollution in the environment, in the decimation of whales and birds, especially water birds, whose immune systems may have been compromised by the pollution, and in human health, in unexplained cancers, immune suppression, infertility and other reproductive and developmental problems like birth defects and learning disorders. The earth has no assimilative capability for PBTs.

So how can we deal with these dangers? Not the way we deal with other potential public-health risks. Our laws, regulations, public-health systems, were set up on a paradigm (a structured approach to world facts, and theories) that doesn't apply well here. The paradigm we use now, which Thornton calls the "risk paradigm," assumes,

- first, that if something goes wrong (sickness or environmental damage), we'll know it (i.e., that there are clear ways of knowing if damage has been done);

- second, that the body and the natural environment can absorb small amounts of bad stuff (stuff that would cause problems in large amounts) without any risk at all (these small amounts are called "acceptable," and if a factory discharges no more than that, it is not doing any harm);

- third, that risks to the body and the environment are time limited (that is, if nothing's gone wrong in a certain amount of time, then the risk is past and nothing will happen later); and

- fourth, that in any case, there is a certain amount of risk we are willing to bear in return for the benefits of whatever's causing the risk

On these assumptions, the risk paradigm tells us to allow organochlorines to be manufactured and sold, subject only to restrictions on the rate at which they may be deposited into the environment. (The "risk paradigm," as Thornton describes it, seems to be an application of the "liberty paradigm": Citizens have the right to make and sell what they like unless the public authority can prove that they are doing harm to their neighbors and to the public interest. If it can prove that, the public authority may restrict the activity, but the restriction must be kept to the absolute minimum necessary to prevent the harm.)

But none of these assumptions work with organochlorines, so the risk paradigm cannot apply. First, of course we'll know, at least eventually, if we get cancer, but cancer is overdetermined: it can come from too many causes, only some of which are environmental, and the base rate of occurrence is one in three. We'll never know (absent some clear correlation of particular cause and particular effect, like that between smoking tobacco and lung cancer) if a particular case, or even a particular cluster, of cancer was caused by any environmental factor, let alone organochlorines. And there does not seem to be any way at all (absent some particular disease, like HIV-AIDS) to determine if an immune system has been compromised; immunosuppression is always a hypothesis after the fact of unexplained sickness and death.

Second and third, if the bad stuff accumulates in the body or the environment—if it is persistent—then even really small amounts will add up to really large amounts eventually, and be harmful, and there will never be a time when the risk is past: it just gets worse. "Acceptable levels" of discharge ultimately reach unacceptable levels.[7] Nor can we "test" the chemicals that are actually ending up in our system. Even if every individual chemical that was ever deposited in the lake, in greater or smaller amounts, were tested and found safe, at least in small amounts, there is no way to test the combination of all of them, which might come from pesticide residues in the streams that feed the lake, fertilizers draining from the lakeside lawns, dioxins deposited in the lake from families burning plastic trash in their back yards, atmospheric deposition of the remnants of a chemical spill on the highway miles away, and leachate from the town's landfill. Although the paradigm can handle individual risks, it cannot handle a global risk, a global accumulation of vast numbers of "acceptable" discharges that never go away, especially when many of them are not suspected.[8]

Finally, it is not the case that we can make an intelligent decision about "voluntarily accepting" a risk when the materialization of that risk is both terrible and mysterious, essentially unknown. Thus a new paradigm is required.

The suggested alternative paradigm is the "ecological paradigm," one that puts the integrity of the body or ecosystem first, in an effort to protect the health of these complex systems over the long term from subtle threats, as well as over the short term from patent ones. The first element of the ecological paradigm is the "Precautionary Principle," which is simply common sense: if we don't understand fully how a complex system works, and we are trying to preserve it, for heaven's sake don't let stuff that might be dangerous get into it. It counsels a ban on any substance that poses a potential risk to the system, even in the absence of scientific proof of harm. This standard is no different from what we use for pharmaceuticals: until you can show that the new drug is effective and safe, a process requiring years of clinical trials, you can't sell it. In general, as individuals we already use the ecological paradigm when dealing with our health (for example, there is probably a level of heroin use that will not do your son or daughter any harm, but you might hesitate before giving your blessing to this "acceptable level" of heroin).

Alone, the Precautionary Principle has little practical heft; it counsels an attitude (caution) but doesn't say what to be cautious about. For guidance in the regulation of organochlorines, some more specific principles are required. Three of these are "zero discharge," "clean production," and "reverse onus." The first two, zero discharge and clean production, are two sides of the same reform, amounting essentially to the redesigning of manufacturing facilities. First, try to eliminate materials known to be harmful from the manufacturing process entirely; second, make sure that every ounce of potentially harmful material that is needed in the manufacturing process is recycled in the factory or locked into the product—there shall be no waste to spread abroad. These principles apply to manufacturing, whether of organochlorines themselves (pesticides) or of products that incorporate them or use them in the process of manufacture, and all they require is that the loops be closed, which makes good economic sense as well as good environmental sense.

Reverse onus is a relatively new principle for evaluating chemicals, mandating transparent evaluation of chemicals (by, it is assumed, the present regulatory regime). It is no longer assumed that a chemical is "innocent until proven guilty," that is, safe until shown to be harmful (a standard that does well for humans in our courts but is misapplied when it comes to pesticides) but rather that chemicals, now on the market or new, are harmful as a class if they are of the type that has been shown to be so in the past, such as organochlorines, and they must be shown to be safe. Companies must pay for these evaluations but, because they have a financial interest in the result, cannot be part of the process.

Most important, we must change the way decisions are made. The decision to make materials or phase them out must rest with those who are impacted by the decision: ordinary citizens. We must be skeptical of both industry and government scientists and technocrats who have a vested interest in making or taxing a product. In fact, we must migrate from a technocracy making allegedly knowledgeable and beneficent decisions on behalf of a governed public to a public acting as government, making decisions that control the effects of a technocracy on their lives and those of their descendants. Government should empanel public-interest scientists and nonscientific members of the general public to pass judgment on materials and the plants that make them.

Together, these principles focus new attention on the chemicals industry—directed to the processes of manufacture rather than on the end-of-pipe solutions used to keep discharges down to "acceptable" (but not demonstrably safe) levels, and setting a new, higher (maybe impossibly high?) standard for regulatory approval. The evaluation of the "safety" of products, as for the nuclear industry, must take into account the methods available for disposing of the products when they are no longer useful. Is there a safe way of disposing of all the organochlorines? If not, the Precautionary Principle would require us to forgo organochlorines, since the hazard can never effectively be mitigated. In practice, the answer is, in fact, no.

In conclusion, then, since many chlorine products are inherently dangerous throughout their lifecycle and since there are no truly safe (self-contained) ways of using chlorine chemistry in manufacturing, the ecological paradigm would require the gradual phasing out of the manufacture and sale of organochlorines in all their uses and applications (and of chlorine chemistry in general) and necessitate the discovery of and phasing in of new nonchlorine alternatives. Not all environmental (or health) problems would be solved by this "chlorine sunset," and in certain areas chlorine would have to continue to be used (water purification ranks first among these), but a major danger to our health and future would be removed if we could reduce the industrial use of chlorine to the extent possible.

Events since the publication of *Pandora's Poison* in 2000 bolster Thornton's argument. In December of that year, the initiative to ban organochlorines became the subject of an unusual meeting of delegates from 122 countries in Johannesburg, South Africa. Held to discuss persistent organic pollutants (POPs, as mentioned earlier), the meeting was chaired by John Buccini, a Canadian government representative to the United Nations Environmental Program (UNEP). The consensus of the meeting was that our environment had suffered enough at the hands of the manufacturers of these harmful substances and that at least the 12 most lethal of them should be banished from the earth. For the record, the 12 worst offenders included eight pesticides (DDT, aldrin, chlordane, dieldrin, endrin, heptachlor, mirex, and toxaphene), two industrial chemicals (PCBs, used for insulation, and hexachlorobenzene, a pesticide), and two unintended byproducts of industrial processes, dioxins and furans. All contain chlorine. (Dioxins and furans do occur "naturally," that is, in the absence of industrial use of chlorine. They are released when any trash, wood, or other organic matter is burned at low temperatures or under other conditions of incomplete combustion. However, they are anthropogenic as well, produced under certain manufacturing conditions and in thermal processes involving organochlorines.)

The treaty that arose from the Johannesburg meeting on POPs called for the immediate end to the use or production of several of them, whereas others were granted a stay of execution for one reason or another: for example PCBs are difficult to remove safely from electrical equipment, and destruction technologies are not universally available (however, they must be eliminated by 2025), and DDT remains in use because no equivalent exists for controlling malarial mosquitoes. In the end, the treaty will contain dozens of nation-specific exemptions, mostly to allow longer phase-out periods. As of this writing, 80 countries have ratified the treaty, and it is now in force. The world's environmental opinion, represented by UNEP, now stands adamantly opposed to the industrial use of chlorine chemistry.

Con Exposition: The Chlorine Industry Is Innocent and Valuable, and We Cannot Do without Its Products

The best people to describe and defend practices under attack are the practitioners themselves. The users of chlorine chemistry have a trade association, the Chlorine Chemistry Council (C3), that works to advance the technology and the fortunes of the chlorine manufacturers and users generally; accordingly, the materials for this section are generally taken from their website.[9]

Chlorine chemistry began in the late nineteenth and early twentieth century. Bleaching powder became available in the second half of the nineteenth century, but chlorine gas, elemental chlorine, only became available in this country after 1893, when the first chloralkali facility came on line in Rumford, Maine. The central process for the production of chlorine, electrolysis of brine, requires large amounts of electricity, so the first plants were set up near sources of power. In 1906, Hooker Chemical established a very large plant near Niagara Falls, not far from a canal site built by William Love and later abandoned, which would later serve as a disposal area for waste chemicals. The electric current divided the brine into sodium hydroxide or caustic soda, for which there were many uses and a large demand, and chlorine gas, whose markets developed slowly. Chlorine's early commercial history is somewhat checkered. The first city to purify its water with chlorine, setting the United States on a path to eliminate most water-borne disease, was Jersey City, New Jersey, in 1908. But one of the first major uses of elemental chlorine was as poison gas (in several forms—pure chlorine, mustard gas, phosgene) in World War I.

When the defeat of Germany in that war released German patents for general use, chlorine chemistry acquired some peacetime uses (even as international treaties made unacceptable the use of chlorine as poison gas). In the mid-1920s, organochlorines for cleaning and degreasing appeared; in 1929, Monsanto introduced PCBs for several functions, primarily as insulators; and in the 1930s DuPont brought CFCs on the market as refrigerants. Polyvinyl chloride plastics and DDT as an all-purpose insecticide, especially in the tropics, came into their own during World War II. The 1940s and 1950s were a golden age of expansion for the industry, as chlorine-based pesticides became standard for agricultural use and organochlorines were adopted nationwide as products and intermediaries. Over the next decades, expansion continued, especially in the manufacture of PVC, which was used to make a huge variety of products, from underground pipes to plastic toys, which replaced traditional materials such as wood, metals, and cement.

First on every list of irreplaceable contributions of chlorine chemistry has to be the disinfection of drinking water. Diarrheal disease, caused almost entirely by pathogens in the drinking water, claims the lives of 2.5 million people a year, most of them children. Cholera, hepatitis, and typhoid used to be the worst killers in the crowded cities of the world, and they still are, where safe drinking water is not available; 10 percent of the diseases of the developing countries are traceable to bad water. Few substances will kill all pathogens; chlorine molecules, with their ability to bind with the outer surfaces of bacteria and viruses, breaking down the cell membranes and killing the germs outright, is one of the few options for water purification. In general, this application is perfectly safe; chlorine all by itself is not a persistent or bioaccumulative material. When dissolved in water it yields materials (hydrochloric and hypochlorous acid) that are also found in nature. And chlorine, unlike ozone or other candidates for water purification, lingers in the water all the way to the tap, knocking off other pathogens as they enter the water supply in between the treatment plant and the final consumer. At the end of the process, the chlorine can be removed by simple aeration. The chlorination of drinking water has been called the most significant contribution to public health in the twentieth century. At this time, about 1.1 billion people still lack access to safe drinking water; chlorine and chlorinated disinfectants like common bleach can render the water safe, a life-saving solution limited only by funding and infrastructure for delivery.[10]

Next on the list of essential functions of the industry would be the contributions to health care and medicine. Eighty-five percent of all pharmaceuticals, including many antibiotics, contain chlorine as an essential ingredient or use chlorine chemistry in the synthesis of the molecule even if chlorine doesn't appear in the final product. Pharmaceuticals whose manufacture depends on chlorine include drugs for heart disease, cancer, AIDS, and malaria; for those concerned with terrorism, they also include the drugs used to treat anthrax.

Perhaps a greater contribution is the inexpensive (hence disposable) plastic material used in every aspect of the delivery of medicine in a hospital—the miles of vinyl tubing, bags for blood and medications, X-ray films, and countless other fabricated devices. The major worry of any hospital is sterility—the ability to keep its equipment and materials, especially those that come into direct contact with patients, free of pathogens. High-temperature sterilization of glass bottles and syringes, which the plastic replaced, was expensive and often failed. Plastic supplies, arriving sterile from the factory and discarded immediately after use, are the patients' best guarantee that they will not leave the hospital with more diseases than they came in with.

A third major contribution to public health is the development of pesticides to control the insect vectors of disease, most notably the anopheles mosquito that carries malaria. Used indiscriminately for protection of crops, DDT engendered insect resistance and accumulated in the bodies of the predators, such as the peregrine falcon. Not surprisingly, DDT has a bad name. If used only inside houses, to kill the mosquitoes where they hide during the day, it provides highly effective protection against malaria. Nations where malaria is a serious threat have not seen fit to ban the insecticide. For one last set of examples of the omnipresence and necessity of chlorine chemistry, we could find none better than PVC, or vinyl, a compound of many uses. Outside of medical devices, the uses that have made the greatest difference in our lives are found in the construction industry. This century holds out the possibility of eliminating substandard housing and providing affordable and decent housing for everyone, largely because of PVC piping and vinyl siding and windows. For all underground water delivery and sewerage removal PVC piping is light and easy to handle, tough enough not to crack under a load and with enough flexibility to maintain its integrity when earthmoving equipment is used in the area around it. It is chemically inert in that environment and reacts with none of the liquids it is used to transport; it will not rust, corrode, or develop pits to harbor pathogens; and it lasts, underground, for 100 years or more. Vinyl siding and windows have replaced the aluminum replacement siding and windows that were so popular twenty years ago; they are safer, more attractive, less expensive, and more energy efficient.

Plastics, most of which are made using chlorine chemistry in one way or another, are also used in a thousand applications throughout the house, from the shower curtains to the mixing bowls, products of that enormous and profitable industry envisioned by Sam Wainwright in *It's a Wonderful Life.*

To finish the list, we may note that chlorine chemistry follows us into outer space, as part of the alloys that make advanced aircraft and rockets possible, included in Kevlar and other fibers used in space suits, essential to making bullet-resistant glass for the armed forces. Chlorine chemistry is also crucially involved in innovative processes, producing ultra-pure silicon for solar cells (photovoltaics) and silicon chips, super-strength polyaramide fibers, the material of bullet-proof vests, and titanium metal and aluminum for aircraft fuselages, jet engines, and spacecraft.

The source of all these products is an enormous industry, employing tens of thousands of people at more than 500 companies at 650 plant sites. In Western Europe alone, chlorine chemistry provides jobs for approximately 40,000 people. In the United States, the production of chlorine and caustic soda is estimated to have generated sales revenue of $16 billion. Those figures do not include revenue and employment in all the industries that use chlorine chemistry as part of some other production—chlorine is used in over half of all industrial chemical processes; 85 percent of pharmaceuticals, as noted earlier; and 96 percent of crop protection chemicals. The largest end use for chlorine chemistry, 34 percent, is the versatile vinyl; organochlorines form the next largest group, about 20 percent. (Purifying water accounts for only 6 percent of production.)

In principle, "substitutes" could be found for all the uses of chlorine or we could simply do without. Practically, however, matching the cost and effectiveness of the literally thousands of products made as a result of chlorine chemistry constitutes a mind-boggling task. For the environmentally minded, it should be noted that most of the "natural materials" substitutes it might occur to us to use are in short supply and that their acquisition would do considerably more environmental damage than whatever damages might be attributed to chlorine chemistry.

Consider three examples. First, cast iron used for pipe requires extraction and smelting of iron ore, an energy-intensive process that also is associated with generation of dioxin. Cast-iron pipe will corrode over time and leak. Second, substitutes for vinyl siding include high-maintenance wood (at great cost to our forests, even if theoretically "renewable,"), stucco or fiber-cement board (some dioxin is generated in the energy-intensive high-temperature manufacture of cement), or aluminum (which is refined using both chlorine and caustic soda, products of chlorine chemistry). Third, organic (naturally occurring) pesticides exist—but insects develop resistance to those, too, and wide use of organic pesticides might render them useless for the small but important organic-gardening and farming sector. And no one has suggested a workable substitute for the chlorine in our water supply, not one that will protect the water all the way to the tap. Chlorine has made our water safe, our hospitals safe, our transportation lighter and more fuel-efficient, and it has filled our households with conveniences. Much of our technological future hangs on this industry.

Having heard the industry's arguments, who on earth would want to attack the products of this whole industry, citing some speculative and future "dangers" that would require the industry to go out of business (peacefully and beautifully, as a "sunset"), flatly in the face of chlorine's obvious and immediate contributions to safety? Joe Thornton would, so to Joe Thornton the argument now turns.

Con Rebuttal: Thornton's Criticisms are Systematically Wrong

The industry's defense against Thornton's attack is two-pronged. The first prong is a studied point-by-point rebuttal, found on a branch of the C3 website[11] called "pandoraspoison.com/industry_views." That's plain enough. (The running head for the several installments at this website is "The Truth About Chlorine: A Response to *Pandora's Poison*.") The industry's opinion of the book is quite clear:

> By recycling thoroughly debated theories and largely disproved allegations, the book's author, a longtime Greenpeace campaigner, ignores reality and merely repackages ideas and positions that have been proselytized by Greenpeace and other like-minded organizations for more than 20 years. . . . These arguments have the marked appearance of desperate, eleventh-hour attempts to "change the rules" because the facts simply don't fit the extreme hypotheses put forward by the author and his confederates.

The second prong of the reply takes the form of a rather handsomely illustrated treatise on the efforts that the chlorine industry is making worldwide, under the heading of the chemical industry's commitment to Responsible Care, to reduce the industry's "footprint," the cumulative impact that its operations have on the natural environment, and to retool its operations to lower emissions of all kinds from their plants. We will present the prongs one at a time.

The "response" portion is a simple attack on *Pandora's Poison* and, as noted earlier, recognizes few bars on holds. The author is accused of pretending to be what he is not (an ethicist, as opposed to a Greenpeace polemicist), of parading long-refuted claims as new, of reckless disregard for the truth and for the characters of the scientists he defames, and of endangering the public by spreading panic that might trigger actions not in the interests of humanity. (Persuaded by environmentalists like Thornton, Peru ceased chlorination of its water for a while and got a four-year cholera epidemic as a consequence.)

In the substance of the rebuttal, the industry points out that it is misleading and wrong to characterize all organic products of chlorine chemistry as POPs or inextricably connected with POPs. Thornton's theoretical argument to that effect is appealing, but environmental data demonstrate otherwise. Despite the growth of the chloralkali industry, environmental releases of virtually all the so-called Stockholm POPs have been declining for years. Intentionally manufactured Stockholm POPs have already been phased out in many developed countries. Emissions of byproducts of production and combustion—dioxins and furans—have been declining for years—well over a 90 percent reduction since 1970. Similar reductions are seen in food samples and human tissue samples over the same period. And this has been occurring in times when the chlorine and daughter products industry—particularly the main product, PVC—has been growing.

Thornton argues that chlorination makes materials more persistent, toxic, and bioaccumulative. With respect to persistence, this ignores chlorine's ability to create reactive intermediates—chemicals on the path between raw materials and final consumer products. In fact, these materials are the exact opposite of persistent—they are, by definition, reactive.

His arguments about increased chlorination leading to increased toxicity is at best only partially true, since the least toxic dioxin of all has more chlorines than the most toxic. It is true that in some cases increased chlorination generates increased oil-solubility and bioaccumulation. On the other hand, this is not the source of the utility of chlorine chemistry for pharmaceuticals or antibiotics. Chemists know that judicious addition of various chemical entities, including chlorine, to a base molecule can affect its pharmaceutical properties, either up or down.

The U.S. EPA created a tool called the "PBT Profiler." This tool, using the kind of chemical classification that Thornton would embrace, identifies only about 25 chlorine-containing materials in commerce that might have PBT or POP characteristics. The Stockholm POPs are included in that list and have already been phased out in the United States. The POPs issue is of minimal significance.

On Thornton's reasoning, we should see a long-term deterioration of the nation's health since the introduction of chlorine products early in the twentieth century. But where's the deterioration? Instead, we see an advance in life expectancy, with strong indications of vigorous health until older ages. More and more people are living to 100 years of age; by now we have about 70,000 of them, and we may expect their numbers to increase. At least we should expect, on Thornton's fearful predictions, that fertility problems should be rampant—with all those endocrine disruptors in the water, who can have babies any more? Yet fertility problems are apparently declining, just as infant mortality and birth defects have in the general improvement of the health of the public. Deaths from infectious diseases, of course, are well down, largely due to improvements in medical care and vector elimination for which chlorine products are in part responsible. Most gratifying, death rates from childhood cancer are down 40 percent. So if Thornton's looking to chlorine compounds to explain all our sickness and death, he's out of luck; there's nothing there to explain.

Further, the "chlorine sunset," that is, the measures he suggests to solve the terrible problem that we just showed is nonexistent, is nothing but a ban on all chlorine chemistry, deceptively presented. For starters, his suggestions for substitutions are largely unworkable—"going back to" wood siding for houses the way we made it in the "good old days" of the early twentieth century is not a bad idea if you don't mind losing the rest of the redwood forests, but "going back to" the glass bottles and repeatedly sterilized rubber tubing for hospitals is an invitation to disaster. Given the thorough penetration of chlorine chemistry through all aspects of our economy, and the wide acceptance of its products, just how does Thornton intend to implement his "sunset"? First, he will have to "educate" the public, who at this time have no idea how widely chlorine chemistry is involved in their lives, let alone that it is dangerous. Another word for *educate,* in this context, is *frighten:* he has to get the public scared enough of chlorine chemistry, sufficiently aware of its "dangers," that they are willing to give up very large numbers of conveniences and protections in a gradual phase-out. But once they are that "aware," why will they tolerate the 5-, 10-, 15-year phase-out? If it's dangerous, get rid of it now! That sentiment, expressed by an aroused public, would be very difficult to damp down with promises of a "sunset."

But then, the effects of a real ban would be so extreme that the same public might reject it altogether, which is, when you think about it, a rational response. Never mind the theoretical advantages of the "ecological paradigm" over the "risk paradigm," if there are any. What the people would be expected to absorb is a change from a civilization relatively free, in the developed nations, of lethal infectious disease, with well-stocked hospitals and more food than we can (or should) eat, to a civilization where the inexpensive conveniences are suddenly costly, where pharmaceuticals and hospital equipment are in short supply and people can't trust their water—all in the name of unseen, unfelt, possible "risks" that someone decided were too much for us to bear. People simply won't take it, and there goes one fine experiment in social engineering down the drain. In short, the last thing Thornton should want is success; the consequences of succeeding in his mission are at the start too awful to contemplate, and at the end, a thoroughgoing rejection of Thornton and all he and his confederates stand for.

Much of the ecological paradigm, especially as it relates to precaution, is already embedded in our regulatory system and in good industrial practices. After all, the United States is a signatory to the Rio Declaration, which includes the most common voicing of the Precautionary Principle: Lack of complete certainty should not trump cost-effective action to prevent harm. In fact, most chemicals invented never reach the marketplace. Pharmaceutical companies make thousands of candidate compounds and reject more than 99 percent of them for even Stage 1 testing, mostly because of toxicity. Of the more than 30 million chemicals given an identification number by the Chemical Abstracts Service, about 80,000 are allowed in commerce because they were registered as potentially having commercial value; about 15,000 are manufactured—not emitted to the environment, mind you, manufactured—to the extent of a ton's worth each year. Moreover, pharmaceuticals and pesticides must, by law, undergo rigorous testing, and chemical companies are required to notify the government in advance of manufacturing and placing new chemicals into commerce.

Finally, there is a practical problem with the "who decides" part of the environmental paradigm. Thornton is quite right that citizens are stakeholders in decisions that impact their lives and environment. But to argue, first, that people who actually understand a technology have no place in the decision-making process if they are from industry; second, that "public interest" scientists—presumably Joe Thornton himself—are neutral and wise; and, third, that those with no technical background should be making the decisions is incredible. It is the functional equivalent of having ordinary citizens design and operate the space shuttle because they have no vested interest in human flight. Would you fly on a mission so operated?

The other prong of the chlorine defense is an articulate commitment to "sustainability" as part of an effort to satisfy the "triple bottom line" of enlightened industry: protection of the environment, social responsibility, and profitability. The publisher of the industry statement on sustainability, the World Chlorine Council, was formed to respond to the concerns about chlorine chemistry raised at the Earth Summit in Rio, in 1992. It moves from a brief recapitulation of chlorine's roles and benefits in the world to a description of the admitted environmental challenges posed by chlorine chemistry.

First, the industry is actively involved in reducing its "footprint," its impact on the natural environment in all respects. It is succeeding in that effort: The Canadian Chemical Producers show that "the total emissions of chlorinated compounds have essentially been cut in half in Canada—from approximately 4,100 metric tonnes in 1992 to 2,000 metric tonnes by 1998."[12] Similarly, the European chlorine industry association found that from the period 1985 to 1997, while production was increasing, emissions of chlorinated substances to the air were reduced by 70 percent and emissions to water by 85 percent, and it's getting better. During a period of industry expansion in the United States, while production rose 20 percent, emissions of chlorine compounds fell by 65 percent. It may not be possible to be perfect—zero, as in "zero discharge," is a very low number—but improvement certainly appears possible.

Second, the industry is actively attempting to lower its energy use. One major initiative is "cogeneration," otherwise known as combined heat and power (CHP). This process attains efficiency by producing electricity from combustion of natural gas, then using the waste heat directly in chemical processes at the plant. Energy is always lost in transfer; but CHP plants can obtain efficiency of 70 percent, as opposed to 32 percent efficiency of electricity generated at a utility. Hydrogen, a side product of the electrolysis of salt, is captured and either sold or burned to offset energy use.

Third, in the spirit of the Stockholm Convention, the chlorine industry has implemented and continues to implement the use of Best Available Techniques (BATs). Older technologies for making chlorine involved the use of a liquid metal, mercury, as one electrode in the electrolysis cell. Although emission of mercury from chloralkali processes is not as large as that from combustion of coal, it has been responsible for stark and egregious incidents, such as the poisoning at Minamata in Japan. The BAT for chloralkali, as defined by the European Integrated Pollution Prevention and Control Bureau, specifies cells that do not use mercury; in fact, in the developed world mercury-based production is being phased out in favor of more modern processes.

The chlorine industry, in short, is one of the most progressive in the world in its attempts to forge sustainability from a very uneven record in the past. Possibly in part because of the worldwide attacks on chlorine chemistry—let us be honest—and the prospect of ignorant and misguided regulation and legislation that opposition might produce, the industry has adopted a full-court press to make the use and production of chlorine and its products the cleanest on the earth.

From both of these lines of rebuttal, it should be clear that Thornton has totally failed to prove his point. The "crisis" of health and environment that he wants to solve with his "sunset" isn't there, so no solving is necessary. Moreover, any "sunset" adopted as he wants it adopted (and it isn't clear just how he would implement it at all, let alone "democratically"), will be terrible for the economy and for human health. Then, left to its own devices, we find that the chlorine industry, acknowledging past (and present) failures, is working very hard, harder than any other industry, to protect the environment from emissions. The greatest likelihood is that a full attack on the industry, with an eye toward ending it, would first end any efforts to make it cleaner, and hence would be counterproductive. But there is no need to challenge, on environmental grounds, an industry that is working so hard to do precisely what Thornton wants it to do, to reduce dangerous emissions and to get to sustainability.

Pro Rebuttal: All the Arguments Above
Fail to Answer Thornton

Let's start by paring down the range of required replies. *For the foreseeable future,* those who would sunset chlorine chemistry as part of industrial processes concede that there is no usable substitute for chlorination of drinking water. In certain small contexts, especially urban areas, ozone treatment may be sufficient, and in some small rural plants ultraviolet treatment may be sufficient. But wherever water has to be transported over large distances, where there is danger of contamination, chlorine saves lives and should be used. You will notice, from the industry's own figures, that only 6 percent of the chlorine extracted for production ends up in the drinking water. Maybe someday there will be a substitute, but not now. We may remove the specters of typhoid, cholera, and dysentery from their positions on chlorine's defensive bastions. Meanwhile, we might explore further means to cut down on the production of trihalomethanes (THMs) and other organochlorines from the interaction of chlorinated water and the organic material with which it comes into contact.

After that, defense of chlorine's bastions gets a bit more vulnerable. First, Thornton does not need to take every vinyl (for instance) product and show that there is an equally satisfactory and inexpensive substitute for it, so there would be no loss at all in our consumption-happy lives if vinyl disappeared from the market. Maybe there would be products that would not be available. Generally, if products become unavailable, we cope rather well. For instance, elephant ivory, which had been readily available for a century, disappeared from the market a few decades ago, when in order to preserve the species we decided to end the ivory trade. Very few riots have broken out in the streets on that account. (Incidentally, the first plastic invented—cellulose nitrate—was the first substitute for elephant-ivory billiard balls. This shows the creativity of the plastics industry even before it *was* an industry.) We innovate, we do without, we find substitutes within existing strictures (if forests are protected by law, and wood is unavailable, we do not revert to wood, we do something else), or we reconceive the need and the product to satisfy it. Consider the most compelling case: pipe. There are three viable and often-used alternatives: concrete, ductile iron, and polyethylene. If the issue is corrosion and flexibility, then polyethylene is the answer. In Europe, polyethylene pipe has about the same market share as PVC. Solutions exist. Well managed, eliminating uses largely by attrition, a chlorine sunset should not produce any disruption at all.

Second, the blithe assumption that no health problems appear to be afflicting us here and now is dangerously shortsighted. There is a curious spate of syndromes affecting children—children each of us knows—that were far less prevalent in the past. Asthma. ADHD. And did children need antidepressants in the 1960s? Moreover, the animal kingdom is sending out disturbing messages, even allowing for the reductions of certain POPs in the environment. The pesticide atrazine, a product of chlorine chemistry, on the market despite all protestations about our careful system, is hugely controversial with respect to interference in sexual differentiation of amphibians. Out there in the waterways, female snails are growing penises and birds are growing stunted and malfunctioning beaks, while dolphins beach and die in increasing numbers for reasons we cannot figure out. Not surprisingly, threats to health lying invisibly in the environment hurt the simpler organisms before the complex (who have elaborate physical buffering systems) and hurt organisms immersed in the contamination before they hurt those at a remove from it. So we humans won't suffer first. Other forms of life will. But when the canaries start dying in the coal mine, you don't point out that you're not a canary. You get out of the coal mine. And if the mine happens to be the natural environment around you, and you can't get out of it, you figure out what's killing the canaries and you get rid of it. Much of the evidence suggests that the organochlorines are the culprits.

Third, the admirable (if late-blooming) efforts to keep their industry as clean as possible are well-meaning but not sufficient. A substance that accumulates in the environment and does not go away in any human span of time must not be put into the environment, period. Zero is a very low number, but it is the only acceptable one. A clean industry, one in which all products are part of the ecological web and at worst all harmful contaminants in the manufacturing process are kept within the plant, recycled, or packaged for other uses, is a worthy goal but at present apparently impossible.

And let's do examine the record. Mercury plants could be shuttered tomorrow. The only thing preventing it is money. Emissions of vinyl chloride and other carcinogenic organochlorines could be reduced by 30–50 percent tomorrow. The only thing preventing it is money. Companies make alternative products but prefer to milk older technology. The only thing preventing change is money. Without a palpable threat investment seems ludicrous to industry. To catalyze action the chlorine industry must be put on a shut-down program and made an example to others unless it can truly deliver the step-change in performance needed now and the truly continuous improvement after. But it can't, or won't, and its members will tell you so. Only a phase-out gets to zero—a sensible number reached with a sensible program.

Their fundamental argument is: we went through a bad patch where we didn't know better, but that's changed and things are getting much better now. What they don't recognize is that's not good enough. A drum of poisonous waste is poisonous. A glass of fine wine with a teaspoonful of poisonous waste is still poisonous. Zero means zero, and enough is enough.

Summing the Debate

So ends the debate. Who wins? Some observations are in order.

First, interestingly, in their major uses, as protectors of our water supply against the lethal organisms that cause typhoid and cholera, and as killers of the insects and other ugly things that devour our food crops, organochlorines' indictment is their mission: they kill things, destroying the cell membranes of targeted disease organisms and confounding the guidance systems of the target pests, and they persist in the environment, staying around to kill the next generation of disease and pest invasion. That's why we like them. On the other hand, their tendency to persist means that if there is any damage they do at all to the non–target species, they will be doing it for a very long time. The scariest part of the POPs damage is that it is subtle, hard to detect, equally hard to attribute to any one cause. When we see environmental damage, we don't know if it came from interactions with POPs or from some entirely unrelated cause.

Plausible cases can be made on both sides, but there seems to be agreement that at least the most hardened POPs offenders are slated for elimination.

For all other materials, a burden of proof has to be assigned. When we find endocrine damage to a species of frog in a waterway where there are detectable traces of organochlorine pesticides, should we (1) assume that the damage may be natural, just something that happens to frogs, or due to many causes, including the weather, and continue tests to see how the pesticides may be involved, letting the pesticide continue to be sold until we have proof that the pesticide is causing the harm and that the inconvenience of removing it from the market is outweighed by the convenience for the frogs, or (2) assume that the pesticide is doing the damage and ban it while tests continue, tests that may eventually show that the pesticide did no harm and that its use may be resumed? The answer to that question makes a great deal of difference to the companies that manufacture pesticides, and possibly to us. That is where "reverse onus" comes in: assumption (1), from the liberty or "risk" paradigm, places the burden (onus) on the public authority, or plaintiff, to show that the damage is linked to the pesticide, whereas assumption (2), from the ecological paradigm, places the onus on the company to show that the substance is absolutely safe for all life indefinitely—and if the substance is a pesticide, that will be very hard to do.

This last statement explains why no one has won the debate or can hope to win it at this point. A burden of proof is not factually or logically discovered, it is assigned, one of the clear human choices in any discovery process. In addition, a standard of proof must be defined. Even in our court system, whereas the burden of proof remains strictly on the prosecutor or plaintiff, the standard of proof varies from "more likely than not" in civil cases to "beyond a reasonable doubt" in capital cases. When precaution can be applied in commensurate proportion to the question at hand and when a *standard of safety* can be agreed upon by reasonable stakeholders and authorities, we advocates of public health and safety will make progress. In many ways, the regulatory systems now in place use this very paradigm. Refinement may be needed, but a solid foundation exists.

The way we make these choices will determine the status of chlorine chemistry—possibly all chemistry and maybe all human activity—for all future debate. The terrible fact is that the economist in the old joke is right: there is no such thing as a free lunch. Modern life in the developed world carries obvious benefits. It brings comfort and wealth that are the envy of the developing world. But it brings substantial costs as well. Certainly monetary costs, but also complex aesthetic costs, involving stress and pace of life. If something is 99.999 percent safe but carries a 0.001 percent risk, how much should we worry? There is no objective standard for "good enough." It is a value judgment to be made by individuals and agreed to functionally in societies. The dilemma of chlorine chemistry offers exactly these two clear horns, and we must choose one or figure out how to reconcile the two. The choice we Americans as a people make about the future of this industry will determine how we evaluate it and all others for safety and usefulness.

THE CONSTRUCTION OF A
SUSTAINABLE INDUSTRY

Is it possible that there is a way between the horns of the dilemma? Could chlorine chemistry be used and contained in such a way that the objections could be overcome on all sides? The industry's literature suggests some moves in this direction, and we can continue the discussion with chemists currently working in the industry. Central to the move to a sustainable industry is the chemical industry's code of ethics, Responsible Care.

The ten guiding principles of Responsible Care cover the industry's obligations to protect the safety and health of its employees and of the general public, in all aspects of its operations. They also spell out the industry's commitment to the protection of the natural environment, both in present operations and in response to discovery of past messes (like Love Canal), and a commitment, novel at the time of the adoption of the principles, to transparency in its operations. Among the principles, beyond the general obligations to protect the environment, the one that interests us most is the second: "To provide chemicals that can be manufactured, transported, used and disposed of safely." Read one way—"To provide [only] chemicals that can be" etc., "[and not to provide them if they cannot]"—it translates as the Precautionary Principle. Read several other ways, it articulates an aspiration, not a rule. We suspect that the phrasing of the principle was deliberately ambiguous, in order to guide an industry that was famous for unsafe practices toward safer practices and then to describe the purpose of an industry that has achieved that level of safety. The principle calls attention to four areas of risk that the industry must address: (1) Manufacturing: can the manufacturing process be carried on without danger of poisoning for the workers, and without harmful emissions that will hurt the neighborhood or the natural environment? (2) Transportation: can we get the chemicals from here to there without disastrous accidents and spills? (3) Use: in their normal use, including uses that spread them through the environment, can the chemicals be shown to be safe for that environment and the people in it? (4) Disposal: when use is finished, can the chemicals and the products made from them be disposed of in a way that will not pollute the natural environment, now or in the future? Let us further examine these four areas of risk.

Manufacturing: What are the possibilities for a completely clean plant, a plant where nothing was emitted as waste? Raw material goes in, product comes out, and everything else is either recycled within the process itself or sequestered as raw material for some later process? Nothing at all would go to the dump. This waste-free process is in theory possible, since the organochlorines that so worry Thornton are all made up of atoms that are constituents of other things. Viewed appropriately, bacteria that degrade a material are equivalent to industrial syntheses that use the material and transform it. As 3M proved so many years ago, paying close attention to the waste stream in order to find reusable parts of it can be profitable to the company as well as better for the world. It is not clear that plants that produce organochlorines as an end product (pesticide plants, for instance) can yet operate without organochlorine emissions. Part of the question comes down to cost. Improvements could be made, but the cost of making them would far exceed any possible return, so they won't in fact be made. As a result, no one has developed the technology for a completely clean plant; since it has no future, it's not worth it. Given infinite capital, or infinite access to free energy, the research on plant processes would be worth it, and it would be done; right now there is no way to do the research.

Transportation: At some point products have to be moved from where they are made to where they will be used. The question is, Which products, and how? Typical industrial forms of transportation vary in scale from transformation on-site, to pipeline transfer between sites, to railcar-load quantities, to truckloads. Complicating the Responsible Care ethic for transportation (and to a greater or lesser extent that for the other steps in the process) is vulnerability to unauthorized use or terrorism and the need for security. But security correlates with control. For materials of concern, the greater control during transportation, the better the security. Consider the four types of transportation again, and recognize that they are listed in declining order of capacity per individual load, cost of operation, and control over the operation. To the extent that materials, especially hazardous materials, can be transported in secure pipelines to nearby facilities or used on-site without further shipping, there is greater control and greater security. This is the direction industry appears to be moving, in any event, both for lower transportation costs and reduced risk.

Use: Can we ever make pesticides and other organochlorines safe for the environment? The major proposals on the table now seem to turn on three considerations. (1) Recall, if the pesticide does not kill the pest or the antibiotic does not kill the invading pathogen, the stuff is useless. It's got to stay deadly. And until we get cell-specific attackers, that means it will kill other species too, like the birds and the innocent bacteria in the body. (2) The chemical in question also has to persist in the environment to do a lot of good, but we can make it safer by structuring it so that it breaks down relatively quickly. Already we have plastic bags that deteriorate in sunlight. We can make and use only the organochlorines that are ultimately unstable in sunlight or otherwise degradable, or medicines that are metabolized into innocuous products so that they will in fact be assimilated into the ecosystem spontaneously. (3) Chemical products have to be destroyed ultimately by nature and the waste transformed into things that are usable by nature. To this end researchers are discovering and potentially growing or modifying organisms that can initiate the first and usually most difficult step of the biodegradative process; that is, organisms that can digest the otherwise lethal substances. These genetically modified organisms pose ethical questions of their own, but it seems the organisms themselves may be very useful in polluted areas. The questions, of course, must be addressed.

Disposal, or more correctly, *"End of Service Life":* Clearly disposal of many organochlorine pesticides is an issue even today. If a sustainable future exists for these molecules, it exists because they have been made photo- or biodegradable, and thus disposal is really the same as use.

The possibilities of recycling plastics from packaging into other packaging or other useful articles are many, various, ingenious, and at this time technically feasible and not very profitable. Perhaps it is fortunate that for the major organochlorine plastic, PVC, very little is used in packaging. The durable materials like pipe and siding do not have the same recycling issues as nondurables like packaging, at least not today. Over time, however, those materials will lose their serviceability and the issues will change. One building material, PVC-coated wire or cable can be recycled in significant amounts. The valuable copper from that wire/cable is recovered. The PVC insulation is somewhat more problematic for recycling than the copper, however.

Recycling technologies for durable PVC are, in principle, the same as those for packaging. The material is ground up, washed, dried, remelted and reformed into articles. Unlike packaging, reuse of durables can be a viable second-life strategy. Careful deconstruction of houses wherein whole windows or lengths of siding and pipe are removed allows for that reuse. The next 15 years will tell whether demolition waste comes under the same disposal pressure that packaging waste did in the early 1990s.

Plastics still have carbon in them, so why can't we develop a similar bug to eat plastics? Possibly we can. Famously, the dictum "waste equals food" is true all over nature—where natural landfills or sewage treatment plants are unnecessary, for every piece of waste given off by any organic process is promptly taken up and metabolized by some other organic process.[13] Humans alone produce waste that cannot be used by anything. But it has been pointed out that nature has had millennia to figure out how to use the waste produced by animal excrement or demise;[14] we have no reason to believe that every new form of excretion instantly had a consumer and user to recycle it into the biosphere. If we leave plastics, with their reconfigurable carbon-containing molecules, in the landfills indefinitely, no doubt an organism will evolve to eat them, and the making and shedding of plastic containers will join the inexorable and unending process of recycling carbon. (The chlorine in the organochlorines will probably end up as some sort of salt.) But with the recombinant-DNA techniques we have available to us, maybe we do not have to wait for evolution to catch up with Styrofoam; maybe we can engineer some of those plastic-eating bugs ourselves.

As noted earlier, the possibilities of recycling plastics are many, various, ingenious, and at this time not very profitable. Ground-up plastic bottles have shown up in fiberfill jackets; processed plastic has shown up as garden lumber; recycled plastic can be used to make tiles, wall covering, and a host of other products. In the present economic climate, efforts to keep the plastic out of the landfills falter and die. However, changes in a very few laws, plus a minimal application of tax incentives and subsidies, could change all that (as it could for newspapers, office paper, wood scraps, metal, cloth, etc.). There is a real hope that with incentives in the right place, the products of chlorine chemistry would no longer reach the landfills or incinerators, where, under some conditions, they threaten the environment.

CONCLUDING OBSERVATION

The problem posed for human society by the processes and products of chlorine chemistry are no different from those posed by any new process or product—genetic modification of food crops, for example. It's just that in the chlorine industry, the debate is present and joined, and the economic and environmental stakes are very significant. How do we decide? The technology has proved its usefulness. We have observed some impact on the environment from its unintended (and some of its intended) effects, but we do not always know how to evaluate the impact; and we do not know how to weigh the proven benefits of the technology against the identified risks it seems to pose. The answer comes down to an assignment of the burden and standard of proof, and that choice, dear reader, is political. Remember to vote.

QUESTIONS FOR REFLECTION

1. How would you find out what things you ordinarily use are the products of chlorine chemistry? Try making an inventory, accompanied by possible substitutions.

2. To what extent is our acceptance of products a matter of "social trust"? What would it mean to "trust" business, government, or science? Is such trust justified? Why or why not?

3. What is "risk"? What kinds of risks do we take in the course of an ordinary day? (Consider all types,

for example, not just what risk is involved in crossing the street but also what risk is involved in skipping a class.) What makes risk "acceptable"?

4. How do we know what we think we know when it comes to risk in our environment? What counts as a sufficient standard for *safety* (in automobiles, foods, air quality, or anything else)?

NOTES

1. IJC 1994.

2. First serialized by the *New Yorker,* then published by Houghton Mifflin, the only house that would touch it.

3. Joe Thornton, *Pandora's Poison: Chlorine, Health, and a New Environmental Strategy* (Cambridge: MIT Press, 2000).

4. Ibid., p. 2.

5. Ibid., p. 5. To conceptualize "parts per trillion," think "one drop in a train of railroad tank cars ten miles long." Thornton takes this comparison from a "risk communication" pamphlet issued by the Chemical

Manufacturers Association (now the American Chemistry Council) (Covello, 1988) apparently intended to show industry spokespersons how they could minimize the appearance of risk from their effluent.

6. Ibid., pp. 5-6.

7. Ibid., p. 9.

8. As described, the question becomes logically unanswerable. We only know that something has "caused" something else to happen when we have a differential effect: some people are sick, others are not, so what caused the sickness? If *everybody* is, or

might be, just a little bit "sick," there is logically no way we could ever know the cause or even, since their condition is now "normal," (i.e., is now a norm) that they are in fact sick. Anything that explains everything, explains nothing. Thornton's argument sometimes veers in that direction.

9. http://c3.org.

10. The authors of the chlorine chemistry exposition cite the Johannesburg Summit 2002 and the World Summit on Sustainable Development, United Nations Department of Public Information, October 2001, for the figures on disease and drinking water. See "The World Chlorine Council and Sustainable Development," available at http://c3.org.

11. http://c3.org.

12. "World Chlorine Council," p. 6.

13. "Waste Equals Food: Our Future and the Nature of Things" is the title of an article by William McDonough, environmental architect and industrial chemist, that appears in J. Laddon, T. Atlee, and L. Shook, eds., *Awakening: The Upside of Y2K* (Spokane: The Printed Word, 1998), available online at http://www.ratical.org/co-globalize/waste=food.html.

14. William F. Carroll, President, American Chemical Society, personal communication.

8

Are We the Problem?

Addressing the New Population Dilemma

INTRODUCTION: CHINA—FOUR FACES OF
THE POPULATION PROBLEM

First of all, it is obvious when we examine the world's population problem that there are just too many Chinese. The U.S. Central Intelligence Agency (CIA) estimates that as of July 2004, there were 1,298,847,624 people in China;[1] that's about 200 million more than in India, the country whose population holds second place. (The United States is third, with upwards of 290 million; hardly in the same ballpark.)[2] On the map, China appears to be a very large country, but much of it is in fact desert, its livable areas clustered along the coast and the rivers. About 45 percent of China's land (in the southeast of the country) holds about 95 percent of its population. With one quarter of the world's population inhabiting that area, China can be considered to be very crowded.

A second point: China's attempts to address its population problem have created some new ones. In order to stabilize its exploding population, China adopted a "one child" policy in 1978, strongly encouraging young adults to marry late and to have only one child per family. The policy was unevenly enforced even at its outset, but attractive perks (medical care, housing, and education, for instance) were attached to signing and abiding by a "one child" contract, and eventually the policy began to show results in the demographic trends. The major result, intended by the policy, was to slow the population growth. Officials claim that 300 million births (more than the population of the United States) have been prevented by the policy between 1980 and the present. The next result, unintended but inevitable in the cultural context of China, is a preponderance of male births; now that ultrasound is available, with elective abortion easily accessible, the cultural preference for boys shows up as a ratio of 117 male births to 100 female births (the global norm is 104 males to 100 females).[3] Foreseeing social instability if large numbers of men cannot find wives, China is now offering families cash to birth and raise girls.[4] The third result of the "one child" policy was better foreseen, but in the long run more difficult to deal with. Every country relies on its workforce, men (especially) and women between the ages of 18 and 65, to support the children and the aged. In China, more than in the West, there is a strong presumption that the children will support the parents in their old age. Meanwhile, access to advanced medicine has prolonged life in China, as it has elsewhere. When the "one child" policy has had two generations to work in China, situations will arise in which two young marrieds, just coming into the workforce, will find themselves solely responsible for supporting 4 parents and 8 grandparents—12 aging loyal Chinese with expensive medical and housing bills to pay. Recognizing the injustice, China is beginning to supplement the income of aging couples who obeyed the "one child" policy and now find themselves in financial distress.[5] But how long can *that* go on without bankrupting the state? As a population accustomed to socialist guarantees of care gets older, without the children to support it, where does China go from here?

Third, after 50 years of Socialist injunctions to selflessness and sacrifice in service to the People, the Chinese are entering the contemporary market world of competition and consumption, and frankly, they like it a lot. The stabilization of its population led to prosperity, lifting millions out of poverty and changing the diet for the better, or at least for the richer.[6] Since 1980, China has been the fastest growing economy in the world. It has already overtaken the United States in the production of steel, grain, and red meat. It wants to become, like the United States and Western Europe and Japan, an automobile economy. Right now the United States is saturated with automobiles, containing almost as many cars as it does people. Japan is close to saturation, with one car owned for every two people. Should China reach that rate of car ownership, it would have a fleet of 640 million cars. What will that number of automobiles do to China's cropland? Lester Brown takes a stab at the answer:

> Assuming the same paved area per vehicle in China as in Europe and Japan, a fleet of 640 million cars would require paving nearly 13 million hectares—most of which would likely be cropland. This would equal almost half of China's 28 million hectares of riceland, which produces 122 million tons of rice, the principal food staple.[7]

The desire for a car, a private car (forbidden under China's socialist government, until a few years ago), is universal. Part of the lure of the free market society is the possibility of one's own personal transportation, the liberty to go anywhere, anytime, according to one's own free choice. Yet automobile use is problematic for the natural environment, in many ways that are familiar to us—emissions adding to greenhouse gases, consumption of scarce fuel imported from unstable areas of the world, the clogging of landfills with castoff junked cars and tires—and in some ways that are not. One problem of affluence in China that does not trouble the American mind is brought up by Lester Brown in the passage above: in their need for paved roads and parking places, about one-fifth of an acre per car, the automobiles will compete harshly for scarce land in a crowded country: the place where the people need the roads and parking lots is where they live, and that's in the southeast, in the traditional cropland of China. This aspect of the new prosperity brings us to the fourth face of China's overpopulation, the loss of its land.

China is rapidly becoming an environmental disaster area, with expanding deserts, catastrophic dust storms, rivers that do not empty into the sea, and aquifers rapidly disappearing, with less and less arable land to grow its food. This aspect of China's population problem is not a category unto itself but emerges from the first three already described. Lester Brown grimly places China at the "leading edge" of the "deteriorating relationship between the global economy and the earth's ecosystem" that threatens the food supply.

> A human population of 1.3 billion and their 400 million cattle, sheep, and goats are weighing heavily on the land. Huge flocks of sheep and goats in the northwest are stripping the land of its protective vegetation, creating a dust bowl on a scale not seen before. Northwestern China is on the verge of a massive ecological meltdown.[8]

The economy of China has expanded four times over in the last quarter century, with incomes rising to match; the people want more and better food, especially food higher on the food chain—meat to supplement the rice and vegetables. That means more cattle and sheep, and it means more grain to feed them to supplement the grass they can eat in summer. There are two problems with putting more meat into the Chinese diet. First, the most obvious place to graze the animals is in the interior, the north and west of China, away from the centers of population. But these areas have very little water, and the huge herds (106 million cattle, 298 million sheep and goats)[9] are stripping the vegetation, which cannot recover. The wind does the rest of the job, taking off the topsoil and blowing the dirt east to the sea. Millions of tons of topsoil can be lost in a single day, with no prospect of reconstituting itself. The dust storms of late winter and spring are now the terror of South Korea; on April 12, 2002, a dust storm originating in China shut down Seoul for days. Even in Japan, farther away, the people complain "about the dust and 'brown rain' that streaks their windows and windshields."[10] The deserts are expanding: "the Gobi Desert expanded by 52,400 square kilometers (20,240 square miles) from 1994 to 1999, an area half the size of Pennsylvania."[11] The desert is now within 150 miles of the capital. The storms are turning the herdsmen, no longer able to make a living, into environmental refugees, sending them into the cities to seek jobs and food. The ultimate displacement may be measured in tens of millions—and in China, there is nowhere to go.[12]

The other thing wrong with the expansion of flocks and herds to provide a U.S. diet for the people is the well-known contraction factor: 10 pounds of plant protein produces only one usable pound of beef protein, which means that if the Chinese want to eat more meat, they must not only find grazing lands for the cattle, but they must grow a lot more grain to feed them enough to bring them to market. And grain, as we recall, is the problem. China had barely enough fertile land to feed its people before they got rich, when the diet consisted entirely of wheat or rice and home or locally grown vegetables. Now there are pressures from three directions: (1) there are more people in China, even while growth has slowed, so more people need to be fed; (2) the people demand a more expensive diet, so more grain needs to be fed to live-stock, especially since the traditional grazing lands have turned to dust bowls; and (3) as the Chinese embrace the automobile, more farmlands are being built over or paved over. "Who will feed China?" Lester Brown asked in 1995.[13] If the answer is, the world grain markets, where China can now well afford to do business, the price of grain will rise precipitously—in China, in the United States, and in the developing nations. But then, who will take care of the poor who will no longer be able to buy bread?

PAUL EHRLICH'S BOMB AND THE AFFLUENT SOCIETY

The Lamentable J-curve

There are, at this writing, 6,390,482,140 members of our species inhabiting planet Earth.[14] At the outset of the twentieth century, world population stood at less than 2 billion. By the time the century was over, it had reached 6 billion. That's 4 billion people added to our planet in 100 years. In 1650, only 350 years ago, our population was only 500 million. If that kind of increase continues, we are looking at absurdly huge numbers of people, enough so that we may soon have only a few square feet apiece to stand in. None of this fear is new; it has been a staple of environmental ethics since 1971, when Paul Ehrlich published *The Population Bomb*.[15] What will happen if the population keeps growing unchecked? Lester Brown draws the con-necting arcs:

> As a species, our failure to control our numbers is taking a frightening toll. Slowing population growth is the key to eradicating poverty and its dis-tressing symptoms, and, conversely, eradicating poverty is the key to slow-ing population growth. With time running out, the urgency of moving simultaneously on both fronts seems clear.[16]

Let's take another look at those numbers. If we look at selected years and the length of time it took the population to double, from then to now, we get an interesting picture:

TABLE 8.1 World Population Growth

YEAR (A.D.)	POPULATION	DOUBLING TIME
1650	500 million	200 years
1850	1 billion	80 years
1930	2 billion	
1950	2.5 billion	35 years
1985	5 billion	

Or, look at it this way: It took from all of human history to 1804 to reach 1 billion.

123 years, to 1927, to reach 2 billion

33 years, to 1960, to reach 3 billion

14 years, to 1974, to reach 4 billion

13 years, to 1987, to reach 5 billion

12 years, to 1999, to reach 6 billion[17]

The curve that represents human population growth is called a *J-curve,* not because it looks much like a J but because it doesn't look like anything else but what it is, a description of exponential growth. If on a standard graph you plot the amount of whatever you're interested in (the number of people on the planet, in this case) on the vertical axis and time on the horizontal axis, a J-curve lies low along the horizontal for most of the graph, then rises slightly, then rises faster, until at the end of the graph, it goes into a sheer vertical rise. If you want to see what a J-curve looks like, plot the following graph: plotting wealth in dollars on the vertical axis and one month of days along the horizontal axis, and schematize the classic uncle's promise: "If you'll be a good boy, I'll give you one penny on the first day of the month, two pennies on the second day, four pennies on the third day," and so on, doubling the amount of pennies every day, until the end of the month. It will take almost a week to get to a dollar. How much will the nephew have at the end of a 30-day month? You'd be surprised. (How much will he have at the end of a 31-day month? Twice as much.) When you finish plotting the accumulation of pennies, you'll have a population curve.

Population growth is usually described by two statistics: (1) the *growth rate*— the difference between the birthrate and the death rate, between those born per thousand population and those who have died per thousand—which number is usually expressed as a percentage (for example, if 80 people were born to a population of 1,000, and 60 people died, in one year, the growth rate would be 20 per 1,000, or 2 percent) and (2) the *fertility rate*—the average number of children born per woman over her lifetime in a given country. Why did the U.S. population's growth rate increase so rapidly over such a short period of time? The generally accepted explanation is that the Industrial Revolution resulted in what might be called a health/sanitation/medical revolution that produced a decline in the death rate. The fertility rate remained the same, as did the usually large size of the American family, but with fewer people dying each year, the population rapidly increased. Globally, in the industrialized North,[18] in the early to mid-1800s, the per capita income and expectancy increased with the advent of factory jobs, improved sanitation, clean drinking water, and better health care, including, eventually, vaccines and antibiotics. These and probably many other factors contributed to the decline in the death rate over a relatively long period of time. Essentially the same thing happened much later in the South, in the countries containing the largest percentage of the world's population. The rapid growth of population due to the decline of the death rate hit the South harder than the North for two reasons, the first of which involved timing: In the South, the advances in health care and sanitation occurred abruptly, primarily after World War II, with the spread of vaccines and antibiotics. "It took 100 years for deaths to drop in Europe compared to the drop in 30 years in the developing world," and the rapid decline in death rates in the South "brought unheard of population growth rates to Africa, Asia, and Latin America."[19] Although fertility rates remained as they had been, averaging about 6 per woman in her life time, actual survival rates increased dramatically, resulting in the doubling of the population every 20 years and a host of social and economic implications, including maintainenance of the food supply, expansion of the educational system, reallocation of jobs, and environmental degradation. (The North was not particularly successful at addressing the last two concerns.) The second reason the South was affected more adversely by the decline in the death rate was that conditions were never right there to bring about the other population trend, which we will examine in the next section.

The Hopeful S-Curve

Early in the analysis of the population crisis, census analysts realized that there was another population trend counterbalancing the J-curve. In the industrialized nations, after the first spurt of growth, the population was not growing very fast at all: the normal family of six-plus children was being replaced by families of two children, and the population was stabilizing at replacement rate. How come? Three reasons top the usual list: first, we didn't need as many children to get the work done; as farm hands moved to the city there was less need to bear more children to tend the crops. Second, with medical advances, parents had real hope of seeing their children surviving to adulthood, so they did not need to birth as many to be sure of having children to care for them when they were old. Third, with (slowly) increasing educational opportunities, women became (a bit) more independent; eventually social independence was possible for women as long as they were not burdened with young children, so those desiring independent social status made the necessary arangements. The sum of these effects was that a drop in the birthrate (fertility) also occurred, which resulted in a declining population growth rate. Generally, it takes about a generation for a decline in the death rate to realize a decline in the birth rate, a development termed *demographic transition*.[20]

This demographic transition happened in the North; it didn't happen in the South. Because improved living conditions, resulting in increased life expectancy in the North, spanned many generations, the social changes leading to fewer children per couple happened gradually. But the South was confronted with the economic and social necessity to defuse the population explosion immediately or face dire consequences. Easier said than done in a democracy with reproductive freedom, such as India, with a population of over a billion, a fertility rate of 3.3, and a population doubling time of 39 years. By contrast, in a country under authoritarian control, population control is more easily achieved, as in China, with a population of 1.3 billion, a fertility rate that has dropped from 5.5 to 1.8 in 40 years, and a population doubling time of 79 years.[21]

The appropriate curve for describing population growth is not, then, as researchers had thought for years, the lamentable J-curve. Rather, in an undeveloped society, population remains steady for long periods of time, then soars exponentially as technological advances such as basic sanitation and water purification take hold and people stop dying, or at least dying as young as used to be expected; eventually population growth resumes a stable, elevated, rate. Thus in developed lands, population growth follows a J-curve through the first, technologically induced demographic transition, then retreats to stability at a higher rate as the new family-limiting factors kick in, presenting the so-called *S-curve* (although it looks as much like an S as the J-curve looks like a J).

Now, if all the nations in the world went through this demographic transition, from the J- to the S-curve, the world population would stabilize, which would be a boon indeed to humankind. Or would it? Numbers aren't the only measure that matters.

I = PAT

From an environmental perspective, the problem with population growth isn't just how many people there are, it's how much damage each person can do to the environment. Humans roamed the world for 40,000 years without doing much harm, but once they settled in, organized technologies around fire, organized agriculture around plowed fields, and began to accumulate goods, they started imprinting their indelible mark on nature. If people continue to use resources at the present rate, resource depletion, deforestation, ecosystem destruction, and worldwide pollution will persist, fulfilling the pessimists' gloomiest predictions.[22]

To determine the environmental impact of humans, John Holdren and Paul and Anne Ehrlich have proposed the equation, $I = PAT$, whereby I = environmental Impact, P = Population, A = Affluence per capita, and T = the effect of the use of the Technology that supports that affluence. The T can be a positive or negative number: in general, the more advanced the technology, the more damage caused in the process of doing something. Let's take a few examples.

For instance, if we are talking about the damage done by logging the steep slopes in the redwood forests of the northwest United States, there is a real difference between the nineteenth century method of cutting the forest—four men on a long saw cut the tree down (over several days), lop the branches off, and haul the trunk using mules—and the twentieth century method—bulldozers clear a road, huge mechanized chain saws cut down a dozen trees in the space of a morning, and tractors haul the logs to the trucks. Mechanized logging not only results in the removal of more trees, with less chance for recovery of the forest, than the older method; it also results in the destruction of all young trees in the area and the destruction of the vegetation that secured the soil, causing mudslides. These remove the topsoil built up over millennia that would be needed to reforest the slopes, while silting up and destroying the ecosystems of the streams that cut through the forest. Mechanized logging ruins logged areas for future lumbering and kills all the fish in the vicinity at the same time, occasionally destroying small towns in the process. Meanwhile, because the trees are cut down indiscriminately, many are lost, shattering on impact with the ground, useless for any human purpose. In the nineteenth century, fewer trees were felled because the available technology did not permit intensive logging and the methods used had little adverse impact on the land around the tree. Also, because the process of tree removal was slower, the ecosystem had more time to recover. All other things being equal—the human desire to cut down trees, the laws, the market—the timber industry did a lot less damage to the environment in the nineteenth century than in the twentieth. Even per tree, the old technology does less damage than the new. However, if the value of the trees, or lumber, were set high enough (most easily by restricting the supply through environmental regulation), technology could re-emerge as a force for good. Required by law to do no damage to the land, the timber companies would have to snake out the logs by helicopter, which would have even less environmental impact than the mules.

For another example, recall the plight of the North Atlantic fisheries described in Chapter 3. The nineteenth-century Gloucester fishing boats, fishing "blind" (with no help from sonar or GPS) with hooks and small nets from small boats, could never exhaust the fishery. Technology now shows the fishers (in much larger boats) where the fish are and provides them with bottom-scraping, fish-devouring nets that disrupt the nurseries of the next generation. Progress in saving the fisheries could be realized instantly simply by prohibiting trawl nets and the larger boats from the fishing grounds; and prohibiting the use of satellite tracking; and limiting the right to fish to the old sailing schooners. On the other hand, if we Americans were ever to discover the political will to attempt to restore the fisheries, we could use satellite technology to demarcate the breeding grounds, develop no-fish areas on a daily basis, and communicate these sites to the fishermen.

Except for the possibility of using advanced technology to develop alternative energy sources (see Chapter 9), the T-for-Technology in the human equation is inevitably positive at this time—that is, it adds to the problem, rather than ameliorating it. Where the newest technology is used, the environmental damage is greatest. The calculations of the equation are rough and approximate, but we can make a good guess as to the comparative measurements. We can see immediately that one American with his energy-intensive and con-sumptive ways causes much more environmental degradation than does a Masai herder in Kenya. Using the I = PAT equation,

One American has the Impact of:

70 Ugandans and Laotians

50 Bangladeshis

20 Indians

10 Chinese

<u>plus</u> 2 Japanese, 2 British, 2 Frenchmen, 2 Swedes, and 2 Australians.

Indeed, as researchers have claimed, "Viewed in this light, the United States is the world's most over-populated nation."[23] One study, using these variables, found significant differences in the influence of each in different countries. For instance, population growth was considered the most important factor in increasing carbon dioxide emissions in Mexico and in Ghana (where afflu-ence actually decreased during the specified time period); in the United States, while population and affluence increased, carbon dioxide emissions were constant (due to improved technology); and in Poland and China, afflu-ence was considered the most important factor having an environmental impact.[24] Although the $I = PAT$ equation is by no means precise, it doesn't need to be to capture the truth of the interaction between people and the environment.

$I = PAT$ has considerable implications for foreign policy. Robert Kates states the case as follows:

> For over two decades the same frustrating exchange has been repeated countless times in international policy circles: A government official or scientist from a wealthy country would make the following argument: The world is threatened with environmental disaster because of the depletion of natural resources (or climate change or the loss of biodiversity), and it cannot continue for long to support its rapidly growing population. To preserve the environment for future generations we need to move quickly to control global population growth, and we must concentrate the effort on the world's poorer countries, where the vast majority of population growth is occurring.
>
> Government officials and scientists from low-income countries would typically respond:
>
> If the world is facing environmental disaster, it is not the fault of the poor who use few resources. The fault must lie with the world's most wealthy countries, where people consume the great bulk of the world's natural resources and energy and cause the great bulk of its environmental degrada-tion. We need to curtail over-consumption in the rich countries which use far more than their share, both to preserve the environment and to allow the poorest people on earth to achieve an acceptable standard of living.
>
> This argument has being going on, in one form or another, for years.[25]

The more people there are to share the planetary pie, the smaller the piece per person will be. But the North with 25 percent of the world's population uses 80 percent of the world's resources; the United States alone, with 5 percent of the world's population, uses 30 percent of the world's resources. There can be no justice in a world where 10 percent of the world's population control 80 percent of the world's wealth.[26] The women in the developing world (and their children) have suffered the most from these inequities.

Population = Poverty

The connection between population growth and poverty is well documented and fairly obvious. But let us take a look at a few statistics from an issue of <u>Popline</u>:

> About 1.2 billion people live on less than one dollar a day. . . .
>
> . . . approximately 57% of the world's population in the 63 poorest countries live on less than two dollars a day. . . .
>
> . . . 1/6 of the world's population [16.6%]—mainly in Europe, North America and Japan—enjoy 80% of the world's income and live on an average of $70 a day [Report from World Bank]. . . . [27]

Another way of visualizing the population/poverty equation: Suppose the world were a small village of 100 people. What would it look like? There would be:

> 57 Asians, 21 Europeans, 14 from the Western Hemisphere—North and South—and 21 Africans;
>
> 70 nonwhite, 30 white
>
> 70 non-Christian, 30 Christian
>
> 6 would own 59 percent of all the wealth in the community, and they'd all live in the United States [Note: There are wealthier individuals all over the world—in the Cayman Islands, for instance, and in Saudi Arabia—but the wealth is concentrated in the United States]
>
> 80 would live in substandard housing
>
> 70 would be illiterate
>
> 50 would be malnourished[28]

The S-Curve Revisited

"Remember the population bomb, the fertility explosion set to devour the world's food and suck up or pollute all its air and water?" Donald McNeil asks, in the Sunday *New York Times* on August 29, 2004. It hasn't been defused. But since Paul Ehrlich wrote, in 1971, much of its power has dissipated.

> Birthrates in developed countries from Italy to Korea have sunk below the levels needed for their populations to replace themselves; the typical age of

marriage and pregnancy has risen, and the use of birth control has soared beyond the dreams of Margaret Sanger and the nightmares of the Vatican.[29]

In 1968, the United Nations Population Division predicted that there would be 12 billion of us by 2050; now, given current trends, the UNPD estimates that world population will level off at 9 billion. Where are all the missing babies? Many have died, mostly of diarrheal diseases due to contaminated water supplies (see Chapter 7, on chlorine chemistry), and many were aborted. Abortion is now available worldwide, and in many cultures abortion to prevent the birth of a girl is acceptable (see Introduction, above). But those deaths in no way account for the sudden decrease in fertility. The major reason for the drop in fertility proves that Thomas Malthus was wrong: families can, indeed, control the number of children they have, one way or another, and there are many reasons for families to want to reduce of the size of their brood in this changed world. First, more opportunities for women exist: where women are educated and eligible for interesting and remunerative employment, they have less interest in having many children. Second, there are more opportunities for children and therefore an incentive for families to conserve wealth and income by limiting their obligations. Third, an urbanizing world does not need many hands to run a farm, and a city has less room for children. But fourth and most important, parents now have good reason to think that their children already born will survive to adulthood, so there is no need to have "insurance" babies.

> . . . simple public health measures like dams for clean water, vitamins for pregnant women, hand-washing for midwives, oral rehydration salts for babies, vaccines for youngsters and antibiotics for all helped double world life expectancy in the 20th century, to 60 years from 30.
> More surviving children means less incentive to give birth as often. As late as 1970, the world's median fertility level was 5.4 births per woman; in 2000, it was 2.9. Barring war, famine, epidemic or disaster, a country needs a birthrate of 2.1 children per woman to hold steady.[30]

The most spectacular drop in fertility has occurred in Italy, traditionally home of large families and regnant Roman Catholicism. By the year 2000, Italy's fertility stood at 1.2; but for immigration, its population will drop 20 percent by 2050. Denmark's fertility dropped below replacement in 1970 and stood at 1.7 in 2001. Even in rural Albania, the birth rate fell from 5.1 to 2.1 between 1970 and 1999. The same decreases can be tracked across the Middle East and North Africa, exploding the myth of Muslim fertility. In Asia, China's fertility rate is lower than that of France, and South Korea's has dropped to 1.17.[31]

The population problem has not gone away; as suggested at the beginning of this chapter, it has fragmented into many problems, each of which will take global effort to solve. First, there are regional population explosions that present the same problems that Paul Ehrlich foresaw in the 1970s—in India and Pakistan, for instance. Second, as in China, there is the problem of support for an aging population—the population profile has changed from the classic pyramid (few people in the highest age brackets, most in the lowest) to a demure cylinder, and yet continuing medical advances raise the life expectancy in developed nations to as much as 100 years. We have more old people and fewer younger people to support them. Third, as in South Africa, we have the AIDS problem—a hollowed-out demography of aging individuals and orphans, as the working-age population succumbs to a disease that is still deadly where health care is poor. But most important, we have the knowledge of $I = PAT$: as the human world gets richer, even as it slows its expansion of numbers, the drain on the earth's resources continues. Confronted with the changes in the population predictions, McNeil tells us, "Dr. [Paul] Ehrlich, a professor of population studies and biology at Stanford, says he was 'pleasantly surprised' by global changes that have undermined the book's gloomiest projections."

> But Dr. Ehrlich still argues that the earth's "optimal population size" is two billion. That's different from the maximum supportable size, which depends on the consumption of resources.
>
> "I have severe doubts that we can support even two billion if they all live like citizens of the U.S.," he said. "The world can support a lot more vegetarian saints than Hummer-driving idiots."[32]

THE ROLE OF THE INTERNATIONAL COMMUNITY

Still under the sway of Ehrlich's 1971 model, the United Nations has addressed overpopulation as a global issue on several occasions. Population issues were given a thorough airing at two U.N. conferences on population, one in Cairo in 1994, and the other on women, in Beijing, in 1995. It was at these conferences that the role of women as crucial players in solving global problems became apparent, arguably for the first time in the history of international conferences.

At the first U.N. conference on population held in Bucharest in 1974, the North pressed the South to control their population, while the South argued for equitable distribution of resources. It was here that the North came up with the slogan that "development is the best contraceptive," which became a mantra for policy makers from industrialized countries in following years. Ten years later at the Mexico City conference the United States, embroiled in abortion controversy at home, declared that population was a "neutral issue," that market forces would solve our problems. But at Cairo, the Clinton administration reversed the U.S. stand, supporting advocates for women and the environment. From this conference came support for improved women's education, improved health care for women and children, improved prenatal care, access to reproductive services, empowerment of women, support for adolescent needs, and support for sustainable development.[33] There was a general consensus that family-planning programs by themselves would not solve the problem of population growth, that addressing underlying social problems, such as illiteracy and the status of women, was an essential element of the solution.[34]

The 1994 agreement that the "most appropriate and effective way to stabilize population growth" is to reduce poverty, improve health care, promote education, and "raise the status of women" was indeed unprecedented, a far cry from the limited family-planning approach.[35] But the 1999 U.N. meeting to assess the progress toward the 1994 goals went considerably further, recommending "unrestricted access to safe abortions in countries where it is legal," sex education at all school levels, and "contraceptive advice" to sexually active teenagers. Predictably, some Muslim and Roman Catholic countries voiced objections. The conference also addressed the AIDS pandemic and the need "for access to preventative measures" especially for adolescents, while preserving parental rights, "cultural values, and religious beliefs."[36]

What could a new United Nations–sponsored conference on "population" address? Surely the focus of the conference should not be only on world fertility, which is plunging. Instead, a multi-targeted approach should be taken. There are still countries whose problem of overpopulation exists largely because the reforms outlined above have not taken place: women still do not have access to employment and education, nor freedom in reproductive choices. According to the $I = PAT$ formula, then, the focus should be threefold: first, to continue those reforms enabling the families of the world to control their size; second, to teach simplicity of lifestyle to the affluent world so that it will rein in consumption and lower its drain on world resources (to "live simply, that all may simply live"); and third, to launch a worldwide research and development project to develop the technology that will save, rather than waste, our resources.

UNITED STATES POLICY: A FOOTNOTE

Aspects of U.S. policy of all types—affecting trade, foreign aid, scientific study, the arts and the humanities, and support for research projects here and abroad—are governed by ideology, more than any communist country's ever has been. In the United States, ideological power has tended to center on what has been called by its supporters "the pro-life movement," although, as the only American social movement in this century or the last to praise murder as an appropriate means for advancing its goals, its product is more likely death than life. The pro-life movement has been around for a half-century and more, concentrating in its early years on opposition to legal abortion of any kind and opposition to access to contraception of any kind. At that point it was driven solely by the Roman Catholic Church and was only marginally political, preferring to accomplish its ends through proselytizing the medical profession. In its 1965 decision in *Griswold v. Connecticut,* the Supreme Court, against fierce faith-based opposition, struck down laws forbidding the sale and use of contraceptive devices.[37] In 1973, the court spoke again in *Roe v. Wade,* concluding that constitutional provisions protecting privacy also protected the right of a woman to seek a legal abortion in the first trimester of pregnancy.[38] That decision made abortion legally obtainable anywhere in the United States during the first trimester of pregnancy, and it did it overnight, which was a bit too fast for a divided nation. The pro-life movement promptly gained a national constituency and has been wreaking havoc in U.S. law and policy ever since. At home, the political power of the movement has interfered with funding for women's health; rural clinics; and, most publicly, stem-cell research aimed at finding cures for Alzheimer's and Parkinson's. Abroad, controversy over population policy in the United States manifests itself in denials of U.S. government funding for agencies that provide family-planning aid around the world. It has held up payment by the United States of its dues to the United Nations (because the United Nations supports clinics that offer family planning); it has held any foreign-operations bills hostage, demanding guarantees that no help will go to clinics, agencies, or nations that counsel abortion in any circumstances; it has even defaulted on dues to the International Monetary Fund. During the Reagan and Bush administrations, government policy went so far as to ban funding to any organization that could not guarantee that none of its employees would ever mention the words "contraception" or "abortion," a provision known as a "gag rule."[39] President Clinton rescinded the rule by executive memorandum in 1997, but ever since then a group in Congress has been trying to reinstate it.

Addressing the state of the argument in the United States at that time, Dr. Nafis Sadik, Executive Director of the United Nations Population Fund, remarked, "By harnessing the energy expended in debating abortion and using it to prevent unintended pregnancies, we can make enormous progress toward ending the debate altogether."[40] By simple extension, the pro-life contingent in the U.S. Congress strongly opposes U.S. funding for the United Nations Fund for Population Activities (UNFPA), on grounds that some UNFPA money goes for reproductive assistance in China, where there had been (often exaggerated) reports of forced abortions. In 1998 pro-life advocates succeeded in cutting U.S. funding, prompting Representative Carolyn Maloney to claim that "1,200 women and more than 22,000 infants will die" because of the decision. She "maintained that 'UNFPA is in no way connected to abortion' but rather provides health care counseling and contributes to women who otherwise remain ignorant about their own health as well as that of their children.' "[41] The trouble with ideology is that you throw out the baby (quite literally) with the bathwater. As a final sad ending to this footnote, U.S. policy on funding health care to combat AIDS abroad has recurrently been made contingent on promises that advice to teenagers on the prevention of HIV infection (a sexually transmitted disease) would include only exhortations to abstinence from all sexual activity and would under no conditions mention condoms—even though the purpose of the condom would be the preservation of health, not the prevention of pregnancy. Ideology can commit people to strange and useless views of human nature and possibility, and is the swiftest destroyer of compassion. Somewhere in its collective future, the United States must learn to reject the temptations of absolutist ideology and orient its policies to the world as it actually is. Of all the expensive habits we have acquired in the course of our prosperity, dogmatism is the one luxury that we will never be able to afford.

QUESTIONS FOR REFLECTION

1. The "population question" comes down to a preference for one of two worlds—a world in which reproduction is strictly controlled and most people can enjoy a comfortable lifestyle and a world in which reproduction is not controlled and some regions of the earth are permanently poor. On a "pro and con" scale, outline the benefits and costs of each. What policies would be necessary to bring about the first sort of world?

2. The problem that the entire developed world will soon face is demographic graying: an older population, with many retirees. The burden of supporting the retirees will fall on a smaller number of workers, a burden worsened by medical progress that keeps the elderly alive much longer at much greater cost. What policies might relieve this burden?

3. African leaders have complained that Western (Northern) notions of "population control" seem to target mothers of color much more than whites. Is this policy racist, even if unintentionally so?

4. The population problem would be reduced if we could control any item in the $I = PAT$ equation. Can you think of how we might reduce, for instance, the contribution that affluence makes to the environmental impact of population?

NOTES

1. Statistics available online at www.cia.gov/cia/publications/factbook/geos/ch.html. I wonder why the CIA is interested.

2. Latter two figures drawn from WallStreetView: www.wallstreetview.com/population.html.

3. Robert Marquand, "China Faces Future as a Land of Boys," *Christian Science Monitor,* 3 September 2004, p. 1.

4. "China Offers Parents Cash for Girls," www.worldpress.org/Asia/1923.cfm.

5. Marquand, "China Faces Future," supra.

6. Lester R. Brown, Plan *B: Rescuing a Planet in Distress and a Civilization in Trouble* (New York: Norton, 2003), p. 86.

7. Ibid., p. 86. Brown cites calculations by Janet Larsen, Earth Policy Institute, based on *Highway Statistics 1999,* U.S. Department of Transportation, and on *Production, Supply and Distribution,* U.S. Department of Agriculture (electronic database updated May 2003).

8. Brown, *Plan B,* p. 11.

9. Ibid. p, 12.

10. Ibid. pp. 12-13.

11. Ibid., p. 13.

12. Ibid., p. 13, citing a U.S. embassy report fetchingly entitled, *The Grapes of Wrath in Inner Mongolia.*

13. *Who Will Feed China* (New York: Norton, 1995).

14. U.S. Census Bureau, World POPClock Projection, available at www.census.gov/. That figure is accurate as of September 3, 2004.

15. New York: Ballantine Books, 1971.

16. Brown, *Plan B,* p. 176

17. David Foster, "Billions More Will Leave Century Than Entered It," *Albany Times Union,* 27 June 1999.

18. As we proceed we will be using "North" to represent the world's less populated, industrialized, rich countries, generally located north of the equator, i.e., the United States, Canada, Western Europe, Japan, Australia, and so forth, and "South" to represent the more populated, less industrialized, poorer countries, generally located south of the equator, that is, much of South America, Asia, and Africa.

19. Robert W. Kates, "Population and Consumption," *Environment* (April, 2000): 13.

20. Alene Gelbard, Carl Haub, and Mary M. Kent, "World Population Beyond Six Billion," *Population Bulletin* (March 1999): 4ff., published by the Population Reference Bureau, Washington, D.C., for a more detailed explanation of demographic transition.

21. "The Century of Population," in *1999 World Population Data Sheet,* p. 1, and *2000 World Population Data Sheet,* p. 6, published by the Population Reference Bureau, Washington, D.C.

22. Robert Livernash and Eric Rodenburg, "Population Change, Resources, and the Environment," *Population Bulletin* 53, no. 1 (March 1998): 2.

23. Paul Ehrlich and Anne Ehrlich, *Healing the Planet* (New York: Addison-Wesley, 1991), p. 7ff.

24. Livernash and Rodenburg, "Population Change," p. 8.

25. Robert W. Kates, "Population and Consumption," *Environment* (April 2000), pp. 10, 12.

26. Joel E. Cohen, "Population Growth and Earth's Carrying Capacity," *Science* (July 1995): 341.

27. "1.2 Billion Live in Absolute Poverty," *Popline* (May–June, 2000). *Popline* is a publication of the Population institute.

28. Statistics drawn from editorial, "Bridging the Gap between the Haves and Have-nots," *Glens Falls [NY] Post Star,* 30 June 2000.

29. Donald G. McNeil Jr., "Demographic 'Bomb' May Only Go 'Pop!' " *New York Times,* 29 August 2004, Week in Review section, pp. 1, 12.

30. Ibid., p. 12.

31. Loc. cit.

32. Loc. cit.

33. Lincoln C. Cen, Winifred M. Fitzgerald, and Lisa Bates, "Women, Politics and Global Management," *Environment* (January–February 1995): 4.

34. Worldwatch Institute, *State of the World 1995* (New York: Norton 1995), p. 177.

35. "UN Assesses the Success of ICPD [International Conference on Population and Development]," *Population Today* (January 1999).

36. Paul Lewis, "Conference Adopts Plan on Limiting Population", *New York Times,* 3 July 1999, p. 12.

37. *Griswold v. Connecticut,* 381 US 479 (1965).

38. *Roe v. Wade,* 410 US 113 (1973).

39. "Committee to Deliberate Mexico City Policy," *Popline* (September–October, 1997).

40. "Informed Choice, Not Inflamed Rhetoric", *Popline* (May–June, 1997).

41. "U.S. Funding for UNFPA Is Sacrificed", *Popline* (September–October, 1998).

9

Fueling the World

What Are the Alternatives for Energy?

INTRODUCTION: 400 MILES ON
A TANK OF GAS

One of America's favorite cars seems to be the Hummer H2, the second in the series of sport utility vehicles (SUVs) based on the army's Humvee (strictly speaking, the HMMWV, for High-Mobility Multipurpose Wheeled Vehicle). For those who have been living in a cave for the last decade, SUVs are "light trucks," low-mileage cars with high road clearance so that, in theory, they can be taken "off road" on weekend trips through the wilderness. They're not the smartest car to buy: they are expensive to buy and to maintain, and they are less safe than standard cars because of their high center of gravity—they tend to roll over in a crash. According to 2003 figures, in an accident, you're 11 percent more likely to die in an SUV than in a regular car.[1] The H2 is the ultimate SUV. It weighs 6,400 pounds, which is nice for the owners, for it puts the Hummer easily into the category of Truck, for which a tax deduction may be taken on its purchase if the vehicle is to be used for business (the minimum weight for the category is 6,000 lbs.; the tax deduction was aimed to help out small farmers and small construction businesses, but dentists and lawyers often have to carry heavy things too.) So in return for paying $45,000–$60,000 for the car, Hummer owners are able to deduct about $38,000 from next year's taxes.[2] The general public gets no such benefits from the H2; the H2 releases about 40 pounds of smog-causing pollutants for every

15,000 miles driven.[3] The only way to reduce those pollutants is to reduce fuel consumption—use as little fuel per mile as possible. Hummer H2s are not very good at that—estimates of fuel efficiency range from 10 to 13 miles per gallon.[4] But they help the American economy; right now, they are Detroit's hottest sellers.[5] (Within a short time, they are projected to be a significant part of the market in China.) You'd think that with that lousy mileage, they'd have to stop at every filling station, like a 4-year old child. But no: part of their enormous weight is in their 32-gallon gas tank, so they can go almost 400 miles on one tank of gas, just like a Ford Taurus, which gets about 21 miles per gallon with an 18-gallon tank.[6] The difference is in the gas efficiency.

Of course better engineered cars are available. There have been electric cars for some time, tooling around quietly on enormous batteries. However, the batteries are heavy and expensive, and they have to be recharged; the maximum range for an electric car is about 200 miles.[7] So the auto industry came up with another candidate for a low-emission car, a gas-electric "hybrid." Most of the driving is done on the emission-free, battery-powered electric motor; the 1.5-liter gas engine is used for acceleration, driving fast on the highway, or recharging the battery. The hybrids—the Honda Insight, the Toyota Prius, and the Honda Civic—like the H2 and the Ford Taurus, can also go 400 miles on a tank of gas, but the gas tank holds only 10 gallons. In the summer, the Prius gets 48–50 miles per gallon with an average driver; in the winter, about 42–44 miles per gallon.[8] That saves a lot of money, and the number of hybrids on the road continues to increase. Imitation is the sincerest form of flattery, and Detroit is now coming out with some partial hybrids, including some "hybrid SUVs," that can get maybe 17 miles per gallon instead of 12 but otherwise use the electric motor mostly to run the accessories.

Where lies the future of the car? About 70 percent of our oil consumption is used for transportation.[9] We know how to bring about efficiencies that will cut that consumption drastically, but we have not yet discovered the political will to bring about the necessary reforms in incentives (for instance, eliminating that tax rebate for the purchase of SUVs). Beyond transportation, where lies the future of America, which is totally dependent upon energy brought from foreign shores to run our dwindling factories, to fuel our electrical grid, and to heat our houses and workplaces as well as fuel the cars that take us from one place to another? If we took oil consumption seriously at all, the SUV would be off the market and we would all be driving hybrids. Yet oil consumption is one of the most serious problems facing the American people. Why the disconnect? Why can't the problems caused by careless consumption of oil be stated and faced by a rational nation?

How big is the problem? "Humanity's way of life is on a collision course with geology," Tim Appenzeller concludes in the June 2004 issue of *National Geographic,* "with the stark fact that the Earth holds a finite supply of oil."[10] The world consumes nearly 80 million barrels *a day,* and consumption is still going up. The United States alone consumed 7.191 billion barrels of oil in 2002, compared to 1.935 billion each for China and Japan, 985 million for Russia, and 949 million for Germany.[11] On the production side, U.S. oil production is declining even as consumption advances; in 2002, the gap was about 5.2 billion barrels, and by 2025 (at present rates) it will be close to 8.4 billion barrels, more than our total consumption now.[12] The way the United States consumes oil turns out to be emblematic of the U.S. approach to energy generally. In the following section, we will consider the problematic state of the production, use, and externalities of conventional sources of energy—coal, oil, natural gas, and nuclear power, with an addendum on hydropower. Then we will examine some alternative sources of energy that researchers are currently exploring.

THE BLACK-HOLE QUESTION
OF CONVENTIONAL FUEL

Fossil fuels—petroleum, natural gas, and coal—provide about 86 percent of all commercial energy in the world.[13] Hydropower and nuclear power provide virtually all of the rest, with emerging alternative energies (wind, solar, etc.) and "biomass" (burning wood for fuel) holding down tiny percentages. Let's consider the costs and benefits for the major players in the energy game.

Fossil Fuels

We have plenty of coal (fossilized plant material, buried and condensed under pressure until it is almost pure carbon). Seams can be over 100 yards thick and can extend over 10,000 square miles. There may be 10 trillion metric tons of coal under the ground. Proven reserves—mapped, measured, ready to be mined—can last for 200 years, but there are many reasons not to want to dig them up.

The first could be the mining itself. In general, mining kills every person who tries it. "Between 1870 and 1950, more than 30,000 coal miners died of accidents and injuries in Pennsylvania alone, equivalent to one man per day for 80 years."[14] Those who survive the exploding gases, cave-ins, and fires live to succumb to black-lung disease, a fatal clogging of the lungs resulting from years of exposure to coal dust. Long before death comes disablement, an end to active life. Is coal worth the sacrifice?

Human lives are not the only sacrifice. The cheapest and easiest way to dig the coal is simply to remove the land from on top of it, however much there is; in Appalachia, mining companies scrape whole mountaintops off, dump them into the valleys on either side of the mountains, killing any life in the streams and polluting them forever. Laws require "reclamation," but this is rarely accomplished; decades after the mine has closed, the land still steams with acid, and there is no life in the streams and lakes.

Burning of the coal continues to aggravate the impact on the environment. First, all fossil fuels pour carbon dioxide and other greenhouse gases into the air and contribute to global warming (see Chapter 1 for a discussion of that problem). Second, the natural radioactivity of the coal is released in burning,

along with the toxic metals (uranium, arsenic, lead, cadmium, mercury, rubid-
ium, thallium, and zinc) that had been absorbed by the plants in their lifetimes
and are now released. "You are likely to get a higher dose of radiation living
next door to a coal-burning power plant than a nuclear plant under normal
(nonaccident) conditions. Coal combustion is responsible for about 25 percent
of all atmospheric mercury pollution in the United States."[15] (Arsenic, too: in
one area of China, there was so much arsenic in the coal that chili peppers
dried over coal fires contained an arsenic level 50,000 times the amount permissible in drinking water in the United States. At least 3,000 people were suffering from severe arsenic poisoning.)[16] Then, there is the acid rain. Sulfur
oxides and nitric oxides are formed during the burning and filter through the
atmosphere. When they come in contact with water vapor or clouds, they seize
the water and turn into sulfuric acid or nitric acid, then come down with the
rain to destroy life in the waters, lakes, and brooks.

They don't just destroy the woodland lakes. They destroy the marble in the
public buildings, parks, and sculpture exhibitions all across the eastern part of
the United States; property damage from air pollution is between $5 billion
and $10 billion annually in the United States alone.[17] Health is impacted; the
atmosphere foul. Given these penalties, maybe we don't want to pursue the
coal with very much enthusiasm.

Oil presents similar dilemmas, plus a few of its own. It too was laid down
during the Carboniferous Age, primarily from the sediment remains of billions
of small organisms, creepy crawlies, and mollusks. Not all oil is in the form we
know it, a flowing black liquid; much oil is in "oil shale," rock containing
organic compounds that turn to oil in high heat and pressure, and "tar sands,"
oil in the form of tar in huge sandy deposits. Some estimates of how much oil
there is in the world count these reserves, some do not. "Available reserves" is
more an economic than a geological construct: given the time, and the money,
all reserves can be transformed into oil. But at what cost?

Costs include health and environmental costs, in the contributions that oil
burning makes to respiratory ailments (like asthma) and global warming. They
also include political costs. The nations of the Persian Gulf own about two-
thirds of the proven oil reserves in the world. That makes them politically very
important to us. But they are not always friendly to us—some displeasure in the
1970s led to a massive embargo on the part of the Organization of Petroleum
Exporting Countries (OPEC), led by Saudi Arabia, and the American economy
went into a tailspin. And there is little stability among them: in 1990, citing
ancient grievances, Iraq invaded neighboring Kuwait, American troops became
involved, and by the time it was over, Iraq had blown up 600 oil wells in Kuwait,
consuming at least 5 billion barrels of oil. Even more was lost, leaking into the
sand or into the Persian Gulf, compromising farming, fishing, and shipping in
the bargain. A standard textbook sums up the situation:

> By some estimates, the cost of supporting regimes that ensure us access to
> oil supplies, and maintaining military forces to keep that oil flowing
> smoothly, amounts to a subsidy of at least $50 billion per year. Adding the

environmental and health costs of refining and using that oil shows that the real cost of gasoline is probably four or five times what we pay at the pump.[18]

And the situation is getting worse. As gas prices soared past $50 per barrel in October 2004, Jad Mouawad of the *New York Times* pointed out that OPEC was stronger than ever. To be sure, many more recent oil sources exist outside OPEC and far from the Middle East, but 61 percent of the oil reserves, the great untapped stores of oil beneath the ground, are in Saudi Arabia, Kuwait, the United Arab Emirates, Iraq, and Iran. Add the other members of OPEC (Venezuela, Nigeria, Algeria, Libya, Indonesia, Qatar), and control by OPEC rises to 75 percent. The non–OPEC sources—Russia, the U.S., Brazil, Kazakhstan, Norway, Mexico, and China, among others—will have pumped their oil dry by 2030, whereas OPEC will have at least some oil well into the next century. The United States had moved to secure control of those oil sources early in the last century and for years had a fine working arrangement with Saudi Arabia, a joint company named Aramco, that allowed the United States a share in the ownership and profits of Arabian oil. Aramco was nationalized in 1980, and the other Gulf states have severely limited any foreign ownership or influence. They have us over a barrel.[19] John Cassidy makes the same point in the *New Yorker:*

> By 2020, according to the Department of Energy, domestic oil producers will be meeting less than a third of United States needs, and the Gulf countries will be supplying up to two-thirds of the world's oil.[20]

So far the officials of OPEC have not chosen the route of plain extortion—sending the price of oil to $100 a barrel and increasing their profit accordingly. Instead, they have kept it within a tolerable range—explicitly in order to make sure that we, and their other customers, do not find it economically necessary to develop alternatives.[21] Yet there may be good reason to develop those alternatives anyway: first, the price of oil will go nowhere but up, and the oil is under the complete control of people who do not always wish us well, second, as Thomas Friedman points out, the high price we are paying for oil supports terrorism, even as we spend more American dollars and American lives to try to end it;[22] third, oil use contributes to various forms of pollution that alternatives might avoid; and fourth, we will have to develop those alternatives anyway at some point in the future, and it will surely be better to do it now while we have oil to buffer our experiments.

Oil is a not only a very expensive indulgence, it is running out. Of the 4 trillion barrels of oil thought to lie under the earth or the seas, only about half are ultimately recoverable, and 465 billion have already been consumed. Immediately recoverable reserves at this point amount to about a trillion barrels, only enough for about the next 40 years at current consumption. Oil extraction will peak soon—within the next 15–30 years, this generation will see the "oil peak," when the supply of oil will start to dwindle, and the world will be changed.[23] And we won't have it all to ourselves any more: China is expanding oil use by about 10 percent per year, and soon half of OPEC oil may be going to Asia.[24]

After the reserves are gone, if demand is still high and growing, where will we get oil? Reckless suggestions persist, like turning oil companies loose in the Arctic National Wildlife Refuge (ANWR) to go after its small oil reserves (about a million barrels per day, or less than 4 percent of U.S. oil consumption, until supplies run out). More serious are the suggestions to exploit the vast hydrocarbon reserves in Canada's bituminous "tar sands," mostly in sparsely populated Alberta, which are estimated to exceed the ANWR reserves by a factor of 40. The energy picture is attractive, but the land left behind by this terribly toxic and destructive extraction would not be attractive at all; Canadians would rather not go that route. Similar hesitations surround the suggestion to extract liquid hydrocarbons from the "oil shale" of the western United States. (Oil shale is really sedimentary rock rich in "kerogen," an organic material that turns liquid and acts like oil, when heated to about 900° F.) Exploiting this resource requires the complete destruction of some of the last unspoiled lands of the continental United States and the production of untold amounts of toxic waste. Is this really a good idea?

Natural gas is probably the most environmentally sound of the fossil fuels, and the most preferred as a source—it is convenient, cheap, and clean burning, producing much less greenhouse emissions than coal or oil. We have enough of it, at current rates of usage, for about another 50 years, and would have more if we could persuade oil producers not to burn it off as waste while they are drilling for oil (with which it is often found). It is difficult to ship; fortunately, reserves are found near most U.S. markets, and the former Soviet Union has abundant supplies for Europe.

But there's lots of natural gas also in the western states of the continental United States; it's trapped in coal seams, often in conjunction with oil, in huge deposits scattered from northern Montana down through Wyoming, Colorado, Utah, and into northern New Mexico. It is held in place by overlying aquifers, and that's the problem with it: to get it out, you have to pump the aquifer dry, removing all the natural water from the area (leaving, after a while, Sahara-type deserts) and creating a huge mess of waste water, contaminated with minerals, salt, and other poisons. Then the natural gas can be recovered, and with the soil stripped away, so can the coal and oil. No life can survive for long where this type of mining is carried on. Ranchers and hunters, not usually allied with the tree-hugging types, have banded together with environmentalists to prevent this peculiarly damaging extraction.

The trade-offs for fossil fuels are well known and very similar: the fuel is there, or will be for the next little while. We know how to burn it; it does its job well. But in use, the burning of any fossil fuel poisons our atmosphere— coal more than oil, oil more than natural gas—but it all contributes to the greenhouse effect. The costs of purchasing the oil from the Gulf states are unacceptably high even now and may get much worse. The costs of energy independence by extraction of our own resources, however, are the most problematic. We can have fossil fuel for the next two centuries—if we are willing to destroy every inch of virgin land we have, in Alaska and in the lower 48. The costs in human life are immense; the costs in the destruction of ecosystems millennia old are unendurable.

The Strange Case of Nuclear Power

Other forms of energy have shown promise. Most famously, after U.S. president Dwight D. Eisenhower proposed the conversion of the terrible power of the atomic bomb into peacetime uses, nuclear energy was supposed to deliver infinite amounts of electrical energy, power "too cheap to meter" for the growth of industry at home and abroad.[25] Nuclear energy has certain undoubted advantages: it is clean and quiet, has no emissions, and produces enormous amounts of energy for its size. It is welcome as a neighbor, nonpolluting, and quietly profitable. Twenty percent of all electricity now consumed in the United States is now produced by 103 plants. The perecentage could have been higher, but bad luck and bad politics have dogged the nuclear industry since its birth. The "anti-nukes" movement, active in forms like SANE (Society to Abolish Nuclear Explosions) in the 1950s and 1960s, simply changed its target to nuclear reactors in the 1960s and 1970s. The rationale for the switch from attacking deadly weapons to attacking peaceful power sources that did less harm to the environment than the fossil-fuel alternatives was apparently a broad-based and justified distrust of government intentions—any and all nuclear reactors could be used, with modifications, to produce new atomic weapons, no matter what the government said, so opposition to atomic weapons should include opposition to nuclear power plants—and an equally justified distrust of large profitable corporations (like General Electric) that made nuclear reactors. The anti-nuke move quickly seized on "safety" as an issue with nuclear power. To live near a plant was to live near a bomb—it might blow up or leak deadly radiation. The safety issue was probably misapplied from the beginning—even the 1986 reactor meltdown at Chernobyl in the Ukraine happened only after 14 separate safety systems had been manually disarmed so that an ill-advised experiment could be attempted in a very imperfect reactor. Nuclear power is safer than most other forms of energy production, in terms of the health of the workers and neighboring citizens, in terms of the likelihood of damaging explosions, even in terms of the amount of nuclear radiation emitted. Coal-burning plants are less safe. The mining of the uranium that fuels the plant is not very clean, but it is no worse than the fossil fuels. Yet the "safety" issue gained traction, and public demonstrations forced the cancellation of plans to build and commission several nuclear power plants.

One of the sticking points for nuclear fuel is the disposal of the wastes spent nuclear fuel retains a measure of radioactivity for years—sometimes thousands of years—after its useful life is over. It should not be disposed of where people can be exposed to it on a regular basis. Right now the "low level" wastes—mine tailings and cast-off clothing from nuclear facilities, for instance—are not disposed of in any systematic manner, and the "high level" wastes, primarily spent fuel rods from commercial plants, can only be stored on the site of the plant or very nearby. Even at that, the political demonstrations from the neighbors will make storage difficult; and although disputes over the suitability of Yucca Mountain for permanent storage continue, there has been no further progress in finding a permanent storage area for nuclear wastes.

It could be argued that the whole anti-nuke movement was a misguided hoax with no good effects, only bad ones. First, the activists demonstrated no real proclivity to using less energy themselves. They continued to involve themselves in high-energy consumption, driving from one demonstration to another, just like the rest of the United States, even as they opposed the use of one of the best forms of energy we have. The romantic back-to-nature aspect of the movement—"Split Wood, Not Atoms"—was appealing, but if taken literally, by replacing all nuclear power with wood stoves, that policy would have destroyed the environment much more quickly than any other course of action open to us. As noted earlier, the safety record of the nuclear industry is better than that of the fossil fuels. It could be a lot better—but the political opposition to any nuclear power at all made it clear that it would not be worth an investor's while to put money into safer experimental designs like the modular High-Temperature, Gas-Cooled Reactor (HTGCR) and the Process-Inherent Ultimate-Safety reactor (PIUS).[26] So the rapid advances in safety and efficiency to be expected with any new technology, not to mention the lowering of price as new and more efficient types compete on the open market, never happened. That may be a shame.

ALTERNATIVE FUELS: AN OVERVIEW

Conservation

The first note to sound in any celebration of energies alternative to fossil fuels is conservation. Unless we learn to conserve fuel, to rein in our endless appetite for energy and our careless habits of wasting it, our consumption will exhaust any supply we put in place. Right now, our technology and habits are so wasteful that most of the energy in fuel is lost as waste heat. This wastage is not necessary; several European countries enjoy higher standards of living than we do but consume 30–50 percent less energy.[27] Conservation techniques are relatively simple. Use compact fluorescent light bulbs instead of incandescent bulbs and get four times as much light (they last ten times as long, too). Reduce heat loss in houses through better insulation, triple-glazed windows, sealed joints, and window coverings. (Superinsulated houses, now available in Sweden, use 90 percent less energy than the average American home.)[28] Caulk around doors and windows. Make sure you get energy-efficient appliances, dishwashers, and dryers. Use efficient air conditioning (or do without). Consider building your new home into the earth, covering it with a sod roof, and constructing it with bales of straw. (The bales must be covered with stucco to seal out water and mice.) Turn off computers, TV, DVD players, cable boxes, printers, modems; even when you think they're off, they're on. Unplug them.

The amount of energy used to charge an electric toothbrush or a cordless phone may seem trivial, but the meter quickly runs up. An analysis done for *The New York Times* by Rocky Mountain Institute, a nonprofit energy consulting and research group, found that energy consumption in an average American home rose 9 percent from 1987 to 2001. Almost all of the growth was due to lights, appliances and other electronic items, which together accounted for about 30 percent of home energy use.[29]

Much more can be saved by industry, but when oil prices are low, managers find it difficult to stay focused on energy savings. (In the early 1980s, in the wake of the OPEC embargo, U.S. industries managed to save about $160 billion per year over their previous energy consumption. Hard to find that sort of effort now.)

Conservation is easiest in the transportation sector. Automobiles and light trucks—very few of them commercial—account for 40 percent of U.S. oil consumption and produce one-fifth of its CO_2 greenhouse gases. "According [to] the U.S. EPA, raising the average fuel efficiency of the passenger fleet by 3 miles per gallon . . . would save American consumers about $25 billion a year in fuel costs, reduce carbon dioxide emissions by 140 million metric tons per year, and save more oil than the maximum expected production from Alaska's Arctic National Wildlife Refuge."[30] As with the factories, fuel efficiencies achieved in automobiles in the 1980s have rapidly been lost due to the popularity of the SUVs. The standard advice is correct: to save fuel and put off global warming, drive less, combine trips, ride a bicycle, car-pool to work, and where you have a choice, use one of the more fuel-friendly technologies (see the Introduction to this chapter.)

The utility companies occasionally finance conservation, just because it is cheaper than building new plants. Instead of adding to the amount of electrical productive capacity, some companies are financing conservation, using schemes whereby customers can earn "negawatts" by avoiding consumption. The United States is not the only country that can profit from consistent and fair conservation schemes. But the United States has the most to gain, since it consumes the most energy. The heart of the problem is finding the political will to address energy consumption head-on: unlike other political issues, it cuts to the heart of the American lifestyle and therefore requires real courage to place before the public.[31] Such mettle in our politicians is rare.

Harnessing the Wind and Water

Hydropower, the power generated by falling water, is one of the oldest and most reliable sources of energy in the United States. Long before electricity was of any use to us, every village built dams across its streams, created ponds, and ran millraces off them to turn the water wheels. The power provided by those steadily turning wheels ran the grist mill and could also be used to turn the woodworker's lathe and to power the saw for the saw mill. When water turbines were invented to produce electricity in the nineteenth century, hydropower became dramatically more efficient; by 1925 it generated 40 percent of the electric power for the whole world. It now provides only 20 percent of the world power but remains crucially important in some places. Norway, for instance, generates 99 percent of its electricity from hydropower.

The dams we Westerners use now, as opposed to the village dams and their attendant mill ponds, carry human and environmental costs that we may not be willing to pay nor able to afford much longer. They have displaced riverine peoples, especially indigenous peoples relying on rivers for traditional fishing, and all the animals of the surrounding area, now flooded by enormous lakes. Whole villages, even the remains of whole civilizations, have been lost. Species, too, must relocate; when displacement occurs in the tropical rainforest (as it does in the Itaipu Dam on the Parana River between Brazil and Paraguay), whole species may be lost that we had no idea existed. Where a dam interferes with patterns of flooding that have fertilized farmlands for millennia, as in Egypt, the environmental damage may be incalculable. Meanwhile, the degradation of the flooded vegetable material behind the dam may poison the waters, and if there are fish (like salmon) that cannot spawn unless they make it all the way up the river, the dam may kill the fish unless "ladders" are provided to allow the fish to get through around the dam.[32]

Here again, technology can save us. There is no more need for huge destructive dams. Rivers can flow freely and turn small turbines at the same time—technology of the so-called "run-of-the-river flow" generation. Low-head hydropower technology can get usable electricity from very small dams, dams that do not flood large areas, dams that a salmon can jump. There are even micro-hydro generators being developed that will provide enough electricity for a single home from the stream in the back yard. The possibilities are there.

Most interesting at this point is the new increase in wind power. When the United Kingdom and Sweden announced in 2003 that they intended to reduce their carbon dioxide emissions by 60 percent by 2050, instead of the 12.5 percent requested by the Kyoto Protocol, their plan to do that included heavy reliance on offshore wind power.

> Coinciding with [Tony] Blair's promise for greenhouse gas reductions, the British government began a new round of licensing seabed locations for thousands of giant windmills. . . . Noting that the U.K. has among the best wind resources in Europe and great expertise in offshore development from North Sea oil, the Minister of Trade predicted that wind could provide up to half of Britain's renewable energy, while also providing 20,000 jobs. The U.K. could become a net energy exporter in 2010 for the first time in 30 years, rather than importing 75 percent of its supply as is predicted in a business-as-usual scenario.[33]

Admittedly, the windmills look weird—417 feet tall, three huge metal vanes, with nothing of Ruysdael in their design. But wind is now the fastest-growing energy source in the world. Germany and Denmark already get about 20 percent of their electricity from wind. Spain—perhaps to provide more targets for Don Quixote—increased its wind energy capacity by 44 percent in 2002.[34]

Wind power has enormous advantages over fossil fuels: "wind farms" (connected windmills placed in one area) are easy to plan and build in comparison to, say, a nuclear plant; there are no fuel costs or emissions, no environmental burden, and they rarely need service—and some people think they are beautiful.

> Theoretically up to 60 percent efficient, modern windmills typically produce about 35 percent of peak capacity under field conditions. Currently, wind farms are the cheapest source of *new* power generation, costing as little as 3 cents/kWh compared to 4 to 5 cents/kWh for coal and five times that much for nuclear fuel. . . . when the land consumed by mining is taken into account, wind power takes about one-third as much area and creates about five times as many jobs to create the same amount of electrical energy as coal.[35]

Two problems attend wind generation. The first is the threat to birds, which may fly into the vanes. Careful design of the windmills, and placement of the towers, can keep this problem to a minimum. (In any case, avian mortality from windmills is considerably less than that from the air pollution from fossil fuel plants.) The second is the need to transmit the power produced over long distances; windy areas tend to be far from cities where the power is needed. High-voltage power lines are not entirely welcome in any neighborhood. An exciting possibility is to create plants on-site that will use electricity from the windmills to divide water into hydrogen and oxygen, to ship to the cities in underground pipelines for assembly into fuel cells.

The Elusive Promise of Solar Energy

Consider that except for very limited energy available from the heat at the center of the earth, all energy comes from the sun. The heat of the sun sets up the convection currents that make the wind blow, the gravity of the sun causes the tides, sun-caused evaporation drives the rain cycle that makes the rivers flow, and above all, the sun is solely responsibly for the process of photosynthesis, by which green plants seize carbon from the air and turn it into fuel—sugar and starch for our bodies, and wood for burning. Fuel wood was, after all, the only source of power for the human race for more than 40,000 years.

> The average amount of solar energy arriving at the top of the atmosphere is 1,330 watts per square meter. About half of this energy is absorbed or reflected by the atmosphere . . . but the amount reaching the earth's surface is some 10,000 times all the commercial energy used each year.[36]

In discussing energy conservation earlier, we talked about "passive" solar energy—obtained, essentially, by constructing your house (or factory or school) so that it faces south, using every scrap of sunlight for light and heat, and then insulating the building so that the heat is not lost. Enormous amounts of energy could be saved if these measures were universally adopted. Special walls, "Trombe" walls, composed of glass blocks containing water, can be placed in the south wall of any building, where they will absorb heat during the day while permitting light to come through and then heat the building at night. Other uses of solar energy tend to be in the experimental stage, like the hot-water heaters that bloomed on suburban roofs during the 1970s energy crisis. (Jimmy Carter put one on the White House roof; Ronald Reagan took it off—it leaked.) Solar cookers have been tried in tropical areas far from electric grids, with mixed success. Another application, currently being tested in the Mojave Desert east of Los Angeles, simply reflects sunlight to a central point to raise the temperature of molten salt, which drives a steam turbine—an application of the technology that allows a magnifying glass to start a fire.

The most hopeful application of solar energy in the future lies in applications of photovoltaic solar energy, whereby photovoltaic cells "capture solar energy and convert it directly to electrical current by separating electrons from their parent atoms and accelerating them across a one-way electrostatic barrier formed by the junction between two different types of semiconductor material."[37] Photovoltaic cells are one of the major areas of advanced research in the energy field, as each generation (about two or three years) of cells increases efficiency and finds new applications. One of the field's great entrepreneurs, Stanford Ovshinsky, figured out how to put sun-powered cells in paper-thin sheets that can be rolled up and taken anywhere. Meanwhile, cells have been built into roof shingles, efficient enough to supply all the electricity for a residence, and advanced amorphous silicon photovoltaic cells are now used for lighthouses, remote villages, ranches, and in many of our calculators and clocks. Japan, lacking coal or oil, now plans to meet most of its energy requirements with solar power.[38]

Fuel Cells

Fuel cells have an enormous potential to power the buildings and vehicles of the future. A fuel cell is essentially a battery that uses a chemical reaction (usually, the reaction of hydrogen and oxygen) to produce electricity. Fuel cells consist of a cathode and an anode (positive and negative electrodes) with a semipermeable electrolyte medium between them. The electrolyte allows ions to pass through it but not electrons. Hydrogen is passed over the anode, where a catalyst (like platinum) strips an electron from the hydrogen atom, making a hydrogen ion, or proton. The electron stays behind, but the ion goes through the electrolyte, attracted to the cathode. The electrons get routed through an external circuit, as an electric current; that's where the useful work gets done. Meanwhile oxygen is passed over the cathode, and when hydrogen ion and electron meet up with the oxygen at the cathode, they combine to form water. Fuel cells first became widely used after the U.S. National Aeronautics and Space Administration (NASA) started using them on spacecraft. They are perfect for the job: they produce electricity with no emissions, and the only byproduct is water—so they become the water supply for the ship. But if their high efficiency, with low emissions, no moving parts, and absolute reliability, make them good for space ships, they're good for other purposes too. They can, for instance, provide a clean fuel supply for whole buildings (a stack of fuel cells adequate to power an average home would be about the size of a refrigerator).[39] More immediately, we may find methanol-fueled fuel cells running our cell phones and pagers very soon. Some utilities have already installed stationary fuel cells to provide backup power in case of crisis.

One of the most important applications of fuel cells will be in transportation. We need, above all, to get cars, trucks, and buses that use fuel efficiently and do not spew greenhouse gases and asthma-triggering particles into the atmosphere. A variety of fuel cell designs—none of them very efficient, yet—are in the process of development for transportation purposes. Already fuel cell buses have been demonstrated in several cities; a fuel cell car is available, but the fuel cells take up a lot of room. Research in this area will continue; there is no market larger than the automotive market, and the rewards will be substantial for the first company that develops a workable fuel-cell car.

TIDES, GEOTHERMALS AND A SUMMING UP

By "alternative" fuels, we tend to mean fuels other than fossil fuels, which have been the reliable drivers of industrial civilization. (The Industrial Revolution could not have happened without coal.) In the wider picture, all carbon, in fact only carbon, is fuel at normal atmospheric temperatures and pressures, at the surface of the earth. For most of human history, biomass—fuel wood, peat, reeds, dung from animals—has been burned for heat and cooking. Wood concentrated as charcoal has been used since ancient times to produce the very hot fires needed for smelting. All over the developing world, in pockets of rural poverty, wood is still the major source of cooking fuel, and it is running out. As population pressures drive people into forests, the forests are disappearing, and families have to search farther and farther from the camps to get the wood for the day's cooking. Historically our most common and reliable source of fuel, wood is disappearing from the modern technological landscape.

On the other hand, technology can harness forces that would have been impossible for our ancestors. The internal temperature of the earth can be used for energy. Steam fields of very high pressure and high temperature lie just beneath the surface of the earth. Wherever hot springs and geysers are found, magma (molten rock) is close to the surface and can be tapped for electric power production and other direct-heating uses. (Iceland heats most of its buildings with geothermal steam.) In California, the Geysers project sinks shafts into steam reservoirs to bring up pressurized steam to turn turbines for electricity. This energy source is clean and useful but only available in a very few places. A much wider potential use of the heat of the earth is sinking large tubes of water into the earth around buildings and pumping water through them; the relatively constant temperature of the earth 20 feet below the surface will help cool the house in summer and heat it in winter; in some places, the cost of heating and cooling the house can be cut in half.[40]

Tide mills, shallow water wheels placed across an inlet from the ocean to turn machinery on the change of tides, have been with us for a millennium and more; one built in England in 1170 produced power for 800 years.[41] Contemporary versions turn the force of the tide into electricity by capturing the tide and holding it behind a dam, essentially creating a small hydropower plant; the Rance River Power Station in France produces 160 megawatts and serves the entire region. Functioning mills can be built any place the tide differential is large enough—at least 12 feet between low and high tide, and preferably more. For the Bay of Fundy, in Nova Scotia, which has a tide differential of more than 50 feet, a huge dam is being contemplated, with concern for the aquatic environment the only obstacle, a very real one. Present tide-mill technology requires a dam that holds back the tide in both directions, then releases it through turbines, as in regular hydropower. In cutting off the shore from the sea, the dam blocks the passage of sea life from the nurseries in the salt marshes to the open sea. This blockage could kill the fisheries.

One avenue of energy provision and use not recently explored is simple contraction, or "micropower": our present system of building huge plants and distributing power over hundreds of miles may make sense in centers of industrial activity but make no sense at all in postindustrial economies like the United States. We would do far better with small plants, preferably wind- or photovoltaic-powered, close to the point of use. As noted earlier, we can now harness even the flow of a good-sized brook to supply the power for one residence. The time may come when most of the energy we use is generated from small power sources spread over many locations.[42]

In sum, the possibilities for alternative energy are very exciting. We can heat our houses with tubes in the earth and turn the sunshine on our roofs into electrical energy. We can design automobiles, trucks, and buses so that they emit nothing worse than water and do not require the destruction of the earth for their fuel supply. Above all, in using sources of energy that are not only renewable but perpetual—wind, tide, and sun—we will no longer have to depend on unstable and hostile nations sitting on large oil reserves.

Yet the greatest source of energy remains energy conservation, and conservation takes political determination, a resource large deposits of which have not been discovered recently in the United States. Once the determination is there, there are a variety of useful incentives that our legislatures at the state and federal level could easily put into place: "feebates" (incentives to purchase and run low-energy appliances and automobiles); tax incentives for the development and installation of alternative fuel suppliers (solar shingles on roofs, for instance); a judicious balancing of "green taxes" and research subsidies to realize new technologies and introduce them to the mainstream of American life, as Janet Sawin, in her excellent paper for Worldwatch, "Mainstreaming Renewable Energy in the 21st Century," describes in detail. It's not a question of rocket science: Germany and Japan have already completely altered their energy consumption by restructuring their taxes and subsidies.[43] Recall the story of the handheld calculators: once the concept was discovered and shown to work, once it was clear there was a market for them, competition and the synergies of many research groups brought the quality of the product up and the price down with lightning speed. The same process will work with hybrid cars and photovoltaic cells: as soon as state commitment establishes a market, American ingenuity will do the rest. But we have to make a start.

QUESTIONS FOR REFLECTION

1. What place would fossil fuels have in a balanced energy regime? Would they be used at all? Why or why not? (Consider the uses of oil in petrochemicals—maybe oil should never be wasted by burning for fuel.)

2. Consider the place of nuclear power in a balanced energy regime. Given the evidence that you can assemble, should we encourage greater use of nuclear power—or ban it altogether?

3. How much energy might we save through energy conservation alone? Do some research and come up with some proposals that would cut energy use in half.

4. What policies (taxes, subsidies, and the like) would you recommend . in order to encourage the development and use of solar energy (passive and photovoltaic energy)?

NOTES

1. Danny Hakim, "Safety Gap Grows Wider Between S.U.V.'s and Cars," *New York Times,* 17 August 2004, Business Day section, p. C1.

2. http://seattlepi.nwsource.com.

3. www.epa.gov/globalwarming.

4. *Business Week,* 23 February 2004; cited online at http://www.honkathummers.com/faq/.

5. Danny Hakim, "In Their Hummers, Right Beside Uncle Sam," *New York Times,* 5 April 2003, cited online at http://www.epic-usa.org.

6. *Businesss Week,* 23 February 2004; cited online at http://www.honkathummers.com/faq/.

7. See William P. Cunningham, Mary Ann Cunningham, and Barbara Saigo, *Environmental Science: A Global Concern* (Boston: McGraw Hill, 2005), p. 432ff.

8. Most of the information on the hybrids is from author LHN's experience driving the family Prius; the rest is from Cunningham, Cunningham, and Saigo, *Environmental Science,* p. 433. The authors claim that the hybrids can go 625 miles without refueling; that's probably true for the two-seater Honda Insight, but for the Prius, 500 is probably tops.

9. Michael Elliott, "Kicking the Big-Car Habit," *Time,* 27 September 2004, p. 5.

10. Tim Appenzeller, "The End of Cheap Oil," *National Geographic* (June 2004): 88.

11. Ibid., pp. 88–89.

12. Ibid., p. 89

13. That fact, and much of the other information in this section, except as otherwise noted, is taken directly from Cunningham, Cunningham, and Saigo, *Environmental Science* (hereinafter C2S), pp. 407–452. Page citations will be given for any information worth checking up on.

14. C2S, p. 410.

15. Ibid., p. 411.

16. Loc. cit.

17. Loc. cit.

18. Ibid., p. 413

19. Jad Mouawad, "Irrelevant? OPEC is Sitting Pretty," *New York Times,* 3 October 2004, Week in Review section, pp. 1, 3.

20. John Cassidy, "Pump Dreams: Is Energy Independence an Impossible Goal?" *New Yorker,* 8 October 2004, p. 42.

21. Mouawad, "Irrelevant.".

22. Thomas L. Friedman, "The Battle of the Pump: Guzzling oil and Fueling Terrorism," Op-Ed, *New York Times,* 7 October 2004.

23. Appenzeller, "End," p. 88.

24. C2S, p. 412.

25. C2S, p. 416. The reference is to Eisenhower's "Atoms for Peace" speech to the United Nations in 1953.

26. Descriptions are available in C2S, p. 419.

27. C2S, p. 429.

28. C2S, p. 430

29. Dylan Loeb McClain, "The House Electric: Cozy but Voracious," *New York Times,* 26 September 2004, Ideas and Trends section, p. 12.

30. C2S, p. 431.

31. "Looking for Energy in the Campaign," *New York Times* lead editorial, 13 September 2004.

32. C2S, p. 447.

33. C2S, p. 429.

34. Ibid.

35. C2S, pp. 448–49.

36. C2S, p. 435.

37. C2S, p. 438.

38. C2S, p. 439.

39. C2S, p. 441.

40. C2S, p. 451.

41. C2S, p. 450.

42. Seth Dunn, *Micropower: The Next Electrical Era,* Worldwatch Paper 151, July 2000, pp. 30–31, citing Amory Lovins, "Energy Strategy: The Road Not Taken?" *Foreign Affairs* (October 1976).

43. Janet L. Sawin, *Mainstreaming Renewable Energy in the 21st Century,* Worldwatch Paper 169, May 2004.

10

Biological Diversity

Saving the Uniquenesses
of the World

INTRODUCTION: THE BEGINNING OF THE
END OR JUST IN TIME?

There is a lot of pressure on Anastasia and Robeki to procreate. There is a desire for their bloodlines to be continued. Many people are listening, hoping, waiting for word of an upcoming blessed event. At this writing, the two have been together on and off for almost a year and a half —since April 2003. They like each other well enough. They are compatible, with an obvious animal attraction between them. But, still, no word of a birth in the future.

Anastasia and Robeki, ages 7 and 10 years, respectively, are Amur (Siberian) tigers, *Panthera tigris altaica,* and they have, in fact, mated numerous times over the past few months; why the pairing has been unfruitful is being examined by the conservation program that manages them. The number of Amur tigers in the wild is dangerously low—too low to be confident that Amur tigers will survive into the next century.

Anastasia and Robeki

Tyger, Tyger burning bright,
In the forests of the night:
What immortal hand or eye,
Dare frame thy fearful symmetry?[1]

Anastasia and Robeki currently live in *Connecticut's Beardsley Zoo*[2] in Bridgeport, Connecticut, far from the native land of their species. Robeki has lived in Bridgeport since December 1997, Anastasia since December 2002. They are part of a Species Survival Plan (SSP) of the American Zoo and Aquarium Association (AZA), formerly the American Association of Zoological Parks and Aquariums (AAZPA). The Amur Tiger SSP is itself part of a partially networked group of international breeding programs, both *in situ* (native ecosystems) and *ex situ* (facilities such as zoos and aquariums), for endangered species.

Like other Amur tigers, Anastasia and Robeki are medium to pale orange with dark brown stripes. They have white chests and bellies and a thick white collar of fur. At their last weigh-ins, about two years ago, Anastasia weighed about 230 pounds and Robeki between 350 and 400 pounds.[3] Both are on the small side for their subspecies, which is generally the largest of the five tiger subspecies. Male Amur tigers may weigh up to 660 pounds, females 200 to 370 pounds.[4]

Anastasia and Robeki have traded, albeit not by their own choosing, the coniferous, mixed, and temperate deciduous forests of their Russian, Chinese, and North Korean homeland, where they would likely roam a combined area of at least 448 square miles, for a 3,100-square-foot (about 0.0001-square-mile) double pen: "the territory size of Amur tigers is quite large, ranging from 100–400 km^2 (39–154 mile^2) for females to 800–1,000 km^2 (309–390 mile^2) for males."[5] Instead of hunting wild boar and elk, they eat Nebraska Brand Feline Diet (horse-meat based, vitamin- and mineral-fortified), prepared for them in the zoo's kitchen.

For diversion from their curtailed lifestyle, Robeki and Anastasia rely on the zoo staff to provide them with enrichment activities—from large rubber balls to cardboard containers scented and disguised as prey and containing "treats." Elizabeth Kudlinski, tiger keeper at Connecticut's Beardsley Zoo until mid-autumn 2004, provides daily and varied enrichment for the tigers. Enrichment is provided for the "indoor" portion of each day, supplemented with less regular outdoor enrichment. Elizabeth explains, "Always indoor enrichment! They are in for a larger portion of each day than they are out—8 hours out, 16 hours in. They don't sleep for the whole 16 hours, even though they are cats!" The tigers are very fond of cedar chips in their areas; they do not like catnip. Other enrichment items include bamboo, beef knucklebones for gnawing, and "bloodsicles"—just what it sounds like: frozen blood! Also enriching are the rearrangement of the pens, including closing gates to limit each animal's access to one side or the other of the double pen or grant full access to both sides for both tigers. Finally, zoo interns are invariably given the task of coming up with new enrichment experiences and activities for the animals—fresh brainstorming for fresh approaches.[6]

There is an electricity to the experience of encountering a tiger, such as Robeki or Anastasia, at close range and for the first time. The experience is even more astounding if an unseen tiger suddenly materializes as its feline motion breaks up the camouflage of tiger stripes in stripes of tall grass. For most visitors, the tiger encounter experience is literally breathtaking. One sucks in the breath and holds it for a moment, standing still and wide-eyed, heart quickening, as the cat passes closely, even though a barrier separates *Homo sapiens* and *Panthera tigris*. One is stopped in place to marvel at the massive head, the beautiful eyes, the dense fur, the enormous paws, the silent stealth and grace of movement, the smoothly rippling muscles, the large and menacing, ivory-colored teeth.

The two tigers are popular with zoo visitors, and people tend to be thrilled to be able to see them. At times, though, a zoo guest questions, cries, rails, complains, goes away angry after viewing what he or she sees as a tiny tiger exhibit. There is a reaction—an objection—intellectual, visceral, or both, to the tigers being caged. The more savvy viewer—savvy about the state of the world's wildlife—while possibly sharing the anger just described, may also be willing to believe two things: that captivity is currently a necessary evil if we are to save endangered species and that professionally managed, accredited zoos, like Connecticut's Beardsley Zoo, have long since transformed from potential devastators of wildlife to centers for conservation, education, animal welfare, and research, in partnership with the scientific community and others in universities, conservation organizations, museums, governments, and research institutions. That savvier viewer, if not of a certain radical animal-rights bent, may direct anger at humankind, and not at the zoo.

Here is how tiger keeper Elizabeth Kudlinski speaks of the tigers when she allows her personal thoughts and feelings to surface:

> I love the cats. I love the tigers. It is really cool to see up close something that would feed on me; well, they wouldn't eat me, but they would play with me for a while! This teaches me respect.
>
> Up close, it is just, WOW!
>
> Sometimes I am sad about penning them up. But then I remember that it has to be done. They are ambassadors for their species. I give them as good a life as possible.
>
> It is great to take care of beings that aren't going to do what I want all the time. This makes me humble and respectful at the same time, because there really are things we can't control![7]

AZA Accreditation

For a U.S. zoo or aquarium to be accredited by the AZA, the zoo must meet many strict criteria, including many concerning animal care. An 81-page document on accreditation standards outlines the requirements.[8] Among the animal care criteria a zoo or aquarium must generally adopt, are a vision[9] and four basic missions, which, newly revised, are conservation, education, research, and excellence in animal welfare (formerly conservation, education, recreation, and research).[10] In some modern institutions not accredited by the AZA, some of the animal care standards and/or one or more of these missions may be lacking. Of some 2,000 licensed exhibitors in the United States, 214 are currently AZA accredited. An elaboration of the AZA mission is as follows:

Our professional association's mission is to provide its members and their
visitors the best possible services through:

- Establishing and maintaining excellent professional standards in all AZA
  Institutions through its accreditation program;

- Establishing and promoting high standards of animal care and welfare;

- Promoting and facilitating collaborative conservation and research programs;

- Advocating effective governmental policies for our members;

- Strengthening and promoting conservation education programs for our
  public and professional development for our members, and;

- Raising awareness of the collective impact of its members and their
  programs.[11]

Michael Hutchins, Director of the Department of Conservation Science of the
AZA and current holder of the William Conway Chair, describes the mem-
bership of the AZA as "constantly raising the bar," regarding the vision, mission, procedures, and processes of the AZA.[12]

The Bronx Zoo,[13] member of the AZA, run by the Wildlife Conservation
Society (WCS) (formerly the New York Zoological Society), has been in the
business of conservation since it opened its gates to the public in 1899—
counting among its successes the saving of the American bison in the first
decades of the 1900s. Yet even here, a visitor to the Bronx Zoo can see a pro-
gression in society's attitude toward wildlife, as reflected in zoo philosophy and
behavior.

Today, the thing that stares me in the face every waking hour, like a grisly
spectre with bloody fang and claw, is the extermination of species. To me
that is a horrible thing. (Dr. William T. Hornaday, director, New York
Zoological Park [The Bronx Zoo], 1914)[14]

Modern zoos, zoos of the past 200 years, have been through three phases.
Entering the Bronx Zoo[15] by the Fordham Road Gate, and approaching the
fountain straight ahead, the visitor is surrounded by a set of three concentric
"rings," the nearest a set of older buildings, that speak of the zoo days of cages
and "houses"—the primate house, the lion house, the bird house, the elephant
house, and so on. The creatures are there for our fancy, our amusement, our
enjoyment; for a zoo, the animals can be status symbols, collected from the
wild—living trophies. The World Zoo Organization, the IUDZG, calls this the
"menagerie" or "living natural history cabinet" stage, characteristic of zoos in
the nineteenth century. The next tier depicts the use, still with us in many
cases, of "displays," an animal and a pond or an animal and a tree or small stand
of trees—static, almost dioramalike. This tier, characteristic of the twentieth-
century "zoological parks" or "living museums," serves to teach us about animals,
perhaps about ecosystems; they are there so we can learn. The third tier, the
most modern, is the "habitat," catering as best it can to the needs of the animals;
this level tries to re-create the animals' natural environment and prides itself
on not collecting animals unnecessarily from the wild to help conserve

their numbers. Such efforts illustrate the twenty-first century trend of the "conservation center" or the "environmental resource center."[16]

At this third level, the needs of the human have disappeared. As described by one of the authors of this text:

> I took my grandson to the Bronx Zoo because he wanted to see the tiger. I had to pay extra to take the special train to pass the tiger exhibit. We got to the tiger exhibit. No tiger. Where was the tiger? we asked. *Sleeping.* Sleeping? Can you wake him up? My grandson wants to see him! *No, can't do that; you will have to come back another time—then, maybe you can see the tiger.*[17]

Outrage! And then, an epiphany occurs—priorities have changed. Animals like tigers at the Bronx Zoo and Anastasia and Robeki in their smaller enclosure at Connecticut's Beardsley Zoo, have needs, like the need for privacy. When these animal welfare needs are put first, the health, including the reproductive ability, of the animals, reaps the benefits.

What Does "Endangered" Really Mean?

What makes a species "endangered?" In the United States, according to the Endangered Species Act of 1973: "The term 'endangered species' means any species which is in danger of extinction throughout all or a significant portion of its range other than a species of the Class Insecta determined by the Secretary to constitute a pest whose protection under the provisions of this Act would present an overwhelming and overriding risk to man."[18]

What about Anastasia and Robeki? Why is their subspecies endangered? Why is the entire tiger species listed as endangered? The World Conservation Union, IUCN for short (formerly, the International Union for Conservation of Nature and Natural Resources), has for four decades maintained "Red Lists" of threatened species, lists of critically endangered, endangered, and vulnerable species. In 1996, the IUCN Red List justified its inclusion of the Amur tiger, one of five extant subspecies of tiger, as follows:

> The Amur tiger's effective population size is estimated at approximately 250 mature individuals, with a declining trend, and no subpopulation estimated to contain more than 50 mature individuals.[19]

Thanks to *in situ* efforts in Russia, the Amur Tiger SSP and other endeavors, the numbers of the Amur tiger have climbed a bit in the past 8 years.

According to the *AZA Tiger Species Survival Plan (SSP), Five-Year Plan (2001–2005):*

> The Bali, Caspian and Javan tiger subspecies were lost between 1937 and 1980, producing an extinction rate of one subspecies every 15 years.

> All five recognized subspecies of tigers need conservation action:
> *Panthera tigris altaica* (Amur tiger, found in the Russian Far East, northern China, and northern North Korea), *P.t. amoyensis* (South China tiger, found in central China), *P.t. corbetti* (Indochinese tiger, found in southern

China, Vietnam, Laos, Thailand, Cambodia, Myanmar, and peninsular Malaysia), *P.t. sumatrae* (Sumatran tiger, found only in Sumatra, Indonesia), and *P.t. tigris* (Bengal tiger, found in India, southern Nepal, Bhutan, Bangladesh and Myanmar).[20]

E. O. Wilson, premier authority on biological diversity and the need for its preservation, discusses that small population size may be a problem for one or more reasons, such as inbreeding depression, effects of predation on small populations, and natural disasters that can wipe out the remaining individuals of a tiny population at one stroke: when a population has genetic weaknesses, "inbreeding starts to lower population growth when the number of breeding adults falls below five hundred. It becomes severe as the number dips below fifty and can easily deliver the coup de grâce to a species when the number reaches ten."[21]

With about 1.5–1.7 million described species living on Earth, and an actual species number of 3 to 60 or more times the described species, there is no across-the-board—across-species, we might say—criterion for a critically endangered, endangered, or vulnerable species—the three international categories of "threatened" species found in the IUCN's Red Lists. In 2000, the IUCN Species Survival Commission (SSC), struggling to form better and better methods of analysis for determining threatened species, compiled the *IUCN Red List Categories and Criteria Version 3.1.*[22]

The Red List Criteria are spelled out carefully in about 30 pages, including five careful criteria for each category. For example, there is general grave concern if a species drops to a single population or populations (groups of interbreeding individuals in one area at one time) of fewer than 50, 250, or 1,000 healthy, fertile adults, respectively, for critically endangered, endangered, and vulnerable status. Healthy, fertile adults form the "effective population size."[23] As numbers dwindle, populations are at greater risk of extinction because of a wide variety of factors, including habitat alteration or destruction, disease outbreaks, impacts of invasive species, and more. With fewer individuals to absorb the impacts of these types of disturbances, small populations are extremely vulnerable. Scientists use the terms "critically endangered," "endangered," and "vulnerable" to reflect how close a given species is thought to be to extinction.

Biodiversity: Biological Diversity

We are talking about biological diversity, or biodiversity—the variety of life forms on our planet. In 1980, Thomas Lovejoy used the term *biological diversity*. In 1986, at the time of the National Forum on BioDiversity in Washington, D.C., sponsored by the National Academy of Sciences and the Smithsonian Institution, E. O. Wilson shortened the term to *BioDiversity,* to make the term easier to use. By popular use, the term soon became *biodiversity*.

Biodiversity refers to the variety of life on Earth. Biodiversity can be discussed at many levels—from diversity of genetic information in an organism to the number of species in an area (or in the world) to the diversity of ecosystems on a continent. In fact, these are the three levels most often discussed.

In this chapter, we are most often referring to "species diversity"—how many species there are in a particular place or in the world.

WHY DOES BIOLOGICAL DIVERSITY MATTER?

Why do we care about biological diversity, the variety of life on Earth? Why do we care about a single species, such as the tiger? With over a million described species in the world, why do we care if a few go extinct? Some reasons that have been proposed include the following:

- Because when a species is gone, it's gone. It is not coming back
- Because, some would say, each form of life has its own right to exist
- Because we use other life for food, clothing, recreation, and more
- Because it refreshes our beings to be around other life
- Because we owe it to future generations
- Because there is value in living things, including value we have not yet discovered
- **Because we can't live without biological diversity. We are so interconnected with the rest of the natural world that we truly will not survive without it. We depend on biological diversity for food, shelter, clean water and air, and for quality of life**

We shall consider some of these reasons in a bit more depth, as we go along.

The Charismatic Megafauna

Remember William Blake's poetic evocation of the tiger, the last stanza of which heads this chapter:

> Tyger Tyger, burning bright, In the forests of the night:
> What immortal hand or eye, Could frame thy fearful symmetry?
> In what distant deeps or skies, Burnt the fire of thine eyes!
> On what wings dare he aspire! What the hand, dare seize the fire?

Some folks like, are fascinated by, are drawn to, snails or bacteria or lichens, worms or algae or protozoans, mosses or liverworts—and other such relatively unsung species. However, most humans gravitate toward the big, "sexy," species—macroscopic plants and animals, flora and fauna, especially animals, especially large, furry ones. Whether cuddly, awe-inspiring, gentle and strong, or fearsome and strong, we are drawn to the charismatic megafauna. Our histories and mythologies are intertwined with theirs as far back as the caves of Lascaux and beyond. Even without the critical roles these creatures play in their environments, our lives would be the poorer without them. Wilson talks about our being drawn to other life as "biophilia" and, in fact, wrote a book about it.[24]

Indeed our fascination with large animals goes back millennia. In the Hebrew Bible, we read about behemoths (elephants) in the book of Job:

> Behold now behemoth, which I made with thee; he eateth grass as an ox. . . . His bones *are as* strong pieces of brass; his bones *are* like bars of iron. . . . Behold, he drinketh up a river, *and* hasteth not: he trusteth that he can draw up Jordan into his mouth. He taketh it with his eyes: *his* nose pierceth through snares. (Job 40: 15–24)[25]

We encounter leviathans (which some researchers presume to be whales and others are certain are crocodiles[26]) in Job, Isaiah, and Psalms:

> Thou didst divide the sea by thy strength: thou brakest the heads of the dragons in the waters.
> Thou brakest the heads of leviathan in pieces, *and* gavest him *to be* meat to the people inhabiting the wilderness. (Psalms 74: 13–14)[27]

(This last also speaks to our long-standing tendencies to fear, conquer, and use nature.)

Some who care about the environment are critical of a strong focus on the conservation of charismatic megafauna, reasoning, with much justification, that there are so many more small and microscopic species that are disappearing, and so many more vanishing nonanimal species than animal species. Species survival plans and similar programs in other countries do not work to save every species, or even every species under the "megafauna" category. However, they are driven by carefully thought-out motives and selection criteria.

AZA conservation biologist Ruth Allard gives current figures: "As of August 2004, there are 106 SSPs, covering a total of 161 species (for example, the Baboon SSP covers five different species)."[28] Currently there is only one invertebrate SSP for a species of snail.

In the mid-1980s it was estimated that if all available spaces in U.S. zoos were devoted to SSPs, then about 300 species might be able to be maintained. Apply that calculation to zoos worldwide, and 900 species might be able to be maintained.[29] Contrast those numbers with 5,483 animal species red-listed as threatened by the IUCN, and add to that 6,776 species of red-listed threatened plants, algae, and lichens.[30] Even if it were their express aim SSPs and their international counterparts cannot save all species. Beyond that, what would we do with 900 or more zoo-bound species? That brings us to wider issues of habitat conservation, and more will be said about this in several places in the chapter.

When AZA's Taxon Advisory Groups (TAGs) are considering species for SSPs, good candidates pass a kind of triage. A species that is likely to become extinct despite human efforts to save it is generally not selected. A species that is likely to "make it" on its own or by other means—in a reserve setting, for example—is generally not selected. A species that will benefit from SSP intervention is a good candidate.[31] The hope of the TAG planners is that SSP-level management will raise awareness about the needs of the SSP species, drawing attention and resources to conservation action on behalf of the species in the wild.

In addition, SSPs

> are being implemented as part of a more holistic effort to preserve species in their natural habitats. Thus, the SSP program seeks to assist worldwide efforts in wildlife and ecosystem conservation through public education, scientific research, training and technology transfer, fund-raising to support habitat preservation, field conservation efforts, . . .[32]

The preponderance of vertebrates in SSPs has two rationales. First,

> Filling key positions in their environments, these animals require considerable space to roam and have relatively low reproductive rates, making them among the most likely species to become extinct.[33]

Second, they tend to be "flagship species," species that will attract public attention that may then support conservation of entire habitat areas.

> For example, the Golden Lion Tamarin SSP focused the public's attention on these colorful, charismatic primates and thus on the plight of the endangered Atlantic Forest ecosystem in Brazil. Areas now under government and private protection provide a haven for a number of species in addition to the tamarin.[34]

Audubon's Editor-at-large, Ted Williams, explains this rationale for one species in particular: "[Florida] panthers are just a little part of what makes panther country so special. They're an 'umbrella species.' That is, you can't have them without having most everything else." [35]

This view is shared by many biologists, but is not without counterpoint. At a recent meeting of invertebrate biologists at the American Museum of Natural History in Manhattan, the reverse was argued: If we preserve the small organisms, the large ones will survive. Dr. Sacha Spector, of the AMNH and Columbia University writes:

> The basis for the assertion is the emerging understanding that the finer spatial patterning of endemism in invertebrates, as compared to either vertebrates or plants, requires a more comprehensive conservation strategy and/or protected area system.[36]

Dr. Spector is saying that, according to a growing body of evidence, when we protect a habitat range for a vertebrate species or a plant , that action does not necessarily properly encompass the ranges of invertebrates for those ecosystems. On the other hand, when we protect a habitat range for an invertebrate species, there is a stronger likelihood of, at the same time, protecting the ranges of the vertebrates from those ecosystems.[37]

Other Biodiversity Groups, Levels of Biodiversity

Although the community of biologists is in the process of revamping what we call the "phylogenetic tree" of life—the family tree of life—based on molecular biology data gathered during the past few decades, it is convenient to describe life in terms of a few major groups. These groups are based on a five-kingdom system of classification proposed by Robert H. Whittaker in 1969 and both embraced and popularized by such biologists as Lynn Margulis, who recognized this as an insightful leap from the older dual-kingdom system of plants and animals.

Monerans are bacteria—of these archaebacteria have more ancient characteristics and eubacteria more modern characteristics. They are one-celled. Whether divided into two kingdoms or kept as one, monerans are the smallest of cells—as with most cells, they are not visible to the naked eye. They come into view, at least with respect to their shape, when magnified about 1,000 times. Alone among the five major groups discussed here, their cells do not have membrane-bound nuclei. They are the modern organisms that give us the best idea of what the first living things may have been like. They are essential to recycling matter on Earth.

Protists, depending on who is doing the grouping, are mostly one-celled organisms, but bigger than monerans and with membrane-bound nuclei. We think of these organisms as protozoans (such as amoebas), micro-algae, macro-algae (seaweeds, certainly not one-celled!), and slime molds (named because of their functional similarities to fungi). In their ecosystems, members of this group run the gamut from "consumer" to "producer" to "decomposer." The former protistan kingdom is currently being divided into a number of kingdoms.

Fungi are the one-celled yeasts and the many-celled mushrooms and other molds. Similarly to bacteria, fungi are important matter-recyclers, or decomposers.

Plants are macroscopic, multicellular organisms. The overwhelming majority of plants photosynthesize, as do the micro- and macro-algae and some groups of monerans, turning sun energy into energy usable both by the photosynthesizers themselves and by those organisms, such as ourselves, that do not photosynthesize.

Animals include sponges; corals, sea anemones, and jellyfish; various parasitic and free-living worms; insects and other arthropods; mollusks; echinoderms; vertebrates, and a number of other groups. It is useful to note that any animal that is not a vertebrate is an invertebrate; thus, invertebrates include some 20-plus major groups of animals. Although all living things in ecosystems are consumers and decomposers in some respects, animals constitute major consumers.

Ecosystems and Biodiversity

Each area of a characteristic grouping of organisms can be thought of as an ecosystem—desert, temperate deciduous forest, tropical rainforest, grassland, and so on. An ecosystem consists of the community of living things that interact with each other as well as the abiotic environment—air, land, and water, with which they interact.

Ecosystems vary greatly in their characteristics. Possibly the most productive (in terms of sun energy converted to chemical energy stored in life) and probably the most diverse (in terms of species) are the tropical rainforests.

Many have estimated that over half the extant species of plants and animals reside in the moist tropical forests:

> ... the greatest diversity of life, as measured by the numbers of species, occurs in habitats with the most year-round solar energy, the widest exposure of ice-free terrain, the most varied terrain, and the greatest climatic stability. ... Thus the equatorial rainforests of the Asian, African, and South American continents possess by far the largest number of plants and animal species.[38]

When we cut out too much of an ecosystem or damage it in some other way, say by removing a species through hunting or gathering or pollution, that ecosystem generally functions less well than it did previously. Energy may not be taken in as efficiently. Matter surely does not cycle the same way. We have likely diminished the food source of one or more organisms, and this tends to have a domino effect of tumbling—i.e., eliminating—other species. On the other hand, when we disrupt an ecosystem, we may cause some species, formerly in check or in balance, to proliferate, introducing a new set of problems. Again, E. O. Wilson observes:

> When we alter the biosphere in any direction, we move the environment away from the delicate dance of biology. When we destroy ecosystems and extinguish species, we degrade the greatest heritage this planet has to offer and thereby threaten our own existence.[39]

And, lest there be any doubt, one reason we might care about ecosystem disruptions is because we are physically, intimately, literally a part of them—part of the matter and energy webs and chains and flow. We gather our particles and energy from the other members of ecosystems and we return these to them. Not only that,

> We evolved here, one among many species, across millions of years, and exist as one organic miracle linked to others. The natural environment we treat with such unnecessary ignorance and recklessness was our cradle and nursery, our school, and remains our one and only home. To its special conditions we are intimately adapted in every one of the bodily fibers and biochemical transactions that gives us life.[40]

We are part of the very ecosystems we are destroying. We may be losing 3 species an hour—about 27,000 species a year.[41]

HOW SERIOUS IS THIS? VERY.

Rates, Causes, and Recovery

What's the fuss, though? Roughly 98 percent of all the species that have ever lived are extinct.[42] And what's the loss of a few species if it means higher human standard of living and comfort and prosperity? The fuss is about the

RATE of extinction. And the either-or presented here—comfort and species loss versus discomfort and species abundance—breaks down in analysis. For evidence, consider the earlier arguments concerning ecosystems.

In 1992, E. O. Wilson wrote:

> If past species have lived on the order of a million years . . . , a common figure for some groups documented in the fossil record, it follows that the normal "background" extinction rate is about one species per million species a year. Human activity has increased extinction between 1,000 and 10,000 times over this level in the rain forest by reduction in area alone.[43]

Others have estimated and come up with a lower current extinction rate. Stuart Pimm, formerly of Columbia University, now at Duke University's Nicholas School of the Environment, and others used habitat destruction rate and paleontological fossil data to make estimates and " . . . reported that the current extinction rate is 100 to 1,000 times the 'natural background rates,' while "paleontologist David M. Raup of the University of Chicago contends, " 'There are very serious problems with that comparison.' He argues that it's likely that Pimm vastly underestimated the rates of extinction in the fossil record and thus is unduly pessimistic about the future."[44]

Wilson holds fast in 2002:

> How much extinction is occurring today? Researchers generally agree that it is catastrophically high, somewhere between one thousand and ten thousand times the rate before human beings began to exert a significant pressure on the environment.[45]

In fact, Wilson goes on to discuss three distinct estimation methods by which his higher rates can be calculated.[46]

How much will we lose? More than most of us might guess, but the actual numbers are contingent upon our actions now and into the future:

> If the decision were taken today to freeze all conservation efforts at their current level while allowing the same rates of deforestation and other forms of environmental destruction to continue, ... at least a fifth of the species of plants and animals would be gone or committed to early extinction by 2030, and a half by the end of the century.[47]

An all-out effort starting now, concentrating on saving areas of high diversity, could leave us with three-quarters of our current species intact.[48] Pimm, referred to above, reaches a conclusion similar to that of Wilson:

> Only about 5 percent of the planet's surface lies in protected reserves, notes Pimm. If human activity destroys or greatly modifies 90 to 95 percent of the land outside reserves, only half the planet's species will survive, he says. That level of habitat destruction may occur as soon as 2100, he says.[49]

Why is biodiversity disappearing? Some biologists cite, "human population" as the underlying cause. Others point to habitat destruction—in turn, caused, of course, by the human population. The prime causes of biodiversity loss are summed up by the acronym HIPPO:

Habitat destruction

Invasive species

Pollution

Population (human)

Overharvesting

For many conservationists the final two terms of the acronym are *poaching* (here included with overharvesting) and *overpopulation*, which highlights the strain that poaching has placed on many species in the wild.

> The prime mover of the incursive forces around the world is the second P in HIPPO—too many people consuming too much of the land and sea apace and the resources they contain. . . . the forces other than human population growth descend in order of importance in the same sequence as the HIPPO letters, from habitat removal as the most destructive and overharvesting the least. . . . [50]

Note the importance of habitat loss to species loss. Part of a body of work, called the theory of island biogeography, states as follows: a 90 percent loss of area in an ecosystem generally leads to 50 percent loss of species in an ecosystem. Conservation biologists are especially worried about the loss of the tropical forests:

> Of all forms of ongoing habitat destruction, the most consequential is the clearing of forests. The maximum extent of the world's forests was reached six thousand to eight thousand years ago, at the dawn of agriculture and following the retreat of the continental glaciers. Today, due to the universal spread of agriculture, only about half of the original forest cover remains, and that is being cut at an accelerating rate.[51]

> The headquarters of global biodiversity are the tropical rainforests. Although they cover only about 6 percent of the land surface, their terrestrial and aquatic habitats contain more than half the known species of organisms. They are also the leading abattoir of extinction, shattered into fragments that are then being severely adulterated or erased one by one. Of all ecosystems, they are rivaled in rate of decline only by the temperate rainforests and tropical dry forests.[52]

The current rate of extinction, whether 100 or 10,000 times the background rate of extinction, is said by many, many biologists to place us squarely in "the sixth great extinction." "Sixth" because, according to the fossil record, in the past 450 million years there have been five other major mass extinctions, with the fifth being the KT extinction that led to the end of the dinosaurs—each of these five extinctions taking 200,000 to several million years for life to recover the previous level of biodiversity, and each having the resulting restored biodiversity be significantly different from the pre-extinction life.

An important difference between previous extinctions and the current purported extinction is that, should our species survive, biodiversity will probably never recover, since we are likely to continue to apply HIPPO-type pressures to Earth.

Recovery of biodiversity levels, should it occur, would take much longer than any human lifetime. Accordingly, in the immediate future, "a mass extinction will result in a bleak world. Scarce in large mammals, it will be overrun with species that multiply in the face of adversity—mostly organisms that we consider weeds and pests. It's the grasses, insects, and rodents that will endure."[53]

The Tigers

Let us return to Anastasia and Robeki's kin. . . . According to the *AZA Tiger Species Survival Plan (SSP), Five-Year Plan (2001–2005),* an estimated 4,400 to 7,700 tigers, of the five extant subspecies, survived in the wild in 1998.[54] In addition to that, there are tigers in captivity:

> There are about 1,100 studbook-registered tigers held in about 225 captive facilities worldwide: 515 Amur, 235 Sumatran, 250 Bengal, 50 South China, and 50 Indochinese. . . . A large number of unregistered tigers are kept in circuses, private facilities and nonparticipating zoos throughout the world, and because of their unknown lineages, will not contribute to any regional captive program. Because these tigers are not registered and are not in a managed program, their numbers and sites are not tracked.[55]

Incidentally, there may be as many as 10,000 privately owned tigers in the United States, about twice the number of tigers in the wild. Because of the problems just noted above, it may be impossible, or even detrimental, to include these animals in such programs as species survival plans, yet such options are discussed among those interested and involved in saving the tigers.

In 2003, the AZA tiger SSP, which currently manages the Amur tiger, the Sumatran tiger, and the Indochinese tiger in the SSP, estimates 400 wild adult Amur tigers inhabit the Russian Far East, on the Russian–Chinese border and in northeast China.[56] According to the AZA annual report of 2003:

> This subspecies is considered critically endangered by the IUCN/SSC Cat Specialist Group and, like all five tiger subspecies, is threatened primarily by habitat loss and fragmentation. Poaching pressure apparently has declined recently due to intensive anti-poaching activities.[57]

Of the 500 or so studbook registered (captive) Amur tigers in zoos worldwide, between 150 and 155 of these tigers in 55–60 U.S. and Canadian facilities are in the Tiger SSP at any one time.[58] The Felid Taxon Advisory group (TAG) currently allots 450 spaces for the tiger SSP. The tigers in the SSP are managed for genetic diversity, which may necessitate sometimes importing animals from the wild.[59]

All five tiger subspecies are in need of conservation interventions. All but the South China tiger currently have programs devoted to their conservation.

Europe, North America, Australia, Indonesia, Malaysia, Singapore, Thailand, and Vietnam all have captive programs.[60]

Other Species

Referring to some of the most endangered species, E. O. Wilson describes a "Hundred Heartbeat Club," animal species with fewer than 100 living members. These include, among others:

> . . . the Philippine eagle, the Hawaiian crow, the Spix's macaw, the Chinese river dolphin, the Javan rhino, the Hainan gibbon, the Vancouver Island marmot, the Texas pipefish, and the Indian Ocean coelacanth. Among many others lined up for early admission are the giant panda, the mountain gorilla, the Sumatran orangutan, the Sumatran rhino, the golden bamboo lemur, the Mediterranean monk seal, the Philippine crocodile, and the barndoor skate, the latter one of the largest fishes of the North Atlantic.[61]

And animals, of course, are not the only endangered groups:

> At least 976 tree species out of the 100,000 known to science worldwide are in similar difficulty. In one extreme category—so close to the edge that conservationists call them the "living dead"—are three species, including the Chinese hornbeam *(Carpinus putoensis),* each of which survives as a single individual.[62]

One might think that food crops would be exempt from such perils. But even here there are grave concerns. As many biologists are aware, modern agricultural methods have driven food crops to ever-increasingly narrow sets of genetics. Such things as seed banks exist, to try to stave off the genetic and species loss, but a power failure here or a natural disaster there, even war and looting, may threaten some of these. Here is but one example:

> In the 1950's, Chinese farmers grew about 10,000 varieties of wheat. Two decades later . . . the number had fallen to 1,000. India experienced a similar loss of rice diversity over the past 3 decades. . . . [63]

In Dollars and Cents and Beyond

It is theoretically possible to frame environmental concerns in economic terms. What would we have to pay for the services nature provides? Clean water, clean air, soil enrichment, waste treatment, fuel production, lumber production, pollination, and more? In 1997, a group of economists and environmental scientists did just that:

> Drawing from multiple databases, they estimated the contribution to be $33 trillion or more each year. This amount is nearly twice the 1992 combined gross national product (GNP) of all countries in the world, or gross world product, of $18 trillion.[64]

Wilson and others point out, however, that it is simply impossible to replace ALL of nature's services with artificial, human-created technologies. This makes the value of nature truly priceless.[65,66]

There are other economic issues to consider. For example, what do we lose when we do not take care of a commodity we expect to be in abundant supply year after year? One of the authors of this text recalls sitting in an ecology lecture in 1977, incredulous that the professor[67] was discussing overfishing the ocean! Overfishing the ocean? Maybe that sounds plausible today, but then it was unbelievable.[68] In 2004, with a $2.5 billion U.S. fish catch and an $82 billion worldwide fish catch annually, the worldwide catch stood at about 90 million tons, a catch that wouldn't grow—and will not, "simply because the amount of ocean is fixed and the organisms it can generate is static," and "fisheries of the western North Atlantic, the Black Sea, and portions of the Caribbean have collapsed."[69]

Those who think that aquaculture can make an enormous difference here may need to think again:

> This "fin-and-shell revolution" necessitates the conversion of valuable wetland habitats, which are nurseries for marine life. To feed the captive populations, fodder must be diverted from crop production. Thus aquaculture competes with other human activity for productive land while reducing natural habitat.[70]

Sometimes we have recognized the value of the ecosystem services provided by a biodiverse area. Into the late twentieth century, the Catskills mountain watershed provided clean water for New York City and bottled water for a large area. Development, with its attendant loss of forest caused "sewage and agricultural runoff . . . [to adulterate] the water until it fell below Environmental Protection Agency standards."[71] What was New York City to do?

> . . . build a filtration plant to replace the Catskill Watershed, at $6 billion to $8 billion capital cost, followed by $300 million annual running costs; or . . . restore the Catskills Watershed to somewhere near its original purification capacity for $1 billion, with subsequently very low maintenance costs.[72]

They purchased forested land and subsidized septic tank upgrades. Now New Yorkers can enjoy both the forested area and clean water, with the flood control provided by the forested area, to boot.

Environmental Economics is serious and plays a key role in sorting out and responding to environmental concerns. Alan Randall, professor of agricultural economics at the Ohio State University and fellow of the American Agricultural Economics Association, was part of the 1986 National Forum on BioDiversity, which gave birth to the term, as now used, "biodiversity." His paper on the topic is published in *BioDiversity* (E. O. Wilson, editor), the proceedings of that forum.[73] Randall points to the importance of mainstream economics, typically utilitarian, anthropocentric, and instrumentalist, in the critical assessment of environmental issues:

The meaningful questions concern the value lost by the disappearance of a chip of biodiversity here and a chunk there. For this smaller question, it is often possible to provide an economic answer that is useful and reasonably reliable.[74]

Randall expects opposition from those who hold more biocentric views of the environment, and he elaborates on the usefulness of mainstream accounting to all environmental veiwpoints, particularly with the "extension and completion of a utilitarian account."[75] Here, accounting

include[s] things that enter human preference structures but are not exchanged in organized markets. This extension and completion of a utilitarian account, where preservation of biodiversity is at issue, is useful because it shows that commercial interests do not always prevail over economic arguments.[76]

Today, there is a growing number of voices finding and touting values to try to save biodiversity. Medicines, foods, fibers, and so on, they say. Look what we have found. Save the ecosystems. We will find more. Growing numbers are trying to harvest ecosystems sustainably; at the same time, burgeoning populations and growing economies are tearing them down. The issues to be considered here are complex and are multiplying, not least of all, arguments over who should benefit financially from the fruits of biodiversity exploration and research—for example, a pharmaceutical company, the indigenous population of an area where a pharmaceutical was found, or the government of the area in question?

Dollars-and-cents evaluations can be misleading. There are species for which we may see no value at the present time. If we do not take care of these, also, we eliminate the discovery and emergence of future value.

No one can guess the full future value of any kind of animal, plant, or microorganism. Its potential is spread across a spectrum of known and as yet unimagined human needs. Even the species themselves are largely unknown.[77]

There are other, less tangible values to biodiverse areas, as mentioned elsewhere—aesthetics, biophilia, spiritual refreshment. Wilson, a scientist, makes the science subordinate and builds to these values in *The Diversity of Life, The Future of Life,* and elsewhere:

Perhaps it is enough to argue that the preservation of the living world is necessary for our long-term material prosperity and health, as I have now done. But . . . there is another, and in some ways deeper, reason. It has to do with the defining and self-image of the human species.[78]

How Are Species Doing?

There are about 1.08 million known species of animals; of those, only about 46,500 are vertebrates; about 4,000 mammals. Estimates of total numbers of extant animal species run from a few million to ten millions to a hundred million or so (but only about 50,000 or so vertebrates). It is well to note that 840,000 of the known species of animals are insects and that total estimates of insect species run from 8 million to 100 million.[79] The IUCN Redlist notes 713 animal species as known to be extinct or extinct in the wild. 5483 are listed as threatened.[80]

There are about 256,000 known species of Plants. There may be 300,000 to half a million or more plant species. There are about 45,000 known species of fungi, but about 1 million to a million and a half species may actually exist. There are about 80,000 known species of protists, half algae and half proto-zoans. There are about 5,000 known species of monerans—eubacteria and archaebacteria, but about 22,000,000 to 230,150,000 species may exist.[81]

The IUCN Red List notes 87 species of plants, lichens, or macroalgae (seaweeds) as extinct or extinct in the wild, with another 6,776 species threatened.[82]

MORE ON THE RESPONSE, LEGISLATIVE
AND OTHERWISE

What have we done?

At one point in recent decades, zoos and aquaria thought of themselves as "an ark." They thought an "ark approach" would work to conserve species. However, zoos came to realize that saving a species with nowhere to put it when it bounced back was an exercise in futility. There has subsequently been a shift in AZA priorities and procedures such that conservation of native habitat is an important part of zoo work.[83]

Species survival plans seem like a drop in the bucket, covering only 161 animals. As noted previously, if all of the zoo space in the United States were used for SSPs, a few hundred animals could be covered, and if all of the zoo space in the world were used, about 900 animals. With only 161 animal species covered by the SSPs, what can be accomplished?

The SSP species *are* flagship species. Saving their habitats does save other species. Many of the SSP species *are* charismatic. Popular interest in these animals *does* encourage popular interest in the related biodiversity-loss issues. Popular interest is desperately needed.

Many regions and countries have their own *in situ* programs. Were it not for a century of work by Russians, at times just a handful of dedicated volunteers, the Amur Tiger would have died out in the wild when the Russian Amur tiger population reached a low of an estimated 30 tigers in the mid-1900s. David Quammen writes about this in his *Monster of God*.[84]

The Convention on International Trade in Endangered Species of Wild Fauna and Flora (CITES) was written after a 1963 meeting of the IUCN. Eighty countries met in Washington, D.C. in 1973, where the treaty was agreed upon; CITES was enacted as a document governing these issues in 1975.

It was mentioned earlier that poaching is a significant piece of overharvest-ing; CITES has made a difference but can be hard to enforce. The people-power is not always there, and the financial incentives can make dealing in exotic animals difficult to resist. When a tiger skin, bones, even sex organs can make the difference between poverty and a comfortable life, animals are at risk.

The Endangered Species Act is actively used in the United States. The U.S. Fish and Wildlife Service (FWS) maintains a list, updated daily, of Threatened and Endangered Species (TESS), and this list also is updated daily. The FWS has recovery plans for many species—from lichens to ferns to trees to arachnids to other invertebrates to fish, and, yes, even to the charismatic megafauna. As of October 1, 2004, the FWS lists endangered and threatened animals as numbering 390 and 128, repectively; endangered plants (and lichens) as numbering 599 and 147, respectively. Recovery plans exist for 415 animals and 609 plants and lichens.[85]

The Endangered Species Act, controversial in 1973 and still controversial, recognizes that species in the United States can disappear, that we can have something to do with causing those disappearances, and that there might be some value to humanity to not having species disappear. CITES, the Convention on International Trade in Endangered Species, was devised in 1975, is administered by the United Nations, and seeks to protect species that would be decimated by poaching or by legitimate trade that might be done without regard for endangerment of species.

Countless NGOs exist, each with its own species or areas of interest in conserving nature.

Extensive plans exist, such as this one, for the Amur Tigers: *A Habitat Protection Plan for Amur Tiger Conservation: A Proposal Outlining Habitat Protection Measures for the Amur Tiger.*[86] The project has the support of the National Geographic Society, the Save the Tiger Fund at the National Fish and Wildlife Foundation, the National Fish and Wildlife Foundation, EXXON Corporation, the National Wildlife Federation, the Wildlife Conservation Society, the Charles Englehard Foundation, the Turner Foundation, and Patagonia, Inc. In addition, the report acknowledges the support of colleagues, such as that supplied by the local Russian people, some who have been studying and working for the tiger' survival for decades. All that effort for one subspecies!

And a growing worldwide network is in place, as evidenced by document after document and conversation after conversation in compiling this chapter—from the IUCN to the AZA to the Nature Conservancy to the Fish and Wildlife Service to *in situ* programs, and the list goes on and on. There are, simply put, many people and many structures in place, and they are dealing with the problem. Add to that legions of educators, researchers, and their institutions.

However, important components are missing: political and social will, a place in national conversations, a place in global conversations—in other words, inclusion in the agenda of national elections and relevance to the day-to-day lives of the citizens of the world, whose priorities are obtaining an education, having a family, having a career, and making a difference in the world in other ways.

ACTION TO SAVE SPECIES—
WHAT CAN WE DO?

We have laws. We have treaties. We can enforce them. We must *manage* wildlife. We have taken over too much of it to not do this, as presumptuous as it sounds.

Michael Hutchins of the AZA makes no bones about the fact that he sees a world of grays, not of blacks and whites. We live in a human-dominated world. We have to manage species. We do not have a choice. We have to deal with introduced species, diseases, even controlling indigenous species when their own now out-of-balance ecosystems cannot control them. Human–animal conflicts are big issues. The needs of animals and of people must both be met. Otherwise wildlife has no chance.[87]

Managing human and wildlife needs is going to require humans and wildlife to rub shoulders if wildlife is to survive. As the August 2004 issue of *Time* discusses in its cover story on saving the big cats,[88] there may be a way out for some species, even such species as top carnivore cats. People are finding ways to share land with species. In the case of the big cats, Anastasia and Robeki's kin, protected areas are not enough. Zoo programs are not enough, but a combination of these with the addition of ways for cats to travel from protected area to protected area—wildlife corridors—this might be enough.

> There is a saying: "After the final no there comes a yes
> And on that yes the future world depends. . . . " (Wallace Stevens, in *The Well-Dressed Man with a Beard*)

Oddly, there is a yes for biodiversity. There are several yeses, in fact.

There are the success stories: bringing back the bison from the brink of extinction, reintroducing wolves in U.S. ecosystems, reintroducing the golden lion tamarin in Brazil.

There have been lessons learned: The California Condor was brought back to find that its native habitat, now sprawling development, is no longer suitable for it. Other habitat is being tried. There are stopgaps, such as the freezing of embryos, eggs, and sperm, for such time as zoo spaces may open up or habitats may somehow be repaired.

And there are ways, still, to make wise choices, such as preserving the biological hot spots of the world, areas where there is abundant biodiversity concentrated in relatively small areas.

> . . . the 17 hottest spots of the world occupy only 1.3 percent of the land surface yet contain a fourth of the planet's terrestrial vertebrate species and 40 percent of its plants.[89]

CONCLUSION

The AZA, a pivotal but largely unsung hero in the fight to staunch the flow of biodiversity loss, is among the many groups that promote "conservation," which has its beginnings in the work of George Perkins Marsh, Gifford Pinchot, and Teddy Roosevelt. Conservation, a utilitarian position, works to promote the greatest good for the greatest number of people in the long run. Note that this approach gives people an edge over the rest of creation, while recognizing our connectedness and dependence.

"Preservation," on the other hand, says that we are but one of many species and takes away the priority of our own species. Preservation can have one of several foci. A biocentric focus promotes the importance of species preservation. An ecocentric (earth-centered) focus in preservation seeks to preserve systems and processes—types of ecosystems, evolution, photosynthesis, and so on. In its focal shift from ark to habitat, the AZA, in the last decades, has moved from an anthropocentric (human-centered) position to one that is at least partly ecocentric. True, habitat may have multiple uses, but the habitat must be largely preserved to remain habitat.

Conservationists, biocentric preservationists, and ecocentric preservationists would strongly distinguish themselves from the "animal rights" position.[90] Animal rights seeks to preserve the individual organism, attributing individual rights to the animal, as we would do for a human being. Saving species has nothing to do with animal rights or sentimental attachment to individuals. Robeki and Anastasia are, according to our programs, important only for their genetics; we care for them so that they may be healthy and free of stress and may breed. Although the AZA attends with great care to animal welfare concerns, individual animals are not important for themselves.

But something very interesting happens when we actually encounter Robeki and Anastasia. They are very special individuals, our distant relatives. We, too, are from those forests of the night, and we feel instant recognition. Whatever the goals of our breeding programs, we know the animals as individuals. Damn such attraction as sentimentality, it is still there. And in the long run, we probably do not want to lose that recognition. As much as the science of ecosystems and the science of species genetics must be used in addressing species loss, we will probably not "reason our way" to saving species, not with science and certainly not with economics. To save the tigers, we are going to need a passion much closer to love. There is much heartfelt work to do, and Wilson and others feel that we are up to the task: Wilson and others point to that.

> In the end, I suspect it will all come down to a decision of ethics—how we value the natural worlds in which we evolved and now, increasingly, how we regard our status as individuals.... The drive toward perpetual expansion—or personal freedom—is basic to the human spirit. But to sustain it we need the most delicate, knowing stewardship of the living world that can be devised.[91]

> I hope I have justified the conviction, shared by many thoughtful people from all walks of life, that the problem can be solved. Adequate resources exist. Those who control them have many reasons to achieve that goal, not least their own security. In the end, however, success or failure will come down to an ethical decision, one on which those now living will be defined and judged for all generations to come. I believe we will choose wisely. A civilization able to envision God and to embark on the colonization of space will surely find the way to save the integrity of this planet and the magnificent life it harbors.[92]

QUESTIONS FOR REFLECTION

1. Why is the tiger so important to us? Consider the role of "wild-ness," danger, lethal strength, and natural beauty in our lives. How much of our appreciation of the tiger might be evolved—a product of our foraging past?

2. There is abundant controversy on whether or not we have a right to keep animals in zoos and aquari-ums. From what you know now, do you think the caging of animals is justified?

3. What more might we be doing to preserve the wild species? Along the same lines, what might we do with zoos and aquariums to make them more effective in their work?

4. Obviously it would be nice to have an attractive variety in Nature. But when applied to species like the snail darter, are the claims of "biodiversity" sufficient to justify overriding important human projects?

NOTES

1. William Blake, *Songs of Innocence and of Experience: Shewing the Two Contrary States of the Human Soul,* with supplementary material by Ruth E. Everett (New York: Avon Books, 1971), pp. 101–102.

2. Connecticut's Beardsley Zoo, 1875 Noble Avenue, Bridgeport, CT 06610-1646, telephone: 203-394-6565, available at http://www.beardsleyzoo.org/.

3. Elizabeth Kudlinski, personal communication, 2004.

4. *5 Tigers: The Tiger Information Center,* updated 2004, available at http://www .5tigers.org/AllAboutTigers/Subspecies/a mur.html, accessed 9 October 2004. The website is maintained by Ronald Tilson, Ph.D., Principal Investigator, Sumatran Tiger Project, and Coordinator, CBSG Tiger Global Conservation Strategy (GCS); J. Tilson, Editor, Webmaster; and A. Alden, Editor, Webmaster.

5. Nowell, K., and P. Jackson, eds., *Wild Cats: Status Survey and Conservation Action Plan* (Gland, Switzerland: IUCN, 1996), available at http://www.5tigers.org/ AllAboutTigers/Subspecies/amur.htm in http://www.5tigers.org/index.html (see n. 4 above).

6. Kudlinski, personal communication, 2004 (see n. 3 above).

7. Ibid.

8. American Zoo and Aquarium Association, "2004 Guide to Accreditation of Zoological Parks and Aquariums and Accreditation Standards," available at AZA Executive Office, 8403 Colesville Road, Suite 710, Silver Spring, MD 20910-3314, telephone (301) 562-0777, fax (301) 562-0888; available online at http://www.aza.org/Accreditation/, accessed 10 October 2004.

9. The American Zoo and Aquarium Association envisions a world where all people respect, value and conserve animals and nature; http://www.aza.org/AboutAZA/Mission Vision/, accessed 10 October 2004.

10. Ibid.

11. Ibid.

12. Michael Hutchins, Director, and William Conway, Chair, Department of Conservation and Science (AZA Executive Office, 8403 Colesville Road, Suite 710, Silver Spring, MD 20910-3314, telephone: 301- 562-0777, fax 301-562-0888), personal communication, 2004.

13. The Wildlife Conservation Society, 2300 Southern Boulevard, Bronx, New York 10460, telephone (718) 220-5100, available online at http://bronxzoo.com/.

14. Robert J. Wiese and Michael Hutchins, *Species Survival Plans: Strategies for*

Wildlife Conservation," (Bethesda, Maryland: American Zoo and Aquarium Association, 1994), p. 10.

15. Wildlife Conservation Society (see n. 13).

16. IUDZG [The World Zoo Organization and The Captive Breeding Specialist Group of IUCN/SSC], *The World Zoo Conservation Strategy; The Role of the Zoos and Aquaria of the World in Global Conservation* (Brook field, IL: Chicago Zoological Society, 1993), p. 5.

17. Lisa H. Newton, personal communication, 2004.

18. Endangered Species Act, § 1532, 1973.

19. http://www.redlist.org/search/details.php?species=15956, accessed 10 October , 2004, from the official IUCN Red List website.

20. Ronald Tilson et al., *AZA Tiger Species Survival Plan (SSP) Five-Year Plan (2001-2005),* Silver Springs, MD, American Zoo and Aquarium Association, 12 January 2001, p. 1; available at http://www.5tigers.org/Research/ssp/reports/ssp5yplan_01_05.pdf ; accessed September 2004.

21. Edward O. Wilson, *The Future of Life* (New York: Knopf, 2002)., p. 56.

22. Available at http://www.iucnredlist.org/info/categories_criteria2001.html, accesssed from the IUCN Redlist Website, October 2004.

23. Ibid.

24. Edward O. Wilson, *Biophilia* (Boston: Harvard University Press, 1986).

25. Job 40: 15, 18, 23, 24; Holy Bible, King James Version (London: Oxford University Press, 1904).

26. David Quammen, *Monster of God: The Man-Eating Predator in the Jungles of History and the Mind* (New York: Norton, 2003), pp. 10–11.

27. Psalms 40: 23–14; Holy Bible, King James Version (London: Oxford University Press, 1904).

28. Ruth Allard (AZA Executive Office, 8403 Colesville Road, Suite 710, Silver Spring, MD 20910-3314, telephone: 301-562-0777, fax: 301-562-0888), personal communication, 2004.

29. Ulysses S. Seal, "Intensive Technology in the Care of *Ex Situ* Populations of Vanishing Species," in E. O. Wilson, ed., *Biodiversity* (Washington, D.C.: National Academy Press, 1988), p. 290.

30. IUCN Red List of Threatened Species: Summary Statistics, http://www.redlist.org/info/tables/table1.html, accessed 5 November 2004 from the official IUCN Red List website.

31. Lisa Tryon (Director of Education, Connecticut's Beardsley Zoo), personal communication, 2004.

32. Wiese and Hutchins, *Species Survival Plans,* p. 22.

33. Ibid.

34. Ibid.

35. Ted Williams, "Going Catatonic," *Audubon* 106(4): 24.

36. Sacha Spector (Manager, Invertebrate Conservation Program, Center for Biodiversity and Conservation, Amercan Museum of Natural History, Central Park West, New York, NY 10024), personal communication, 2004.

37. Ibid.

38. Wilson, *Future,* p. 10.

39. Ibid.

40. Ibid.

41. E. O. Wilson, *The Diversity of Life* (New York: Norton, 1992), p. 280.

42. Ibid., p. xxii.

43. Ibid.

44. Charlotte Schubert, "Life on the Edge: Will a Mass Extinction Usher in a World of Weeds and Pests?" *Science News* 160(11): 169.

45. Wilson, *Future,* pp. 98–99.

46. Ibid., pp. 100–101.

47. Ibid., pp. 101–2.

48. Ibid., p. 102.

49. Schubert, *Life,* p. 169.

50. Wilson, *Future,* p. 50.

51. Ibid., p. 58.

52. Ibid., p. 59.

53. Schubert, *Life,* p. 168.

54. Tilson et al., *AZA Species Survival Plan,* p. 1 (see n. 20 above).

55. Ibid., pp. 1-2.

56. Ronald Tilson, Gerald Brady, Mike Dulaney, and Kathy Traylor-Holzer, *AZA Annual Report of the Tiger SSP, Tiger (Panthera tigris),* 2003, p. 2, available at http://www.5tigers.org/Research/ssp/reports/2003/ AMURTIGERSSPfinal plan03.pdf, accessed 5 November 2004 (see also n. 8 above).

57. Ibid.

58. Kathy Traylor-Holzer (North American Regional studbook keeper for Amur tigers), personal communication, 2004.

59. Tilson et al., *AZA Annual Report,* p. 1.

60. Tilson et al., *AZA Tiger Species Survival Plan,* p. 1 (see n. 20 above).

61. Wilson, *Future,* p. 89.

62. Ibid.

63. J. Raloff, "The Ultimate Crop Insurance: A New Treaty Strives to Save 10,000 Years of Plant Breeding," *Science News* (September 2004): 171.

64. Wilson, *Future,* pp. 105-106.

65. Ibid., p. 106.

66. Alan Randall. "What Mainstream Economists Have to Say about the Value of BioDiversity," in Wilson, *BioDiversity,* p. 222.

67. The late estuarine biologist, ornithologist, and ecologist Salvatore F. Bongiorno. Salvatore was a pioneer of tidal marsh restoration.

68. Joanne H. Choly, personal recollection, 2004.

69. Wilson, *Future,* p. 107.

70. Ibid.

71. Ibid.

72. Ibid., pp. 107-108.

73. Randall, "Mainstream Economists," in Wilson, *Biodiversity,* p. 222.

74. Ibid., p. 222.

75. Ibid., p 223.

76. Ibid.

77. Ibid. p 113.

78. Ibid., p. 128.

79. These data are from Edward O. Wilson and Dan L Perlman, *Conserving Earth's Biodiversity, with E. O. Wilson,* CD-ROM, Island Press, 2000.

80. IUCN Red List, accessed at http://www.redlist.org/, October 2004.

81. Wilson and Perlman, *Conserving.*

82. IUCN Red List, accessed at http://www.redlist.org/, October 2004.

83. Lisa Tryon (Director of Education at Connecticut's Beardsley Zoo; Director of the Bear Taxon Advisory Group), personal communication, 2004.

84. David Quammen, *Monster of God: The Man-Eating Predator in the Jungles of History and the Mind* (New York: Norton), p. 360.

85. Data obtained online from the U.S. Fish and Wildlife Service, available at http://ecos.fws.gov/tess_public/ TESSBoxscore, accessed 1 October 2004.

86. Dale Miquelle, Howard Quigley, and Maurice Hornoker, "A Habitat Protection Plan for Amur Tiger Conservation: A Proposal Outlining Habitat Protection Measures for the Amur Tiger," Moscow, Idaho, The Hornoker Wildlife Institute (now part of the Wildlife Conservation Society), available at http://5tigers.org/, accessed October 2004.

87. Hutchins, personal communication, 2004 (see n. 12 above).

88. T. McCarthy and A. Dorfman, "Saving the Big Cats," *Time,* 23 August 2004, pp. 44-53.

89. Wilson, *Diversity,* p. xxii.

90. Michael Hutchins, Brandie Smith, and Ruth Allard, "In Defense of Zoos and Aquariums: The Ethical Basis for Keeping Wild Animals in Captivity," *Journal of the American Veterinary Medical Association* 223(7): 958-66.

91. Edward O. Wilson., "The Current State of Biological Diversity," in Wilson, *BioDiversity,* p. 16.

92. Wilson, *Future,* p. 189.

Epilogue:
The Future of an Idea

The foregoing chapters give us few grounds for hope for the natural environment. Although small bits of standard progress can be discovered (the development of hybrid cars, the banning of DDT; the American Chemistry Council's "Responsible Care" initiative), most projected scenarios terminate in devastation. The genetically modified organisms, for instance, do not seem to pose any threat to the environment, at least in comparison to most of the other situations documented. But the controversy over the "Frankenfoods" gives us a perfect example of a bad fit between environmental activism and the problem it attempts to address. We need to count on the NGOs of this world, Greenpeace and the others, to home in on real problems, not on artifacts of current economic and political conditions. As we write, the population problem grows worse in the developing nations by dint of sheer numbers, and in the developed nations too, where level of consumption per capita is over the top. There is no morally acceptable way of dealing with the number-of-people part of the problem and no politically acceptable way of dealing with the consumption part. As long as the world's population and consumption grow, nothing else will work in any field. Global warming is increasing: we are watching the ice caps melt and lakes form in the arctic; polar bears not yet dead of PCB concentrations in their fat may starve to death. While tens of thousands protest, the slaughter of the apes continues; the horror felt by the civilized world seems to have no effect on mindless destroyers. The organochlorines, stock for our pesticides and plastics, are widely blamed for the deterioration of the fishing stock in the Great Lakes and for hormonal disruption everywhere. Antibiotic resistance, a condition unheard of a few decades ago, now threatens lives all over the world, raising the ghosts of ancient diseases we thought conquered and dead. The fisheries continue to decline. Logging continues in the national forests and the last reserves of the ancient redwoods.

The only conclusion available to rational and civilized persons is that "sustainable" economic activity, developmental or otherwise, has to be the goal of research and policy now and into the foreseeable future. Yet just at this point the national (and international) effort to preserve environmental gains has run into a wall of opposition. It is difficult to believe that only 12 years ago we elected an administration whose vice president had written a major book on the need to preserve the environment. It is even harder to recapture the entire environmental thrust begun in 1970 at the first Earth Day that motivated all the powerful legislation of the 1970s—Clean Water, Clean Air, Endangered Species, Wilderness Protection. Environmental initiatives undertaken at the outset of the Clinton administration died before coming to birth, and a national mood of "deregulation" set in, sweeping environmental protections toward oblivion. We have just reelected, to our everlasting shame, an administration whose first environmental initiative was to attempt to open the Arctic National Wildlife Refuge to oil exploration, followed by steps to permit roads in all the national forests, systematically weaken clean-air and clean-water legislation, and above all promote the consumption of petroleum, on which the family fortunes of the U.S. president and vice-president depend. What happened in America?

It's a good question. Why this sudden check in the commitment to environmental preservation? The explanations are legion; most have to do with the change in the priorities of the middle class. The first job of the head of the family is to make a living. Charities and long-range obligations, like those to the natural environment, come second. A skillful politician can make it appear that environmental initiatives are a threat to jobs, which they sometimes are in the short run, and improve his own position in the polls by siding with "jobs" and against "tree huggers." Along with fears of unemployment, resentment of "government regulation" lies close to the surface of the American mind, and no one wants to pay the taxes that support public initiatives and agencies. In times of economic and political uncertainty, political gold lies in opposing expensive and job-threatening environmental regulations. Ideologues and politicians have discovered this gold; historians writing the story of the last decade of the twentieth century and the first decade of the twenty-first will document an ugly mood in an ungenerous and short-sighted electorate, trembling at the thought of Arab bogeymen terrorizing their country clubs and unwilling to subsidize any attempts to regulate for the common good in the long run.

If there is a note of hope in the generalized downward trend of the environmental initiatives, it comes from a strange new angle. The cases are almost too young to write, although the new chapter on alternative energies is a start. We try to include some good news in each edition of *Watersheds,* so keep an eye out for the next one.

Item: In the headquarters of the Rocky Mountain Institute bananas and tropical flowers manage to grow in the Colorado cold, which reaches temperatures of −47°F. The building has no furnace. How is this possible? Because of special insulating windows that receive all light and hold all heat and that are oriented toward the sun. You don't need a government subsidy to build such a headquarters—savings in the cost of heating bills paid for it in the first year of operation. We could build all our houses this way. Further, if we put photovoltaic cells on the roofs of those houses, we could make electricity. Houses could be like trees, producing more energy than they consume. If all of us did this, the energy crisis would be over, now and forever.

Item: *Technology Today*, alumni magazine of MIT, hardly a radical sheet, featured an article on the fuel cell cars of the future. Only, the future is now—prototypes are zipping around the roads. They're not ready for prime time, the author of the article thinks; like most brand-new technology, they cost too much to build to sell them at a price acceptable to the average consumer and still make money. But they'll get there, probably very soon.

Item: Many European nations have introduced the concept of "extended producer responsibility" to address the problem of solid waste, trash. If you make it, goes the concept, it's yours. When whoever you sold it to is through with it, you'll get it back. You'd better, therefore, make it (1) biodegradable, (2) reusable after upgrade (this especially true for computers, (3) recyclable, or reusable after reassembly with other parts, or you will have a very large trash-disposal bill. If there is, God forbid, lead in your product (as there is in many CRTs), your trash bill for toxic waste will be astronomical. Learn how to make CRTs differently or prepare to recycle all of them. Most hopeful in this new concept of environmental regulation is the powerful incentive it gives all manufacturers to design for sustainability—to design each product with its end use and disposal in mind, knowing that it cannot put any further burden on the earth. Incidentally, we have not heard much about this initiative since the last edition; we'll try to include a chapter on it in the next one.

Item: There are a large number of organizations—many of them working with the IUCN, the World Conservation Union—quietly networking to protect biodiversity so that we do not lose it before we realize how much we depend on it (and would miss it if it were gone, regardless of our need).

These items and others are discussed in *Natural Capitalism*, by Paul Hawken and Amory and L. Hunter Lovins, the prime movers of the Rocky Mountain Institute, mentioned earlier. Amory Lovins and others have more recently written a treatise on how to phase out petroleum consumption, *Winning the Oil Endgame*. It is not likely that its strategies will be popular during the current administration. But there is the hope—although, in the light of the foregoing chapters, we'd best not fall in love with it—that with minimal government intervention, private enterprise will remake itself in an environmentally sustainable mode. Maybe it will, maybe it won't. Stay tuned.

Bibliography

Armstrong, Susan J., and Richard G. Botzler. *Environmental Ethics: Divergence and Convergence.* New York: McGraw-Hill, 2003. ISBN 0-07-283845-0

Attfield, Robin. *The Ethics of Environmental Concern.* New York: Columbia University Press, 1983.

Berman, Daniel, and John T. O'Connor. *Who Owns the Sun?* White River Junction, VT: Chelsea Green, 1996. ISBN 0-930031-86-5

Berry, Thomas. *The Dream of the Earth.* San Francisco: Sierra Club Books, 1988.

Brown, Lester R. *Who Will Feed China? Wake-Up Call for a Small Planet.* New York: Norton, 1995.

Burch, Mark A. *Stepping Lightly: Simplicity for People and the Planet.* Gabriola Island, BC: New Society Publishers, 2000.

Callicott, J. Baird. "Animal Liberation: A Triangular Affair." *Environmental Ethics* 2(1980): 311–38.

————. *Beyond the Land Ethic.* Albany: SUNY Press, 1999. ISBN 0-7914-4084-2.

————. *In Defense of the Land Ethic.* Albany: SUNY Press, 1989. ISBN 0-88706-900-2

Callicott, J. Baird, and Michael Nelson. *American Indian Environmental Ethics: An Ojibwa Case Study.* Upper Saddle River, NJ: Prentice-Hall, 2003. ISBN: 0-13-043121-4

Carson, Rachel. *Silent Spring,* special edition with Introduction by Al Gore. Boston: Houghton Mifflin, 1994 (first published in 1962).

Colbert, Theo, et al. *Our Stolen Future: Are We Threatening Our Fertility, Intelligence, and Survival?—a Scientific Detective Story.* New York: Dutton, 1996. ASIN: 0525939822

Commoner, Barry. *The Closing Circle.* New York: Ballantine Books, 1986. ISBN: 0-345-34505-3

Daly, Herman E., and John B. Cobb, Jr. *For the Common Good: Redirecting the Economy toward Community, the Environment, and a Sustainable Future.* Boston: Beacon Press, 1994.

Dallmeyer, Dorinda, ed. *Values at Sea: Ethics for the Marine Environment.* Atlanta: University of Georgia Press, 2003. ISBN 0-8203-2470-1

Deane-Drummond, Celia. *The Ethics of Nature.* Oxford: Blackwell, 2003. ISBN 0-631-22937-X.

DesJardins, Joseph. *Environmental Ethics: Concepts, Policy, Theory.* Mountain View, CA: Mayfield, 1999. ISBN 1-55934-986-7

————. *Environmental Ethics: An Introduction to Environmental Philosophy,* 2d ed. Belmont, CA: Wadsworth, 1997. ISBN 0-534-50508-2

Diamond, Jared. "The Last Americans: Environmental Collapse and the End of Civilization." *Harper's Magazine,* June 2003, pp. 43–51.

Easterbrook, Gregg. *A Moment on the Earth: The Coming Age of Environmental Optimism.* New York: Penguin Books, 1995.

Eisenberg, Evan. *The Ecology of Eden.* New York: Knopf, 1998.

Elkington, John. *Cannibals with Forks: The Triple Bottom Line of 21st Century Business.* Stony Creek, CT: New Society Publishers, 1997.

Epstein, Richard A. *Takings: Private Property and the Power of Eminent Domain.* Cambridge, MA: Harvard University Press, 1985.

Glick, Daniel. "GeoSigns." *National Geographic,* special issue on global warming, 206, no. 3 (September 2004): 12–33.

Goodpaster, Kenneth E. "On Being Morally Considerable." *Journal of Philosophy* 75(1978): 308–25.

Graham, Frank, Jr. *Since Silent Spring.* Boston: Houghton Mifflin, 1970.

Gudorf, Christine E., and James Edward Huchingson. *Boundaries: A Casebook in Environmental Ethics.* Washington, DC: Georgetown University Press, 2003. ISBN: 0-87840-134-2.

Hardin, Garrett. "The Tragedy of the Commons." *Science* 162(1968): 1243–48.

Hargrove, Eugene C. *The Animal Rights/Environmental Ethics Debate.* Albany: SUNY Press, 1992. ISBN 0-7914-0934-1

————. *Foundations of Environmental Ethics.* Englewood Cliffs: Prentice-Hall, 1989.

Harris, David. *The Last Stand: The War between Wall Street and Main Street over California's Ancient Redwoods.* New York: Times Books/Random House, 1996.

Hawken, Paul, Amory Lovins, and L. Hunter Lovins. *Natural Capitalism: Creating the Next Industrial Revolution.* Boston: Little, Brown, 1999.

Hoffman, Peter. *Tomorrow's Energy: Hydrogen, Fuel Cells, and the Prospects for a Cleaner Planet.* Cambridge: MIT Press, 2001. ISBN: 0-262-58221-X

Lear, Linda. *Rachel Carson: Witness for Nature.* New York: Holt (Owl), 1997.

Leopold, Aldo. *A Sand County Almanac and Sketches Here and There,* commemorative ed., New York: Oxford University Press, 1987.

List, Peter C., ed. *Radical Environmentalism: Philosophy and Tactics.* Belmont, CA: Wadsworth, 1993.

Lovins, L. Hunter, and Amory B. Lovins, with Seth Zuckerman. *Energy Unbound: A Fable for America's Future.* San Francisco, CA: Sierra Club Books, 1986.

Lovins, Amory B., E. Kyle Datta, Odd-Even Bustnes, Jonathan G. Koomey, and Nathan J. Glasgow, *Winning the Oil Endgame: Innovation for Profits, Jobs, and Security,* with Forewords by George P. Schultz and Sir Mark Moody-Smart. Snowmass, CO: Rocky Mountain Institute, 2004.

Lucas v. South Carolina Coastal Council, U.S. June 29, 1992; 22 *Environmental Law Reporter* 21104 (September 1992).

Lucas v. South Carolina Coastal Council, S.C. Nov. 20, 1992; 23 *Environmental Law Reporter* 20297 (September 1992).

Martin-Schramm, James B., and Robert L. Stivers. *Christian Environmental Ethics: A Case Method Approach.* Orbis Books, 2003. ISBN: 1-57075-499-3

McKibben, Bill. *Enough: Staying Human in an Engineered Age.* New York: Henry Holt, 2003.

———. *The End of Nature.* New York: Random House, 1989. ISBN-0-394-57601-2.

Miller, G. Tyler, Jr. *Living in the Environment, 11th ed.* Belmont, CA: Wadsworth Brooks/Cole, 2000.

Montaigne, Fen. "EcoSigns." *National Geographic,* special issue on global warming, 206, no. 3 (September 2004): 34–55.

Morell, Virginia. "TimeSigns." *National Geographic,* special issue on global warming, 206, no. 3 (September 2004): 56–74.

Oelschlager, Max. *The Idea of Wilderness: From Prehistory to the Age of Ecology,* New Haven: Yale University Press, 1991.

Orr, David W. *Ecological Literacy: Education and the Transition to a Postmodern World.* Albany: SUNY Press, 1992.

Passmore, John. *Man's Responsibility for Nature: Ecological Problems and Western Traditions,* London: Duckworth, 1974.

Pojman, Louis P. *Environmental Ethics: Theory and Practice.* Belmont, CA: Wadsworth, 2004. ISBN: 0-534-63971-2

Quammen, David. *Monster of God: The Man-Eating Predator in the Jungles of History and Mind.* New York: Norton, 2003. ISBN: 0-39305140-4

———. *The Song of the Dodo: Island Biogeography in an Age of Extinctions.* New York: Simon and Schuster, 1996.

Reaka-Kudla, Marjorie L. et al., eds. *Biodiversity II.* Washington, D.C.: National Academy Press, 1997. ISBN: 0-309-05584-9

Regan, Tom. *The Case for Animal Rights.* Berkeley: University of California Press, 1983.

Rolston, Holmes III. *Environmental Ethics: Duties to and Values in the Natural World,* Philadelphia: Temple University Press, 2003. ISBN: 0-87722-628-8

Sagoff, Mark. *The Economy of the Earth: Philosophy, Law, and the Environment.* New York: Cambridge University Press, 1988.

Schumacher, E. F., *Small Is Beautiful: Economics As If People Mattered.* New York: Harper and Row, 1973.

Sideris, Lisa H. *Environmental Ethics, Ecological Theology, and Natural Selection.* New York: Columbia University Press, 2003. ISBN: 0-231-12660-3

Simon, Julian L. *The Ultimate Resource.* Princeton, NJ: Princeton University Press, 1981.

Singer, Peter, *Animal Liberation: A New Ethics for our Treatment of Animals.* New York: New York Review, 1975.

Speth, James Gustave. *Red Sky at Morning: America and the Crisis of the Global Environment,* New Haven: Yale University Press, 2004. ISBN 0-300-10232-1

Sterba, James P. *Earth Ethics: Environmental Ethics, Animal Rights, and Practical Applications,* Englewood Cliffs, NJ: Prentice Hall, 1995. ISBN 0-02-417102-6

Stone, Christopher D. *Should Trees Have Standing? Toward Legal Rights for Natural Objects.* Los Altos: William Kaufman, 1974.

Sutton, Phillip W. *Nature, Environment and Society.* New York: Palgrave MacMillan, 2004. ISBN 0-333-99568-6

Taylor, Paul W. *Respect for Nature: A Theory of Environmental Ethics.* Princeton, NJ: Princeton University Press, 1986. ISBN 0-691-02250-X

Wilson, Edward O. *The Future of Life.* New York: Vintage, 2003. ISBN: 0-309-03739-5

———. *The Diversity of Life.* Cambridge, MA: Harvard University Press, 1992. ISBN 0-674-21298-3

———. *Biodiversity.* Washington, D.C.: National Academy Press, 1989. ISBN: 0-309-03739-5

Index